Praise for *Magical*

"Frater Barrabbas has craft

the Qabalah that is clear, accessible, and ecumenical. The author avoids complex definitions, long and drawn-out history lessons, and psychobabble, focusing instead on supplying information that readers can use and understand . . . *Magical Qabalah for Beginners* does an excellent job of presenting this vital component of Western Magic for the benefit of all esoteric students."

—Chic and Sandra Tabatha Cicero, Chief Adepts of the Hermetic Order of the Golden Dawn and authors of *The Essential Golden Dawn*

"While many introductory books on Qabalah have been published over the years, *Magical Qabalah for Beginners* goes beyond the usual description of the Tree of Life and traces the development of Qabalistic mysticism from its traditional Jewish origins to its significant role in many modern magical systems. Those starting out on the path of learning magical Qabalah would do well to explore this book, which places the system in its proper historical context and at the same time demonstrates how it is currently implemented by the various magical traditions."

—Scott Stenwick, author of *Arcana* and *Mastering the Mystical Heptarchy*

"*Magical Qabalah for Beginners* acknowledges the Gnostic, Neo-Pythagorean, and Neo-Platonic roots of the Qabalah, which makes it more accessible to occultists of all denominations, not only the Abrahamic. Being written by a Pagan, the book uses a language and mindset that also makes it user-friendly to students coming from the various Pagan traditions. While it is well-grounded in the Western Mystery Tradition and the paradigm of the Golden Dawn, and of its successors, it still is innovative and takes off into a new and fresh direction."

—Frater Sincerus Renatus, Senior Adept of the
Rosicrucian Order of Alpha Omega

"A thorough and concise introduction to a subject fundamental for Ritual Magic and the Golden Dawn."

—David Griffin, Golden Dawn Imperator and author of
The Ritual Magic Manual

"Whether you're a Witch, heathen, shaman, or magician, study of the magical organizational system known as the Qabalah can be of benefit to greater understanding of your own path. *Magical Qabalah for Beginners* is the introductory book that I wish we'd had back when I was first being trained in the Craft and couldn't quite grasp this aspect of the occult. Illuminating the history, structure, and practical application of the Qabalah, this work helps 'crack the code,' providing a welcome key to a set of beliefs that opens a door into a world that's long influenced magic in the West."

—Veronica Cummer, author of *Sorgitzak: Old Forest Craft* and editor of *To Fly by Night: The Craft of the Hedgewitch*

Magical
Qabalah
for Beginners

© Paul B. Rucker

About the Author

Frater Barrabbas is a practicing ritual magician who has studied magic and the occult for over thirty-five years. He is the founder of a magical order called the Order of the Gnostic Star and an elder and lineage holder in the Alexandrian tradition of Witchcraft. He lives in Minnesota.

Please visit his blog, fraterbarrabbas.blogspot.com.

Magical Qabalah

For Beginners

A Comprehensive Guide to Occult Knowledge

FRATER BARRABBAS

Llewellyn Publications
Woodbury, Minnesota

FIRST EDITION
First Printing, 2013

Cover background texture: iStockphoto.com/Peter Zelei
Cover design by Adrienne Zimiga
Interior illustrations by Llewellyn Art Department

Llewellyn Publications is a registered trademark of Llewellyn Worldwide Ltd.

Library of Congress Cataloging-in-Publication Data

Barrabbas, Frater.
  Magical Qabalah for beginners : a comprehensive guide to occult knowledge /
Frater Barrabbas. — 1st ed.
      p.   cm.
  Includes bibliographical references and index.
  ISBN 978-0-7387-3244-2
  1. Cabala. I. Title.
  BF1623.C2B384 2013
  135'.47—dc23
                           2012028107

Llewellyn Worldwide Ltd. does not participate in, endorse, or have any authority
or responsibility concerning private business transactions between our authors
and the public.
  All mail addressed to the author is forwarded, but the publisher cannot, unless
specifically instructed by the author, give out an address or phone number.
  Any Internet references contained in this work are current at publication time,
but the publisher cannot guarantee that a specific location will continue to be
maintained. Please refer to the publisher's website for links to authors' websites
and other sources.

Llewellyn Publications
A Division of Llewellyn Worldwide Ltd.
2143 Wooddale Drive
Woodbury, MN 55125-2989
www.llewellyn.com

Printed in the United States of America

contents

Part Two: Practical Qabalah:
Qabalistic Magic Simplified

Why Study the Qabalah?

A long time ago, when I was just sixteen years old, I got to visit the local infamous occult bookstore in the city of Milwaukee, not too far from where I lived. I thought that this store, called Sanctum Regnum, was the coolest place on the planet. I had just recently started calling myself a Witch and affecting all sorts of weirdness and silliness, including wearing black clothes, sporting occult jewelry, and doing other "Witchy things." As I was young and inexperienced, it was still a rather superficial preoccupation on my part.

Sanctum Regnum was a very gothic occult bookstore. It was black and red on the outside and inside, with shelves of obscure and hard-to-find books, swords, daggers, crystal balls, Tarot cards, jewelry, and herbs. It even had a moveable throne in the back, which functioned as a door to the basement where Tarot card readings and other psychic things were going on. It was, in a word, a repository of everything having to do with the occult, magic, and Witchcraft. Needless to say, I was deeply enthralled with it!

Anyway, here I was, at this very special place with strange-looking inhabitants, just soaking it all in as much as I could. I attempted to interact with some of the other customers, and I am sure that I was probably pretty annoying and obnoxious, being an overexcited teenager. I approached two mysterious individuals with long hair, beards, and hippie-style clothing, who were quietly discussing a book that they had opened and were examining together. I walked up to them and said, "So, do you guys know anyone around here who is practicing Witchcraft?"

They turned and coolly appraised me, and my exuberance was quickly squashed. One of them asked me, "Do you know of the Qabalah?" It was an awkward moment for me, and I wanted to lie and say, "Sure, I know lots of stuff," but I didn't. Instead, I said, "Well, actually, no, I don't." At the mere utterance of that admission, they turned their backs to me and continued with their quiet conversation, completely ignoring me.

Needless to say, I felt like a complete schmuck. My feelings were hurt, and I felt crushed. That was my first experience with the Qabalah. I took it upon myself from that moment on to learn and master that arcane subject, to prove to them and anyone else that I could do it, but it was a path and a preoccupation that took many years. Now, nearly forty years later, I can say, "Yes, I do know of the Qabalah!"

Because of that traumatic experience, I can easily understand that the word *Qabalah* evokes all sorts of fantastic and imaginary things. It is a word that is often used to label things that are mysterious, obscure, overly complex, uniquely trendy, and incapable of being understood by ordinary folk. Many are put off by the word itself, since it is a foreign word whose meaning is obscure to English speakers. Also, there are a number of different spellings for this word, as the variations of *Qabalah*, *Qabala*, *Cabala*, and *Kabbalah* would indicate. Merely the fact that this word has different spellings, which would seem to indicate different things to different people, adds to the overall confusion associated with this subject.

Western occultists tend to use the spelling *Qabalah*, but *Cabala* would indicate a decidedly Christian or archaic spelling, and *Kabbalah* is the spelling preferred by scholars and Jewish adherents. Therefore, the spelling itself indicates a different perspective in terms of how the topic is to be presented. Because I am using the spelling *Qabalah*, you can assume that I am taking a nonsectarian and modern occult perspective. We'll take that as a given for the rest of this book.

Defining the Qabalah

So what is the Qabalah, and why is it important? Why bother to learn it, and what benefit will you gain from studying it? These are very serious questions, and if I am going to engage your mind and imagination, they had better be answered in the first few pages or I will lose your interest altogether. I won't stultify you with complex definitions, long and drawn-out history lessons, or attempts to regale you with all sorts of mystic mumble jumble. The Qabalah is actually quite simple and succinct—believe it or not! It has some very specific uses that are revolutionary and remarkable, allowing the average occultist to comprehend and master all sorts of diverse spiritual ideas, systems, and theological aspects. In fact, it can organize and give meaning to nearly everything that is concerned with mysticism, occultism, religion, and magic. If you think that sounds like quite a tall order to fill, you are correct, but the Qabalah does that and much more.

Qabalah comes from the Hebrew verb root *QBL*, which means "to receive or accept instruction, to undertake." What that means is that the Qabalah is a kind of mystical knowledge that is directly received or apprehended from the source, which is the Godhead. Ironically, the word *qabalah* in Modern Hebrew is a very common term because it is used to denote a kind of business receipt or transaction (something received, or giving information). Yet to really understand what the word means, we have to penetrate deeper into its more esoteric meaning. So the esoteric definition of the word Qabalah indicates a kind of oral tradition or knowledge, passed from master to student. That is the meaning which we will use in this book.

Often, arcane books on the subject divide the Qabalah into the mystical or spiritual Qabalah, which is a form of occult speculation, and the practical Qabalah, which is a form of magic or occultism. Since the very beginning of its inception, the Qabalah served the purposes and functions of occult speculation, practical magical applications, and ecstatic spiritual practices. We will be focusing exclusively on the occult speculation and practical magical applications.

The Qabalah has the following basic functions and uses in modern occultism. Keep in mind that these are just the basic functions, so there are likely many more, and with a lot more detail, too. We are going to stick with the basics because this is a book for beginners.

> *Qabalah is a model of the various spirit worlds and how they are symbolically structured.*

This modeling is accomplished through a diagram that is called the *Tree of Life*. It also helps to have a really good imagination and to understand that the spirit world is not quite in the same place as the material world that we interact with on a daily basis.

> *Qabalah is a meta-system and a system of meta-knowledge. It assists in the organization of other religious, spiritual, and occult systems, and it reveals the relationships between those different systems. Meta-knowledge is a form of abstracted knowledge that gives meaning and definition to other attributes of knowledge; in other words, it is a kind of knowledge about knowledge.*

What kind of knowledge, you might ask? The knowledge of reality, of the self and the world in which it exists—this is called *ontology* (the study of reality). This meta-system and meta-knowledge are represented by what is known as "tables of correspondences," where the attributes of the Qabalah are compared to the attributes of every conceivable category in any spiritual, occultic, or religious system. That declaration might seem to be a bit vague or grandiose, but as we proceed together in filling out the details about what the Qabalah is, it will make a lot of sense. I will definitely have to explain all of that in much greater detail later in the book, since it is also a key concept.

Qabalah is a system of cosmology and cosmogony.

Cosmology is the evolution, structure, and constituent parts of the universe. The cosmology of the Qabalah is based on a more spiritual perspective of the universe, so it concerns itself with the phenomena of Spirit and its domain, and how it interacts with the worlds of mind and matter.

Cosmogony is the theory or model about the origin of the universe or how it was created. Keep in mind that the Qabalah promotes the "mind before matter" model with regard to cosmogony, as opposed to the "matter before mind" model that science promotes. What this means is that, like the biblical and other creation myths, consciousness existed as a unified field before the material universe unfolded, and that it had a direct part to play in that unfolding. We would call this unified field of consciousness that existed before any material thing the *Universal Mind* or the *Monad* (first being, or the One) that engaged itself with the design, fashioning, and ensouling of the spiritual and material universes.

Both the occult/religious model (mind before matter) and the scientific model (matter before mind) are correct. They just represent two different perspectives. The occult model is a meta-physical system that promotes the idea that matter is imbued with consciousness and, as a result, sentience and spirit are innate to physical matter. The occult model does not attempt to determine how the material universe was actually formed, since science has done a good job explaining the origin of the universe and everything in it. Problems arise when the mythic concept of creation in the occult model is confused with the actual evolution and derivation of the material universe. As occultists, we need to have a foot in both the scientific and the religious camps, and realize that our perspective changes the way things are defined but not determined. We also need to understand that something that is a myth is neither false nor based on ignorance. Myths are powerful allegorical symbols that explain our reality in a deeper and more spiritual manner.

These are very important points, since they act as the foundation for understanding and making sense out of occult beliefs and practices, and the way that spiritual and paranormal phenomena appear to function in the material world. What is defined by this perspective is a living, knowing universe, endowed with a meaningful destiny and guided by a unified super intelligence. That stands in stark contrast to the random, soul-less, meaningless, materialized, and autonomous universe that science promotes. We will get a lot deeper into these concepts later on.

Qabalah is a practical methodology that makes itself very useful for the practice of magic and what is called "theurgistic ascension."

What might sound like a complex term simply represents a system of practical magic that allows the practitioner to ascend through the planes of the spirit world and obtain union with the One. We will discuss these concepts in greater detail later on, but one thing you should keep in mind is that the Qabalah has many important practical applications. It isn't just a lot of philosophy or mystical speculation.

Magicians use the Qabalah to fashion sigils, talismans, word formulas, acronyms, and ciphers, and to determine the intrinsic numerological relationship between words and phrases. It is also an occult map of the Inner Planes and a system of correspondences. A practical Qabalist is often, but not always, a practitioner of ritual or ceremonial magic who uses meditation, contemplation, and theurgy to ultimately achieve full and total enlightenment, or at-one-ment, with the Godhead. This is the purpose of the Qabalah, and it is also the purpose of most forms of higher magic as well.

To recap the uses of the Qabalah, we can say that it has the following five functional applications:

- Map or model of the Spirit world
- Meta-system and meta-knowledge system
- Cosmology and cosmogony
- Practical system of correspondences, formulas, acronyms, ciphers, sigils, and numerology
- System of magic, meditation, and contemplation

Now that you know what the Qabalah can be used for, I should further explain its importance and why it is critical that an occultist not only know and understand it but also, over time, even master it.

Importance of the Qabalah

Certainly, you could forgo studying or using the Qabalah, and you would still be able to meditate, contemplate, and even work forms of magic. However, because the Qabalah is a powerful meta-system, it can help you put all of the pieces together. It is a system that can help you organize the various occult systems and religions that you have adopted along with the mystical experiences that you might have had. It can even help you understand other religious systems that you might want to grasp without having to become an adherent. In fact, the Qabalah is one of the few meta-systems available to the practicing occultist. It is not the only meta-system, but it is one of the more common meta-systems currently in use.

There are lots of books written about the Qabalah from any angle you could possibly imagine, and perhaps some even beyond your imagination. All of these books will become immediately accessible to you if you manage to learn the basics first. In other words, having a basic knowledge of the Qabalah opens doors that might not be open to those who lack this knowledge.

Additionally, other occult systems are related to the Qabalah, such as the Tarot, astrology, alchemy, hermetics, magic—the list is almost endless. In short, nearly every occult system in the Western Mystery tradition is affected or touched in some manner by the Qabalah. Even though I was goaded into studying the Qabalah many years ago, I also found references to it, whether direct or oblique, in all of the other occult books and materials that I read and studied.

What might turn some people off to the Qabalah is the assumption that it is somehow deeply intertwined with the Abrahamic faiths, and that it is therefore irrelevant to anyone who is a Pagan or a Witch. Once again, this is proven false by the fact that the Qabalah is a meta-system that means many things to many people; it is not the inherent property of any exclusive religious faith. As an occult system, it is part of the Western spiritual tradition, so it is as much a part of our cultural heritage as rock-and-roll and blue suede shoes. We can engage with the Qabalah on our own terms, since there is no absolute, correct, or proper way to interpret or use this system. It belongs to all of us! All we have to do is to figure out a way of sensibly interpreting it, and then using it.

Some Historical Notes

Examining the history of the Qabalah also shows that it was not just the product of Jewish mystical speculation, although that certainly does represent its earliest expressions. Qabalah has its origins in a kind of occultic and magical speculation that began with the late prophetic book of Ezekiel, wherein the first chapter the prophet writes about his vision of the "Glory of God," which appeared as a fiery heavenly chariot with a throne in its midst. The name for that chariot with a throne placed in its center was "Merkabah," and a lot of speculation was centered on the nature of that divine chariot of God.

Other speculations were centered on the multiple domains of the Palaces of God, such as what was represented in the visionary section of the apocryphal first book of Enoch (known as "1 Enoch"). The palaces with many domains were called the "Haikhalot" (palaces) in Hebrew. This many-tiered palace appeared to be synonymous with the levels of the heavens, and perhaps even of hell. This is similar to the many levels of heaven and hell that Dante later wrote about in his epic poem the *Divine Comedy*. There was also speculation about the very first Hebrew word in Genesis, *Bereshith* ("In the beginning"), which spawned an entire cosmogony.

These topics were considered mystical and also as occult speculation, yet they had, from the very beginning, a practical and magical side, too. In fact, as the Qabalah developed, it also spawned magical traditions and even grimoires (magical how-to books). However, the first real exposition of what would later be called the Qabalah in the 12th century was found in a small book called the "Sepher Yetzirah" (Book of Formation), which was written in Palestine somewhere between the third and sixth centuries CE. This book pulled all of the ideas together about the Merkabah, Haikhalot, and Bereshith mystical speculations and added to it ideas that were imported from Greek philosophy, such as *Neoplatonism* and *Neopythagoreanism*. There were even Jewish Gnostic elements in the founding book of the Qabalah, so it was already by this time becoming a repository of classical and mystical thinking that went far beyond what it had started out to be.

As an aside, the terms that I am using, such as Neo-platonism, Neopythagoreanism, Gnosticism, etc. can be found in the glossary at the back of this book. Any concept that I am presenting which might be obscure or based on a foreign word will be succinctly defined in the glossary.

Qabalah, unfortunately, lends itself to an elaborate nomenclature, and a glossary is a very handy tool to keep everything properly defined.

If we consider the history of the Qabalah, how it evolved, and who was using it, we can find that it went through a number of stages, with different people finding great value from it at different times. From the period of the third century to the 13th century, the Qabalah was built up by individuals who were nominally Jewish occultists, since it continued to gather and harness ideas and speculation that were outside of the mainstream of rabbinic Judaism. It reached its height during the 16th century and later began to experience a period of decline, as scholarly rabbis began to question and reject some of its more unorthodox notions.

In the 16th to 18th centuries, the Qabalah became the focus of European Christians, who took up this discipline and brought it into a secular but Christian discourse, thus melding it with astrology, medicine, cosmology, alchemy, nearly all esoteric speculation, and, of course, ceremonial magic. By the 19th century, science had dropped the study of the Qabalah, but occultists continued to develop it. It was in the late 19th century that the 22 paths were associated with the Tarot, and the Tree of Life got its final rendition, the very one that we are familiar with today. In the 20th century, the Qabalah became fashionable and interesting to mainstream Jews, who picked it up from where the 19th century occultists had taken it.

You could almost compare the Qabalah to a piece of taffy. It started out within one religious domain (Judaism), then it was pulled over to another religious domain (Christianity), then to another (Christian occultism), and now it is being pulled back by some adherents of Judaism while others are pulling it toward Paganism and Witchcraft. After all that pulling back and forth, the original piece of taffy has gotten quite large and wide, not to mention that each group that has mutated it has put their particular stamp on it. In our present postmodern world, the Qabalah is still current, relevant, and in wide use by many different people who have many different spiritual and religious perspectives.

The Qabalah is many things to many people; it can be relevant even to those who are Pagans or Witches. The power of employing this meta-system in your personal religious speculation and magical work makes it a very compelling discipline to study and master. All you have to do is remember that there is more than one Qabalah being studied and used in the world.

Learning the Qabalah is a lot like learning how to drive a car and getting your license. It may seem initially very intimidating and daunting, but not doing it makes one dependent on others or the public transportation system in order to get anywhere, especially for destinations that are too far to walk. You can avoid learning how to drive and thereby find other ways of getting around, or you can learn to master your own "transportation destiny"—the choice is yours, of course.

Similarly, you can learn to master the Qabalah and acquire the symbolic key to all religions, occult systems, and high magic, or you can make do with your own finite domain, perhaps relying on others to help you make sense out of everything that you might experience in your occult practice. All of this seems so limiting when you consider that with just a little bit of your time and some effort you will understand many religions and the occult in a more organized and unified manner.

———

Now I believe I have answered many of the questions about what the Qabalah is, how it is used, and why it is important. I hope that you have a pretty good idea about this subject, and that many of the cobwebs, illusions, and misinformation have been swept aside. In their place we have some pretty solid concepts on which to build our discussion of this supposedly arcane topic.

Are you excited about learning more? Is this topic starting to make sense to you? Do you see why you should learn about the Qabalah? If the answer is yes to these questions, then I have successfully concluded the first chapter. I'm sure you want to know what is in the rest of this book and what we'll be covering in the chapters ahead.

This book is divided into two major parts: in the first part, the basic theoretical parts of the Qabalah are covered; and in the second part, the practical aspects of the Qabalah are revealed. The first part is divided into six chapters; and the second part, which is longer, is divided into nine chapters. There is this introductory chapter, which you are already reading, and the epilogue, which of course comes at the end. The following list contains the chapter headings and contents for Part One and Part Two:

Part One

1. Qabalah in five parts. These are: Ten Sephiroth, 22 paths, Four Worlds and the Four Subtle Bodies, Three Negative Veils, and the Tree of Life.

2. A brief and succinct history of the Qabalah in nine parts. We will also examine the history and development of Jewish literature.

3. Ten Sephiroth, in greater detail.

4. 22 Paths, in greater detail.

5. Creation, Unmanifest Godhead, and the Nature of Evil: A thorough discussion of the creation of the spiritual and material universe, the nature of the unknown and unmanifest Deity, and the nature of evil and the imperfection of the material world.

6. Four Worlds and the Four Subtle Bodies: A presentation of the Four Qabalistic Worlds and the Four Basic Subtle Bodies that are associated with them.

Part Two

7. Practical Qabalah: This part is divided into nine chapters, expounding on the topics of practical exercises, using tables of correspondences, and explanations of Gematria, Notariqon, and Temurah, pathworking, theurgic ascension, and a brief explanation of Qabalistic magic.

8. Epilogue—wrapping it all up.

In addition, there is a glossary defining all of the more important terms used in this book, and a bibliography in which I have listed all of the books that I consulted to write this work. I have also listed some additional books that you might want to read to further your studies in chapter 16, where I talk about how to learn the Qabalah.

So, let's start the journey and begin our grand tour of the venerable Qabalah. You are invited!

Part One

Theoretical Qabalah: Basic Elements

two

Essential Qabalah in Five Parts

In this chapter we will succinctly define the Qabalah, and this will help you to realize that it is not beyond your ability to grasp and use. Often, breaking a topic down into its more essential parts makes it much easier to comprehend than attempting to take in the whole thing. Disassembling this topic doesn't mean that we are going to be leaving it that way, however. I will also show you how all the parts fit together to create a seamless whole. I think that this is the best way to approach any complex topic: to organize and break it down into smaller related parts.

Unfortunately, this chapter is probably the toughest one in the book, since I am going to attempt to establish some precise definitions before actually going over the details of the things I've defined. I felt that it was important to write down these definitions before we get into the details so that they could help you organize and determine the scope of the following chapters. I would recommend that you read over this chapter slowly and carefully.

One other thing that I want to bring up as we delve into the details of the Qabalah is the methodology that I will use to represent Hebrew letters using the English alphabet. At times I will just spell out the words phonetically (in lower case), and other times I will use capital letters to show how the word is spelled in Hebrew.

I felt that it would be easier to dispense with using the iconic Hebrew alphabet for this work since that would force the reader to regularly consult a table of Hebrew to English letters. I have also tried to make certain that my spelling corresponds to what is traditionally found in books on the Qabalah. However, there are some peculiarities that we need to note here.

First of all, there are no vowels in the Hebrew alphabet. Vowels are determined by a system of pointing, or marks, placed on, above, or below the Hebrew letter. So that means that all 22 letters of the Hebrew alphabet are actually consonants. The letter *Aleph* is a glottal stop; the letter *Ain* is a laryngeal (from the larynx) voiced fricative (which I indicate by the letters "a'a," denoting the voiced laryngeal constriction, like in the word *Da'ath*); and the letter *Thav* is an aspirated "t" sound.

Chet is a voiceless laryngeal fricative (not like an English "ch" sound, but more like the Scottish *loch*), and the letter *Vav* can be either a silent vowel holder (for "o" or "u") or similar to the English "v." *Beth* can have a hard "b" sound if at the beginning of a word, or a soft "v" sound when it occurs in the middle of a word, unless it is doubled (indicated with a point placed in the center of the letter, called a *dagesh*). The same is true for the letter *Peh*, which can sound like a "p" or an "f."

The letter *Tzaddi* sounds like an inter-dental aspirated "t," which can be simulated by a combination of a "tz" or "ts" in English. *Qoph* is like the letter *Kaph*, but without the aspiration, so its sound is softer and deeper in the throat. The rest of the letters are similar to the English consonantal sounds. Hebrew is typically spoken with an emphasis on the last syllable.

It is really easy to understand the Qabalah if you can look at it reduced to its most essential parts, and there are only five. Those five parts make up the overall structure of the Qabalah, and they can allow us to view it either as a whole structure or each part separately. These five parts are:

• Ten Sephiroth
• 22 Pathways
• Origin from nothing and the Three Negative Veils
• Four Worlds and the Four Subtle Bodies
• The Tree of Life

All of these concepts and themes have their origin in very specific and strategic verses found in the Old Testament, which is called the Hebrew Bible or the Tenakh. Don't let this revelation turn you off, because the source material, although extracted from the Bible, was greatly modified and joined with ideas that have their origin in

Greek philosophy. From the beginning, the Qabalah has always been a mixture of different metaphysical perspectives, which joined traditional Jewish, Gnostic, and Greek philosophical streams together into a holistic discipline.

Ten Sephiroth, 22 Letters, and Emanationism

First off, the word *Sephiroth* needs some explanation before we get any further into discussing these five basic concepts. This word is written in the plural form based on a feminine noun in Hebrew, where the singular form is *Sephirah*. This word means "number" in Hebrew (not "sphere"), although it isn't the typical Hebrew word used for that word. Hebrew writers would typically use the word *misparim* to denote the word *numbers*.[1] Both *Sephiroth* and *misparim* have the same Hebrew root, which is SPhR (to write, to tell, to count, to number), and for that matter, so does the Hebrew word *sepher* (book). However, the word *Sephirah*, which is atypical, would represent a special or esoteric use of the word for *number*. Therefore, the ten Sephiroth are known as the ten special numbers through which the structure of the world was created.

The use of the Decade as a mystical concept of creation was likely derived from Greek philosophy—most notably, from the teachings of Pythagoras, although there are other native Jewish sources as well.[2] The number ten is important simply because the two human hands together have ten fin-

---

1. Gershom Scholem, *Kabbalah*, 23.
2. Scholem, *Kabbalah*, 21.

gers. It is, therefore, a universal system for human numeration. One of the earliest counting systems was based on ten, and the number ten became associated with the ideas of *completeness* and *wholeness*. So having ten Sephiroth could be construed as possessing a set of numbers that was complete and represented the source of all other numbers and numeration in general.

In addition to the ten numbers, there are also 22 letters, which are the letters of the Hebrew alphabet. According to early Jewish sources (Sepher Yetzirah), the 22 Hebrew letters were used to formulate the material world, since to them, a word is a powerful symbol of the thing it represents; through that symbol, a material thing can be made manifest. So numbers (geometry) and letters (words of power) were used by the Godhead to create the material and spiritual worlds. They represent an integral part of the Qabalah and the source of everything that exists. Creation is often depicted as occurring through a process called *emanation* (to issue from a source), which was a term coined in Greek philosophic circles in late antiquity. The first emanation was called the One, or the Monad, since it represented the first thing that was manifested in the mysterious process of creation.

The basic premise of creation, as found in the Qabalah, is that the Monad, through its innate desire to create, caused a series of emanations[3] to occur that evolved in waves, manifesting as the spiritual and material worlds. This method of creation, from highest to lowest, is a process called *involution*, which is a word representing that the

---

3. R. T. Wallis, *Neoplatonism*, pages 61–65.

highest form as Spirit came to reside in a lower form (mind and body). The corresponding ascent by individuals to the One would be considered *evolution*. Thus, creation happened, beginning from the most abstract state of being (as the One), then on down to the plurality of spirits and material forms that exist in our world today.

This process of emanation was grouped together into three levels consisting of dialectic triads, in which the final emanation, as the material universe, became the tenth point and also the fourth level. A dialectic triad is the basic philosophic foundation for determining anything, consisting of thesis, antithesis, and synthesis. A harmonious union between two opposing ideas is found in a third, which blends the previous two together; this is the nature of how everything was created in the Qabalah. These dialectic triads are found repeated in each level of Spirit, Mind, and Soul, and they are called the Sephiroth. The tenth point, which represents the level of the material universe but is not represented by a triad, is also one of the Sephiroth. It exists below, alone, and by itself, in emulation of the One. You could say that the One is reflected in the Many because the lowest level of material existence is modeled on the Monad itself (see figure 1).

Emanation has the mysterious quality of being continuous because it is not limited by either space or time, which means that it occurs simultaneously and everywhere at once. Even though the process of creation through emanation appears continuous, there are still strategic barriers or veils that come between the levels of Spirit and Mind. These barriers are known as the Greater Abyss, which acts

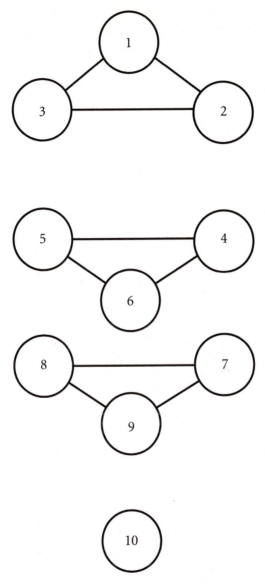

Figure 1: Simple diagram of the Tree of Life

as a chasm between the Spirit and the Mind, and the Lesser Abyss, which acts as a wall between the Mind and the Soul. The Greater Abyss is more notable than that Lesser Abyss because it represents a more formidable gap between states. Yet these barriers are paradoxical in that they exist for those individual spirits seeking ascension and reunification with the One, but don't impair emanations descending from the One. It is for this reason that they are called a *ring pass-not*, because they allow emanations to pass through, but deflect the ascension of souls. So they are temporary barriers relating specifically to the state of one's conscious development.

We can easily recognize in the Sephiroth, as depicted by the progression of numbers from 1 to 10, a kind of mathematically ordered sequence that extends from the One to the Many. Each recognizable stage functions as a lower order copy of the previous higher level, with its overall structure and essential integrity having been inherited from its predecessor. Some have called this progression the *Great Chain of Being*, and it is just another way of labeling this process.

Examining the ten Sephiroth, we can see the influences of Neopythagorean and Stoic philosophies.[4] Neopythagoreans mixed up Pythagoras's concept of divine numbers with Plato's concept of ideals, so that pure numbers were equated as the thoughts (ideals) of the Godhead. In addition, emanation occurred as a mathematical process, in which numbers, as pure ideals, emerged in a gradation of divine forms through a process of sacred geometry. Only in the final expression did matter become built up through a condensation of those ideals. So the idea of numbers

---

4. Scholem, *Kabbalah*, 26.

being involved in the act of creation through emanation can be seen to have its origin in Pythagorean philosophy. This would particularly include the theory of binary opposites and their resultant union in a harmonious third (dialectic triads), which is a result of the perfect union of the pair. These syzygies, which is derived from a philosophical term *syzygy* that means "pairs of opposites," are shown to exist as three pairs in the planes of Spirit, Mind, and Soul, each with a mediating offspring as the resultant third, and this formulation was an apparent deliberate adaptation of Greek mathematical philosophy.

The concept of emanationism was not new when the early Qabalists first used it. The Neoplatonists in the third and fourth centuries had fully developed this idea. It was taken on by Gnostics of the same or later period and used to produce a very elaborate system of emanations. Gnosticism was an early form of religious occultism that practiced techniques to acquire a secret or divine knowledge, which they called *gnosis* (intuitive wisdom). All this occurred two to three centuries before the writing of the first definitive book of the Qabalah, called the Sepher Yetzirah.

But whatever the form, emanationism as a concept denotes a process that could be imagined as waves flowing forth from a perfect source, circling in ever-widening circuits or spheres of lesser incarnations and then, ultimately, returning to itself.

One additional point that I need to make is that in this process of creation, the higher level does not lose any of its powers or become in any way diluted by the process of creating a lower form. It, in fact, remains intact, isolated, and perfectly whole. This is not to say that the higher level is unaware of its product. It is indeed very much aware of it, but it doesn't need to engage with that lower level in order for it to be fully alive and uniquely self-aware. So there are ten Sephiroth or numbers representing this progression from the One to the Many, and these ten stages could be considered the attributes of the One, or the Deity, which is how they are perceived in the Qabalah.

Monism and Creation

Those who are Pagans will doubtlessly point to the concept of the "One" and say that it represents a kind of monotheism or monism that is alien to modern Pagan perspectives. If you are an ardent polytheist, then the concept of a single universal Godhead would be antithetical to your beliefs. Yet the whole concept of Deity is really complex, and in fact it is paradoxical. What do I mean when I say that Deity is paradoxical? Let me explain.

It is quite possible to speak of a Deity as being a finite individual with a known set of characteristics. Often one of these characteristics is gender, since the Deity is known to be masculine or feminine, or have some kind of bias in one direction or another. A gendered Deity can also be compared or made relative to either the archetypal masculine or feminine aspects of Deity based solely on the criterion of gender. Proposing a duo-theological pair of God and Goddess (such as in Wicca) ultimately leads one to the idea of their joining, where they form a union that is greater than themselves, which I would call the One. In some circles of Witchcraft, this Unity is referred to as the Dryghton of ancient provenance.

If we admit that the nature of Deity is paradoxical, then that would make perceiving a distinct god or goddess, a collective god or goddess, or the union of all as the One as simply variations of the same thing—a situation in which they would be coexistent within the mutual concept of the Godhead. Even holding a non-polarized perspective of Deity, such as in animism, would do nothing more than collectively emulate that union where all polarities are ultimately joined together. Additionally, all of these diverse and different ideas about Deity are readily dealt with and easily conceptualized in the Qabalah. So the Qabalah verifies that all of the world's religions and their concepts of Deity are simultaneously valid, authentic, and correct.

The Monad, which is the first thing that manifests, also has a source, and this is where the authors of the Qabalah discussed the mysterious creation of the One from that which is nothing. This is a difficult concept to address, and we will return later to discuss it in greater detail (chapter 6). The Jews believed in a concept of Deity that was unnamed, unknowable, and invisible (not manifest), and it was this unmanifested Deity that was the original source of all that was created, including the One.

Thus the One, although apparently self-begotten and self-determined, had as its mysterious source a triple pre-existing nothingness, called the Three Negative Veils, which were named *Ein* (Nothing), *Ein Sof* (Limitless Nothing), and *Ein Sof Aur* (Limitless Light). The creation of the One from nothing is a controversial occult concept, and certainly one that has been disputed by the hard sciences until very recently. The Three Negative Veils enshroud the One and its products, and they exist as the mysterious and ineffable source that is also nothingness.

While the ten numbers were involved in the creation of everything through the power of the emanation of the One, the 22 letters of the Hebrew alphabet represent the *Pathways* where evolved (individuated) beings may return back to the One. Since these letters are the very devices with which holy scriptures, such as the Hebrew Bible, were written, it is believed that they contain the secret knowledge and the power of creation, and they can also aid in the reunification of individual souls with the One. Some believe that the holy scriptures were actually directly written by the mind of the One for the express enrichment and enlightenment of the many; others believe that they were inspired works written by people.

Therefore, the 22 Pathways are the means through which the holy seeker is able to slowly and spiritually evolve through a process of transformative initiation. Whereas the emanation of the divine numbers is symbolized by the lightning bolt that falls from heaven to earth, the circuitous path of the 22 letters, returning through all of the divine numbers to the One, is symbolized by a great serpent. One major change that the occultists of the 19th century made to the Qabalah was to associate the 22 trumps of the Tarot with the 22 Pathways. This association was actually quite brilliant, and became one of the many contributions that the Golden Dawn (a magical order of late-19th-century Britain) made to the modern occult revival.

Four Worlds and the Four Bodies

In addition to the ten numbers and 22 letters, there are also the Four Worlds. These Four Worlds represent the larger stages of emanation, which can be perceived as consisting of the groupings of the ten numbers or Sephiroth in triadic forms, with the tenth hanging down below. They can also be seen as entire worlds, where each contains their own expression of the ten Sephiroth. Either approach is meaningful, but most Qabalists believe that the Four Worlds are distinct.

These Four Worlds can be seen as representing separate planes of being, where the highest is the plane of the Absolute or World of Emanations; the next is the plane of archetypal meanings; the third is the plane of Mind (Thought) or the World of Formation; and the final is the plane of Matter or World of Action. In some systems of occultism, the four Trees are seen as four distinct levels of being, such as mineral, vegetable, animal, and human, each with its own cycle of involution and evolution. This is a system proposed by the French occultist Jean Dubuis in his works on Qabalah and spagyric alchemy. Variations on this theme can be found in other European occult systems as well.

We can also see the Four Worlds as representing the four elements, where the absolute plane is Fire, Archetypal plane is Water, Mental plane is Air, and the Material plane is Earth. From this association of element to world, one could assume that the progression of the four elements occurred in this sequence. Yet to avoid any additional confusion, the Jewish Qabalists (based on the Sepher Yetzirah) saw the progression of the four elements to be the same as the creation of the first four Sephirah. Therefore, the Monad was considered to be analogous to Spirit, and they referred to it using the Hebrew word for spirit, *Ruach*, which also means "breath."

From Spirit emerged the second Sephirah, which was Air, and this element was thought to be the primal element because it was formless and invisible like the creator. Then Air begat Water and Fire, and the first four Sephiroth were thus made manifest. The primal element of Air created the 22 letters, Water created the cosmos, and Fire created the Throne of Glory and the hosts of the angels. The 22 letters were then used to create all material things. This progression of the four elements is quite different from what I just wrote above, and it remains one of the paradoxes associated with them. Both perspectives could be considered correct and accurate as long as one uses them consistently.

The ten numbers or Sephiroth are also projected through the Four Worlds, producing a kind of graduated spectrum where each Sephirah is defined as being encapsulated by each one of the worlds. You can imagine this concept as a Tree of Life structure existing in each of the Four Worlds, or where each Sephirah of the Tree of Life is divided into four levels. The keywords for these Four Worlds are emanation, creation, formation, and action. (See figure 2.)

Because the ten Sephiroth are projected through the Four Worlds, they leave an imprint upon each world. What this does is to produce a total of 40 Sephiroth. If that seems a trifle bit much, you could also consider that the 22 Pathways could also be projected through the Four Worlds, producing 88 total Pathways. Add that number to the 40 Sephiroth, and we are talking about a total of 128 correspondences! Thank-

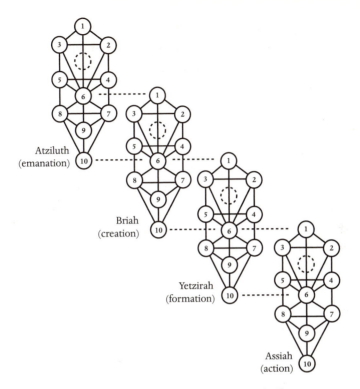

Figure 2: Four Worlds and the Tree of Life

fully, according to the Qabalists, we are only capable of comprehending the 32 correspondences (10 Sephiroth and 22 Pathways) of the lowest world of the Material plane. So that is where we will focus our work.

As you can see, this comprehensible limitation represents the extent of the supposed chasm that exists between us and the Absolute Spirit in terms of levels of conscious evolution. But within each human being is also a godlike entity, and that God/dess within is the primary means to commune and connect with the Source of All. This brings us to our next topic, which consists of the Four Subtle Bodies.

Since there are Four Worlds, it would seem only natural that there should also be Four Subtle Bodies operating in every human being. The Four Subtle Bodies are similar to the Four Worlds, except that the Subtle Bodies are a miniature version of the four cosmic worlds. The difference between them is said to be the difference between what the Qabalists call the *macrocosm* and the *microcosm*, which are completely distinct levels of being; one is on a cosmic level and the other is on the same level as individual beings. Often, Qabalists will elaborate on the number of Subtle Bodies, increasing their number to seven or even 11, but for our purposes, there are just four.

A person's Godhead is called, in Hebrew, the *Yechidah*, and it represents that aspect of Deity which lives inside of us. Think of it as our link to the absolute plane. The next level is the human spirit, which is called *Neschamah*, or intuitive self. The mind is called the *Ruach* (vital animating force) and the emotional body is called the *Nephesh*. These Four Subtle Bodies are relative to the Four Worlds. We will not only examine them in greater detail, but we will also learn how to sense and realize these Subtle Bodies using specific meditation techniques and bodily focus points called *chakras* by the Eastern traditions.

Tree of Life

A succinct device that integrates the ten Sephiroth, the 22 Pathways, the Three Negative Veils, and the Four Worlds together into a single structural design is called the *Tree of*

Life. This model is sometimes called a *glyph*, since it is like a letter or character; it has an intrinsic shape and design, which has a specific meaning.

Legend tells us that the current Tree of Life was originally designed by Moses Cordovero in the mid-16th century, and in fact he supposedly came up with more than one version. That is why if you study the Qabalah from Jewish sources, you might notice a version of the Tree of Life that is somewhat different from the one typically found in modern occult books.

We will get into the details of these versions and what they mean later on, but keep in mind that the Tree of Life is only a model of what all of these Qabalistic elements might look like if they were presented in a unified form. We should never confuse a model for what it represents, just as we should never confuse a map for the specific territory that it is symbolically depicting (see figure 3).

The usefulness of the model of the Tree of Life is that it is able to encapsulate all of the five elements of the Qabalah. It can also be used as a map for the mysterious Inner Planes, that place where spirits and aspects of the Deity reside. We can use the Tree of Life to ascend and descend the four planes of being, and also to understand how thought becomes form and form becomes thought—or how a symbol translates into a material object, and vice versa.

Knowing this secret will aid us in attaining ascension to the One and how to manifest our desires into physical reality. We can also imagine the Tree of Life superimposed on our bodies to help us master our own personal spiritual and magical dimensions. So the Tree of Life is a very

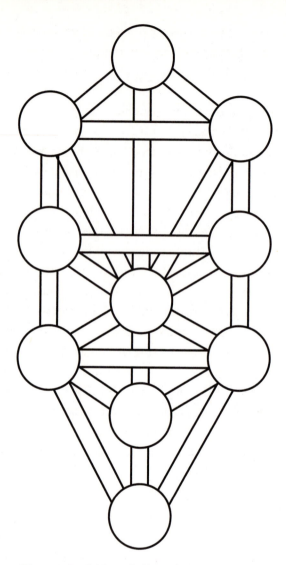

Figure 3: Basic Tree of Life, including Pathways

important and useful tool. In fact, it can be the only actual tool that the Qabalistic magician possesses.

————

We have now covered the five essential parts of the Qabalah, and except for a few mind-bending explanations on creation, emanation, and the origin of everything within nothing, I am hopeful that you have found this chapter comprehensible. Once you break something down into its basic elements, it is pretty easy to understand. The rest of the first part of the book will be spent explaining these five essential parts in greater detail.

Still, I wanted to expand on the topic of the usefulness of the Qabalah and explain what I meant previously by calling it a meta-system, or that it contains meta-knowledge. I think a few other points should also be made to explain what the Qabalah actually contains with regard to its practical application and why it is important for occultists to master. Some of this has been covered in the first chapter, but not to the level of detail that I think any serious student should know. I may have convinced you to read the rest of this book, but I need to show you just how ingenious and important the Qabalah really is.

Defining a Meta-System and Meta-Knowledge

My focus for this section is really about the nature of a meta-system and meta-knowledge as they pertain to occultism. Defining these two terms will also show how the Qabalah is able to function and what any other replacement system must contain in order to be as effective. As a beginner, I am certain that you have no interest or desire whatsoever in fashioning a replacement for the Qabalah. In fact, you might not be convinced that it is either important or even useful. So I will focus on just the essentials of the definitions and not get any deeper than that.

Some of the concepts that I am going to use to define the Qabalah might be a bit difficult to understand, and they might even include elements that we haven't yet covered. If I happen to discuss anything in this section that is unfamiliar to you, then all I ask is that you persevere and move forward for now. You can look up unfamiliar terms in the glossary located in the back of this book. I promise that they will be covered with enough detail for this discussion to make perfect sense to you when you have completed reading this book.

First, I want to tell you there are some very compelling reasons why I value and use the Qabalah. I would like to precisely define the function of the Qabalah to show you why it is good enough just the way it is. Still, the basic foundation for the Qabalah is language, particularly the mysticism of letters and numbers, and their interchangeability in strategic words and phrases.

The Jewish Qabalah has as its foundation the Hebrew language—specifically, Classical or Biblical Hebrew. The reason for using Hebrew is simple: the Qabalah is vested in the sacred scriptures of the Hebrew Bible. Recently, some occultists (beginning with Aleister Crowley) have shown that the Hebrew language can be substituted with any other sacred tongue. That might be wonderful for someone who has an advanced knowledge of the Qabalah and a facility for languages, but anyone who might attempt this task should be aware that there is an important factor associated with choosing a replacement language.

A replacement language for Classical Hebrew should be based on some kind of body of sacred writings that would give it certain mystical and occult affiliations. As I have already pointed out, the numbers 10 and 22 are still important to the Tree of Life model, so any alphabet that has more than 22 letters would have to be somehow accommodated.

Therefore, we can add Greek, Egyptian (Coptic), Arabic, and even Latin, Sanskrit, and English to the range of possible foundational languages used to build a different Qabalah. Once we depart from the dual structures of the ten Sephiroth and 22 Pathways to facilitate building a system with an alphabet, we would then have to change the structure of the Tree of Life itself and even the corresponding number of trumps in the Tarot. So there are built-in limitations if a student wants to fashion a Qabalah using a different alphabet.

Other elements that are found in the Qabalah are a cosmology, cosmogony, occult metaphysics, and the various practices and techniques of the practical Qabalah. Practical methodologies, which we will cover later on, would consist of building tables of correspondences, establishing various spiritual hierarchies, determining the interrelationships of a word-based numerology (called *arithmology* in Greek), and the creation of acronyms, ciphers, and sigils. Some of these practical techniques are not critically important, such as the crafting of acronyms and ciphers, whose usefulness would completely depend on the sophistication and knowledge of the occultist or magician.

I have found all of these practical techniques to be useful and important in my studies at some point, so I would have to completely replace them if I chose to replace the Hebrew Qabalah with something else. I will cover these more sophisticated techniques later in this book (chapters 8 through 16), but for now I want to focus on the nature of a meta-system and meta-knowledge.

What is a *meta-system* and what is *meta-knowledge*? I will admit that I am neither a computer scientist nor a mathematician, so my definitions will not be as precise (nor as confusing) as theirs might be. I will use imprecise words to define these terms as they would be used in defining the nature of the Qabalah. Besides, it helps to keep things simple.

A meta-system is a system that is described by attributes that are themselves abstract objects with their own properties and attributes. The interrelationship between these attributes would form what is loosely defined as a meta-system. It is, therefore, simply *a system that is used to describe or organize a system*. For instance, we could use the seven planets of antiquity to qualify several of the Sephiroth of the Tree of Life, but those seven planets are independent symbols with their own meaning and context (such as in astrology or planetary magic). This is how a system is used to define a system in the Qabalah.

When you think of a meta-system, you can just conceive of it as a huge filing cabinet filled to capacity with various folders and papers containing a myriad of occult, religious, and mystical symbology from every spiritual sys-

tem in the world. Imagine this massive filing cabinet with
ten drawers, one for each Sephirah, and a folder divider
in each drawer representing the associated Pathways. The
folders in those divisions in each drawer would contain all
of the symbology associated with that Sephirah and its specific Pathways. That is probably the easiest way to imagine
the Qabalah as a meta-system.

This definition, as it applies to the Qabalah, provides
the basis for the tables of correspondences and the ordering of the various attributes around the associated qualities
of the ten Sephiroth and the 22 Pathways, making a series
of tables with at most 32 rows. It could also be applied to
the various hierarchies and lists of spirits and gods, which
would also be included as a subset of the tables of correspondences. The tables can also be reduced to focus on just
the ten Sephiroth, or attributes of the four elements, seven
planets, or 12 signs of the zodiac.

Meta-knowledge is defined roughly as information
about information, including the added dimensions that we
should consider: (1) it has a structural organization (modeling and organizing); and (2) it is a way of defining specific
attributes (called *tagging*). Applying this to the metaphor of
the filing cabinet, you can think of tagging as putting labels
on the various folders and organizing them in some kind of
overall sequence. The methodology used for the tagging and
organizing would be called the meta-knowledge of the Qabalistic meta-system.

Additionally, this definition would specifically show
how the model of the Tree of Life relates to the various
attributes associated with the Sephiroth and Pathways,

and also how it could be organized into relationships and attribute qualifiers. Relationships would be specifically the interconnectivity of Paths and Sephiroth on the Tree of Life. Attribute qualifiers are all of the symbols that are grouped with these Pathways and Sephiroth, giving them greater meaning than they would otherwise possess. So there are two ways to represent these inherent qualities of the Qabalah: the glyph of the Tree of Life and the tables of correspondences (as the big filing cabinet).

The model of the Tree of Life also establishes a spiritual hierarchy and organizes the attributes of the Sephiroth and Pathways, showing the extent and the limitation of their interrelationships. (Not all Sephiroth are connected to each other with Pathways, and the Pathways represent specific qualities associated with the Sephiroth that they connect.) The quality of tagging is to be found in the associations that match meta-data (planets, elements, signs of the zodiac, etc.) to the Sephiroth and Pathways, so it is shown in both the Tree of Life and the tables of correspondences.

A key concept here, and one that is probably the most important point of all, is that the Qabalah is not just a bunch of lists or an interesting-looking glyph. The Qabalah encapsulates symbols, and these symbols are either religious or occultic in nature, or both. Symbols should not be confused with signs, which is a common mistake that we all make. Signs are representative; they are, in fact, simple placeholders, like a stop sign or a railroad-crossing sign. On the other hand, symbols such as the Wiccan pentacle, the Christian Calvary cross, or the Jewish hexagram called the Magen (Shield of) David are dynamic living processes or functions.

Symbols are conscious markers for deep-level psychic processes that are transcendental and transpersonal, and, I might add, usually mysterious to most people. Focusing on symbols can give one access to deeper layers of meaning and collective significance. Sources of symbols are numinous, archaic, and inexplicable. With these concepts in mind, we can say something about the collective symbolism of the Qabalah, which contains the symbology of all the religions of the world. The religious symbology of the Qabalah is a living, breathing aggregation of functions, almost like a living body itself.

To access the Qabalah, we need only to access the various symbols of the Qabalah, and we do that through the techniques of meditation, contemplation, pathworking, and various forms of theurgy. This methodology of accessing the symbols of the Qabalah is called the practical Qabalah, and it makes the symbology come alive in our minds. Also, if we accept that the symbolism of the Qabalah is alive, then even organizing these symbols into groups or structures, such as the Tree of Life, will have an unintended and powerful effect.

Therefore, the functional qualities of the Qabalah (such as the definition by attributes and organizing information as a model with specific attribute tagging) would be defined by the terms *meta-system* and *meta-knowledge*. These two concepts are the most important aspects in determining the value of the Qabalah, and they would also function as important qualities for any system that would be used to replace it. A replacement system would have to have the following six elements:

- Stages or phases of emanation (analogous to the Sephiroth) based on pure number
- Alphabetic system of interrelationships (analogous to the Pathways)
- A glyph or symbolic model depicting the structure of the emanations and Pathways along with an implied hierarchy and interrelationships
- Foundational language—typically a sacred tongue of some kind
- Spiritual hierarchy
- Various tables of correspondences—important occult attributes and their associated tags

In addition to the above list of elements, a meta-system and meta-knowledge would be used to determine a cosmology and cosmogony, produce a structure of the inner spiritual planes, and aid the occultist to define a kind of esoteric epistemology (nature and scope of knowledge) and ontology (nature of reality). It would also define the relationship between the ultimate Godhead as the One, and individual human beings as the Many.

Emanation and evolution are both implied by this hierarchy as well as by the definition of the macrocosm and the microcosm. This structure is also recursive, since the glyph of the Tree of Life applies to the cosmic emanations of the Godhead as well as to the psycho-spiritual structure of individual human beings. I would also include the Four Worlds as representing a more direct model of the groupings or structures of the Inner Planes.

More specifically, a system of the Qabalah would also function under the theorem that mind existed before matter. Therefore, if one were to omit using the Qabalah, then some of these qualities would have to be determined using some other kind of philosophical mechanism. Thankfully, we won't attempt such a massive enterprise.

Summary

We have broken down the Qabalah into five distinct elements and have briefly covered each one. Yet there is much more detailed information associated with them. I will therefore be presenting a more detailed presentation on each of these elements in the later chapters of this book. To really understand the Qabalah, we need to examine each of the ten Sephiroth, the 22 Pathways, the Three Negative Veils, and how creation occurred, as well as discuss the nature of the Four Worlds and the Four Subtle Bodies and how all of these elements fit together to form the Tree of Life.

The mysterious process of creation has also been discussed, and I have shown that the underlying forces set forth by the Monad are called emanation (involution) and evolution. Emanation is the mechanism of creation, where a unique unified source dispassionately replicates itself into a lower order. Evolution is the methodology through which individual spirits ascend and ultimately achieve union with the One.

We also examined probably one of the most difficult topics in the study of the Qabalah, and that is its fundamental definition, which we have compared to a meta-system and meta-knowledge. A meta-system is nothing more than a system that describes a system. That definition is succinctly stated as:

A meta-system is a system that is described by attributes that are themselves abstract objects with their own properties and attributes.

Qabalah is a meta-system because the elements that are used to describe its various qualities are themselves defined as parts or attributes of another system. Therefore, the Qabalah appears to pull other distinct systems together into itself—such as elements, planets, astrological signs, and many other qualities. We compared this to a huge filing cabinet, which has ten drawers, inner-drawer dividers, and uses a specific methodology for organizing and labeling the folders, dividers, and drawers.

We also examined the definition of meta-knowledge, which is simply information about information. It is a methodology for organizing and identifying information (tagging). The Tree of Life is a perfect example of how meta-knowledge is established and ordered in an occult system.

A couple of other words to be used during the discussion are *meta-data* and *meta-hierarchy*. Meta-data is a specific description (or set of descriptions) about a certain data element. Meta-data defines the type or class of data (planets, elements, signs of the zodiac, etc.), and it also defines the relationship between these various elements to the Qabalah. A meta-hierarchy is a hierarchy that pulls other unique and distinct hierarchies together into a single larger hierarchy. Such a meta-hierarchy is found in the combination of the ten Sephiroth and the Four Worlds, where different classes of spirits are associated with each level and Sephirah combination.

These definitions help to thoroughly define the nature of the Qabalah. They also define what would be required if someone were ambitious (or crazy) enough to attempt to replace it with another system. I have provided a list of six elements that are essential to a functioning Qabalah, and I have also shown how many different attributes can be linked to the Qabalah through tables of correspondences.

We will be revisiting all of these various concepts again in the later chapters of this book, so if some of them seem a little vague, they will become very familiar as we examine the numerous details of the Qabalah. It might even be helpful if you were to re-read this chapter once you have completed digesting the whole book. I suspect you will then find that these concepts are much clearer and perhaps even quite obvious.

A Brief History of the Qabalah

Before we get too far into the details of the Qabalah, we should examine its history and learn how this system was invented and evolved over time. History can be a very dry subject and often seems not very relevant to an occult topic. Yet the Qabalah is steeped in history, and knowing that history will help you understand the *why* and the *how* of the present-day Qabalah. Knowing the historical evolution of the Qabalah will help you to accurately realize the basic elements of the Qabalah, and that is why we are taking this historical tour.

We begin our story well before the time of Christianity, so for the dating regimen I will use the historical notation of

BCE, and forward from that point in time, CE. Most modern historians don't use the typical BC and AD notations, and neither will I. Legends tell us that the Qabalah was given to Moses when he received the Ten Commandments, or that Adam was taught the Qabalah by either God or his angels. However, the real history is that the Qabalah was invented by human ingenuity over the course of two thousand years.

Qabalah is a system of thought that has a long history, whose roots exist contemporaneously with some of the later books of the Old Testament and the early Palestinian Talmud. When we examine the evolving timeline of the Qabalah, we'll get a better idea about how much this system has actually changed through the centuries.

Sources for the Qabalah are found from an early period, perhaps as early as the seventh century BCE, when various forms of mystical speculation attempted to fill in the blanks that were not part of the Jerusalem sacrificial cult. Certain themes from the scriptures lent themselves to this kind of speculation, such as the magical creation of the world and the various mysteriously recurring manifestations of an unnamed and unknowable Godhead. These speculations occurred centuries before the books of the Hebrew Bible were assembled and made into an authorized religious canon.

Yet the first major milestone in time was when the book called the Sepher Yetzirah was written, which was likely in the Galilee area in the third to sixth century CE. The time of the origin for that book has already been determined by historians, although definitive evidence is lacking. Then sometime after the inauguration of that first milestone, this body of lore was taken to Babylonia in the seventh century, and then, later in the early Middle Ages, to Italy, Germany, and the Provence region of southern France, where it acquired the name of *Qabalah* in the 12th century.

Adherents of the Qabalah migrated to Moorish Spain because it was a friendlier environment and, once there, the Qabalah truly flowered. European, and then Palestinian, Jews later adopted and promoted the Qabalah after they were expelled from Catholic Spain. They spread it throughout Europe, where it reached its peak in the 17th century. It was through the writings and teachings of Isaac Luria (16th century) that the Qabalah came to its place of ascent and universal acceptance; after that, it began to decline.

Yet even as the Qabalah declined in Jewish circles, it underwent resurgence within various Christian intellectual circles, until the late 18th century when it changed hands with Christian occultists, who brought it into a distinctly occult formulation in the 19th century.

Dion Fortune and her group, as well as the Golden Dawn (Mathers and Westcott), Aleister Crowley, and Israel Regardie, added their particular stamp to this body of lore. Occultists have continued to work with it, and it has also recently found resurgence in some Jewish circles as well.

The history of the Qabalah has been researched and brilliantly corroborated by the late Gershom Scholem in his wonderful book *Kabbalah.* I am deeply indebted to the writings of Gershom Sholem, who was one of the few great academic historians on Jewish history and also one of the first to explain the origins of the Qabalah. Unlike many authors, Scholem has admitted that the Qabalah and its various antecedents were employed in occult and magical practices from the very beginning, and that only later were such practices disassociated from the main body of mystical speculation. A useful quote from his book, found in the introduction, sets the whole tone of his rather straightforward work:

> *From the beginning of its development, the Kabbalah embraced an esotericism closely akin to the spirit of Gnosticism, one which was not restricted to instruction in the mystical path but also included ideas on cosmology, angelology, and magic. Only later, and as a result of contact with medieval Jewish philosophy, the Kabbalah became a Jewish 'mystical theology,' more or less systematically elaborated. This process brought about a separation of the mystical, speculative elements from the occult and especially magical elements, a divergence that at times was distinct but was never total.*[5]

This divergence, according to Scholem, produced two opposing but not completely distinct disciplines, one based wholly on speculation (Qabalah *Iyyunit*) and its associated mystical practices such as meditation and contemplation, and another based wholly on practical or magical techniques (Qabalah *Ma'asit*). Those who pursued the practical applications were concerned with determining the names of angels and Godhead attributes, and they promoted occult methods of theurgy, practical spell work, and Goetic (demonic) magic.

---

5. Scholem, *Kabbalah*, 5.

These two disciplines diverged probably sometime around the 14th century, so, before that time, magic and theurgy played an important part in the formation and development of the Qabalah. That Scholem admits the primacy and importance of magical practices and occult speculation to the formation of the Qabalah appears to be quite unique, since many other authors seem to either deny this possibility or to denigrate the obvious practical applications of the Qabalah as a divergent and unimportant later development.

The fact that historians have any clue about the evolution of the Qabalah is due primarily to the voluminous literature that was produced over the centuries. That literature can also be condensed down to several strategic manuscripts, books, and authors representing specific milestones in the development of the Qabalah. The origins of the Qabalah are veiled in speculation and conjecture, but the appearance of these manuscripts and books gives a credible timeline for its development.

We know that by the time the first in a long series of manuscripts was written and disseminated (i.e., the Sepher Yetzirah), the various ideas and concepts of the Qabalah had already achieved a certain level of maturity and refinement. This fact reveals that the Qabalah had already been undergoing many centuries of development before this first milestone was achieved. In fact, it would seem that the Qabalists were attempting to legitimize their knowledge by producing their own versions of this literature.

What seemed to have been taking place was a kind of shadow process in which various Qabalists sought to mimic what was being done by various Jewish rabbinical schools.

In order to understand the evolution of the Qabalah, we need to first document the evolution and development of Jewish biblical literature, since it would seem that the two are linked.

Jewish Biblical Literature

In order to proceed with developing a history of the Qabalah, let us first examine the corresponding history of the Hebrew Bible and Jewish biblical literature. I will define terms such as *Midrash*, *Mishnah*, and *Torah* and demonstrate that Qabalists used these works as models for developing the Qabalah.

The Hebrew Bible is called the *Tenakh*, and it consists of three essential parts.[6] The first and most important part is called the *Torah*, which means "instruction." The Torah contains the first five books of the Hebrew Bible: Genesis, Exodus, Leviticus, Numbers, and Deuteronomy. The second part, in sequential order, is called the *Khetuvim*, which are the lesser books, such as the Psalms, Proverbs, Job, Song of Songs, Ruth, and others, and the third part is called the *Nevi'im*, which are the books of the Prophets, including Joshua, Kings, and Judges. The word *Tenakh* is an acronym for Torah, Nevi'im, and Khetuvim, or TNKh. The canon of the Hebrew Bible was formulated and finalized sometime during the last two centuries BCE, during the Hasmonean kingship.

---

6. See Barry Holtz, ed., *Back to the Sources: Reading the Classical Jewish Texts*, pages 33 and 34, where the Tenakh is discussed, along with its age and component books.

In addition to the Hebrew Bible, there was also a considerable amount of orally transmitted lore regarding various legal considerations, traditions, and even folklore. This oral lore was finally written up after the Bar Kokhba revolt in Judea (132–136 CE), because the religious leaders of the day feared that this knowledge would be lost if it weren't committed to writing. Therefore, a new religious literature was redacted and completed around 200 CE by Judah ha-Nasi and his followers, and it was called the *Mishnah*, which means "repetition" (derived from the verb root ShNH, which means to "study and review"). Many rabbinical scholars worked on the Mishnah, and Judah ha-Nasi was only the last in a long line of multigenerational scholars, called the *Tannaim*, or teachers.

Once the Mishnah was committed to writing, there were many comments and additional considerations that began to be associated with it, and these were compiled into another book, called the *Gemara*, which consisted of writings that presented a deeper and more thorough analysis of the contents of the Mishnah. The combination of the Mishnah and the Gemara was called the *Talmud*, which also contained a lot of historical information and footnotes about the associated scholarship (annotations, controversies, and arguments) that went into the canonization of the Tenakh and the final formulation of the Mishnah.

Rabbinical scholars of the Gemara were called the *Amoraim*, which means "those who say or tell about [the Laws]." Additionally, there were two Talmuds that were developed: the first in Palestine, which was called the Jerusalem Talmud, and the second in Babylon, which was appropriately called the Babylonian Talmud. Of these two Talmuds, only the Babylonian is complete, while nearly half of the Jerusalem Talmud was supposedly lost.

———

Another important book in the body of Jewish biblical lore that was being developed during the same time frame as the Jerusalem and Babylonian Talmud was the *Midrash*, which means "to investigate or study." The Midrash was a body of written lore that consisted of many homiletic commentaries (sermons) and an in-depth analysis of various passages of the Torah.[7] These textual analyses consisted of two kinds: those that were concerned with Jewish religious law (*halakha*) and those that were concerned with non-legal and homiletic themes (*aggadah*).

Also, the Midrash was not a single book, since it was considered more of a process than a theme developed by a single author. The various books of the Midrash were each focused on a single book of the Tenakh, and these were ultimately grouped together as ten Midrashim called the *Midrash Rabba*, or Great Midrash.

Qabalah was powerfully influenced by strategic verses in the Hebrew Bible. Its tenets were formulated by a religious worldview of Judaism, which was also shared by Christianity and Islam. Despite the fact that the Qabalah was founded in the holy scriptures of the Torah, it also freely incorporated methodologies and philosophic concepts that were alien to biblical teachings: the occult prac-

———

7. Holtz, ed., *Back to the Sources*, 177. The period of development for the Midrash was 400 CE to 1200 CE.

tices and philosophies of the Greco-Roman pagan world. The occultic nature of the Qabalah made it a perfect system and methodology for those who espoused an esoteric or theurgic spiritual perspective, yet it was European occultists who adopted and made it into a modern occult tool.

History of the Qabalah in Nine Phases

After considering the evolution of Jewish biblical literature, we can now determine a historical timeline consisting of nine phases for the development of the Qabalah. Each of these phases, except for the first, had a specific literary work representing the ideas, practices, and beliefs current during that period. None of the historians that I have researched have tied the evolution of the Qabalah to specific literary works, but it is implied in all of them, since it is the literary products that these historians have turned to in order to base their conjectures.

It is my theory that as this Jewish biblical literature evolved, so did the corresponding Qabalistic literature. The location and centers for the development of this Jewish biblical literature became the centers for the Qabalah as well. So, during the time when the Jewish rabbis in Palestine were assembling the Mishnah and building up the Jerusalem Talmud, the Qabalists in the same area produced and built up the Sepher Yetzirah. When the focus of religious academia shifted to Babylon and produced the Babylonian Talmud and the Midrash, so too did the Qabalists. Then, when the focus for rabbinic studies moved to Provence and then again to Spain, the centers for Qabalistic development followed suit. At each major location, the Qabalists achieved a literary milestone that produced an additional manuscript (or a series of manuscripts), thereby adding to the lore of the Qabalah.

These nine phases are represented by eight milestone literary creations that profoundly shaped the development of the Qabalah. These works consist of the following list of books or authors: Sepher Yetzirah, *Raza Rabba* (Great Mystery), Sepher Bahir (Book of Illumination), Sepher Zohar (Book of Splendors), the writings of Moses Cordovero and Isaac Luria, *Qabalah Denudada* (Qabalah Unveiled) of Christian Knorr von Rosenroth, *The Mystical Qabalah* by Dion Fortune, and the writings of Dr. Philip S. Berg and Z'ev ben Shimon Halevi. Each of these books and author's writings represents a specific period in the timeline of the Qabalah. I would propose that these stages be grouped in the following manner:

- Esoteric origins (occurring several centuries before the third century CE, Judea)
- Sepher Yetzirah (third–fifth centuries, Judea)
- *Raza Rabba* (sixth–ninth centuries, Babylon during the Talmudic period)
- Sepher Bahir (ninth–11th centuries, Provence)
- Sepher Zohar—Classical Spanish Qabalah (12th–16th centuries, Spain)
- Moses Cordovero and Isaac Luria (mid-16th century, Safed)
- *Qabalah Denudata*—Christian Qabalah (late 17th century, Germany)
- *Mystical Qabalah*—Occult Qabalah (1935, England)

• Berg and Halevi—Jewish resurgence (1970s–1990s, United States)

These nine levels consist of particular periods of development, such as the origins of esotericism (*Merkabah* and *Heikhalot* mysticism), the time of the Sepher Yetzirah and *Qabalah Ma'asit*, then the period of the Talmud, to the time of the classical Spanish Jewish Qabalah, followed by a period of transition during which the Qabalah became the provenance of Christian occultists, and then its final metamorphosis into the modern system used by occultists and modern Jews today. To complete this historical analysis, we should briefly examine each of these periods of the Qabalah. What we will find is that the Qabalah changed over time to become the focus and philosophy of different groups of individuals, some of whom would hardly agree or realize any affinity with those who came after them. (See figure 4.)

Esoteric Origins— Merkabah and Heikhalot Mysticism

The process of expressing an otherwise invisible and unknowable God began to be conceptualized in a mythical and theosophical format. Some scholars believe that the seventh century BCE was the point in time when monotheism began to be formulated in Judaism, while others believe that it was more firmly established after the first exilic period. Regardless of the exact timing, these speculations began to build a body of mystical insights and ideas,

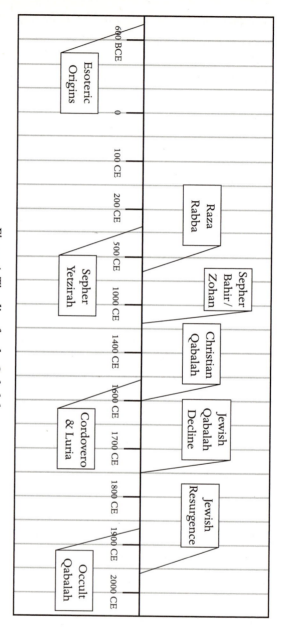

Figure 4: Timeline for the Qabalah

causing the exoteric history and laws of the Jews to become a secret and esoteric universal doctrine.

Perhaps the most striking speculation developed out of one of the more obscure books of the prophets, Ezekiel, who saw a vision of the Throne of God that was placed within a chariot and surrounded by protective angels (Seraphim). One could compare this motif with the Chariot card in the modern Tarot. The Chariot Throne, also known as the *Merkabah*, fueled a great deal of imaginative speculation. So, too, did Jacob's ladder, and the *Bereshith* of Genesis, which produced speculation about the nature of divine creation. (*Bereshith* is Hebrew for "In the beginning" and is part of the first sentence as well as the chapter name of the biblical book of Genesis.)

The *Palaces* of the House of God were as important as the Chariot Throne, known as the *Heikhalot*. Supposedly, there were seven of these palaces arranged in ascending order, which made them analogous to the seven heavens or celestial spheres. The Heikhalot mysticism would play an important role in forming the practical Qabalah, since obtaining access to the various palaces would require ecstatic and magical techniques, and also occult knowledge. The first Book of Enoch has an excellent example of this Heikhalot structure.

A system of detailed exercises was established to produce magical and ecstatic effects used to attain the spiritual state of ascent that would allow a seeker to commune directly with the Deity. It was a sequential process in which the adherent would first access the various Palaces of the House of God, and then he would move on to the very Chariot of God itself. Once these palaces were accessed, he would seek to command spirits through the use of various secret names and seals, and by those same mechanisms, to cast out demons. These practices may be similar to those practiced by the Essenes and other itinerant magical/mystical practitioners.

Most important from this period was the introduction of a body of esoteric literature that discussed in great detail all of the attributes of the various levels of the heavenly palaces (Heikhalot) and the various angelic beings and spirits that reside there, especially their hidden names. Most of these writings exist in a fragmentary form, but one of the most important was the *Reuyot Yehezkel* (Vision of Ezekiel).[8] The main emphasis of these works was not an analysis of the passages found in the scriptures, but they were based instead on actual direct experience with the divine symbols and apparitions of the Godhead.

Examinations of the Bereshith passage, which triggered speculation about cosmology (known as *ma'aseh Bereshith*) and even speculation about the supposed measurements of the various limbs of the mysterious Chariot Driver, are given full expression in esoteric literature. The *Shi'ur Komah*[9] (measuring of the body) was a collection of speculation that sought to measure the *Glory* of the Godhead. It was linked to esoteric interpretations of the biblical book Song of Songs, particularly the descriptions of the beloved, which was called the Body of the Divine Presence (*guf ha-Shekhineh*).[10]

---

8. Joseph Dan, *Kabbalah: A Very Short Introduction*, 15.
9. Scholem, *Kabbalah*, 16.
10. Dan, *Kabbalah: A Very Short Introduction*, 17.

There occurred at this time a blending between the mystical literature of the Merkabah and the Jewish theurgistic literature. The grimoire Sepher Raziel ha-Malach was produced at this time, and it is a prime example of angelic magic based on Heikhalot mysticism, as was the *Harba de Moshe* (Sword of Moses).

Sepher Yetzirah and Qabalah Ma'asit

The advent of the Sepher Yetzirah saw the establishment of the primary concept of 32 emanations with Mystical Names of Power. The practical Qabalah became a system of theurgy based upon an occult epistemology. The influences of Greek Neoplatonic philosophy is apparent in the use of emanationism and represents a borrowing and reinterpreting of both the traditional Hebrew sources and Greek philosophy. Although, according to Scholem, specific Neoplatonic ideas, such as emanationism, deliberately found their way into the Qabalah at a later time.[11] The influences pervading the Sepher Yetzirah would appear to be more associated with Jewish Gnosticism and its incorporation of various Greek philosophical elements and influences, such as the philosophy of Pythagoras.

The Sepher Yetzirah (Book of Formation) is a product of the fulfillment of the esoteric speculation of the *ma'aseh Bereshith* (work of creation), from which it produced a detailed cosmology and cosmogony. It is considered by scholars to be the earliest text that contains detailed and systematic thought on matters that had previously been

---

11. Scholem, *Kabbalah*, 21 and 27.

either unwritten or known only to a select few. As a book, it was brief and concise; yet its influence was to have a massive impact on all subsequent Jewish mystical and occult speculation. Divine wisdom was an important theme for the Sepher Yetzirah, since the creation of the cosmos was evidently accomplished through 32 secret paths of wisdom. These 32 secret paths were defined as consisting of ten numbers and 22 elemental letters, and represented the foundation for all creation.[12]

An important occult and magical concept is implied in the writings of the Sepher Yetzirah. If creation was accomplished through numbers (geometry) and letters (grammar), then the laws of creation would also be the laws of mathematics and language. This idea would have tremendous implications in the application of magic and various occult speculations.

The time period for the origin and composition of the Sepher Yetzirah has been variously given as between the third and sixth centuries CE. The reason for this approximate date is based upon the style of Hebrew that was used to write this book.[13] So the original core manuscript can be attributed to this time period based on the writing style, but other post-Talmudic elements were added later in its evolution. (As of yet, there has been no actual archaeological find that would definitively determine the date of this work.)

---

12. Dan, *Kabbalah: A Very Short Introduction*, 19.
13. Scholem, *Kabbalah*, 26.

Raza Rabba and Talmudic Mysticism

This was a period of great creativity for the Qabalah, but it did not substantively alter the fundamental tenets or produce any new or original doctrines, except perhaps for the invention of Gematria (arithmology). It would seem that the Sepher Yetzirah had become the primary focus for those who espoused a Qabalistic spiritual perspective. Mystical and magical activity shifted from Palestine to Babylonia, but some activity continued in Palestine for some time. Yet in the area of the practical Qabalah and theurgy, a great deal was developed and expanded upon. Practical magic existed side by side with the contemplation on the chariot.

Toward the end of this period, the various sources began to be assembled for the next great leap forward. The book *Raza Rabba* (Great Mystery) appears to have been written at this time, which contained a great deal of magical and occult material. The angelology of this book appears to be a synthesis of an earlier form of Gnostic metaphysics, such as the Aions and the Pleroma (Greek for *Source*). Aions, also called Aeons, and the Pleroma were analogous to the Sephiroth of the Tree of Life. The Pleroma was the totality of the Aions, producing a distinct world that was whole, complete, and separate from the material world. The Greek word *Aion*, which means "time," was promoted as a form of Godhead by Neoplatonists and Gnostics. Three trends can also be traced to this final period of flowering before the center of Qabalistic thought migrated to the West (Italy, Germany, and Provence), and these are the inclusion of Neoplatonism, the transmigration of souls, and the invention of Gematria.[14]

---

14. Scholem, *Kabbalah*, 31.

The transmigration of souls, obviously appropriated from Neoplatonism, was integrated into a Jewish eschatology, and so acquired a distinctly Jewish character. Gematria, and other systems of numerology, were developed to show a link between sacred names, words, and phrases from the scriptures and liturgy; these techniques became known as the theory of names.[15]

Sepher Bahir:
Beginning of the Classical Qabalah

Compared to any period previous to it, this period saw the greatest development of the Qabalah. It was during this period that the Sepher Bahir was assembled and written; the Sepher Zohar was written and disseminated; and the structure of the Tree of Life was determined. Many other elements of the Qabalah that would be recognizable today can trace their origins to this era.

The Sepher Bahir (Book of Illumination) was written as a classical Midrash, and many of its paragraphs began with an attribution to the sayings of a Talmudic sage on a specific passage of the scriptures. Only certain passages were examined in this manner—only those that were pertinent to the Heikhalot and Merkabah mystical speculations, such as the passages from the books of Ezekiel, Song of Songs, and Genesis. In addition, the book analyzed and expounded extensively on various passages of the Sepher Yetzirah, which functioned as the primary source of termi-

---

15. Scholem, *Kabbalah*, 32–33.

nology and inspiration.[16] Much of what had been speculated upon during the Talmudic period found its way into the assembled writings of the Sepher Bahir. This included the newly acquired belief in the transmigration of souls. It is assumed by scholars that the bulk of the development of this book has its origin in the preceding centuries, so that it became a highly specialized and unique expression for synthesizing various Qabalistic beliefs and practices.

———

Three locations became centers of the Qabalah in their time, and these were Provence (11th century to the early 13th century), Spain (12th century to the late 15th century), and Safed in Palestine (16th century). Provence is where the Sepher Bahir was assembled and where the Qabalah was first referred to by its actual name. Provence was also where rabbinic culture achieved a high state of development, and many pagan philosophical works were translated, most notably by Judah ibn Tibben.[17] Many of these translated works were from Neoplatonic sources. It is here that Gnostic speculation was fully wedded with Neoplatonic philosophy within a Jewish mystical framework.

In Spain, there were two different schools of the Qabalah, one centered in Gerona and Toledo, and the other in Castile. These two schools promoted different perspectives in regard to the Qabalah; Gerona and Toledo adopted a more mystical and philosophic perspective, and Castile adopted a more Gnostic, theurgic, and occult perspective.

---

16. Dan, *Kabbalah: A Very Short Introduction*, 22.
17. Scholem, *Kabbalah*, 44.

Gerona (a Catalonian town near Barcelona) was the first location to flower, establishing the basic structure and tenets that became the Classical Qabalah. It was in Gerona that ecstatic tendencies were renewed and propagated.

From this foundational school, two other opposing perspectives began to dominate the practice and teachings of Classical Qabalah. On the one side presided what could be called the rational school of Qabalah (founded by Isaac ibn Latif), whose adherents sought to describe it through a more philosophical and mystical interpretation, removing the obvious occult elements and seeking to use a system of devotion and contemplation to realize its various tenets.

On the other hand, in Castile, the Qabalah was characterized by a school (headed by Isaac ha-Kohen) declaring the opposite perspective, that of Gnostic theosophy, occult speculation, and the deliberate practice of theurgy.[18] It is from this more occult school that the speculations of a Tree of Evil (demonic emanations) began to be developed, which included the creation of a more systematic hierarchy of angelic and demonic spirits, as well as equating the Logos (as found in Greek philosophy) with a new angel called *Metatron*.

Sepher Zohar

The Sepher Zohar (Book of Splendor) was the first successful attempt at producing a Qabalistic Midrash; prior to that great achievement, no one would have dared to have undertaken such an ambitious endeavor. It is apparent that

---

18. Scholem, *Kabbalah*, 52–53.

Moses ben Shem Tov de Leon wrote this monumental work during the period between 1280 and 1286 as an attempt to distill at least two different philosophical schools (Gerona and Castile) into a single unified one, producing a work that merged rational philosophy with Gnostic and occult insights and tenets.[19]

However, even to this day there is some speculation as to who actually wrote this great work. Because this book was characterized as a series of conversations between a rabbi of the Tannaic period (first century CE) named Simeon ben Yochai and his associates, some Qabalists have believed that he was the real author.

This work consisted of a vast multivolume set of homiletics (sermons) on the Torah, and the biblical books Song of Songs, Ruth, and Lamentations. Like the Sepher Bahir, these were not comprehensive commentaries, but instead they focused on strategic passages. However, much of the text of the Torah was examined and commented upon, making it a far greater accomplishment than what had been done previously. The Zohar had the effect of producing a kind of uniquely Jewish mystical-based theology, even though it was also wedded to tenets that were particularly uncanonical.

A few of the most important books of the Zohar can be listed here with a brief description:[20]

- *Midrash ha-Ne'lam* (Esoteric Midrash)—The Esoteric Midrash functions as a subset of the main

---

19. Dan, *Kabbalah: A Very Short Introduction*, 31–32.
20. Scholem, *Kabbalah*, 214, 215, and 217.

Midrash (the first book in the series), and consists of a mixture of short Hebrew and Aramaic expositions on strategic verses in the Tenakh. It includes mostly sections from Genesis, compares the lives of the Prophets to the general fate of humanity, and includes the books of Ruth and the Song of Songs. This book was written mostly in medieval Hebrew and parts of it may have been written before any of the other books.

- *Idra Rabba* (Greater Assembly)—This book consists of a discussion of the mysteries of Adam Kadmon, the primordial and first-created man. The dissertation is conducted by Simeon, with comments and questions inserted by his companions. According to Gershom Scholem, this book is of a superior quality and is the most structured and detailed discourse in the entire Zohar.

- *Idra Zuta* (Lesser Assembly)—This book tells of the death of Simeon ben Yochai and expounds on the closing words to his followers. Scholem has compared this book with a Qabalistic version of the death of Moses. This book was often considered the final book of the Zohar, since it deals with the death of its main protagonist.

- *Heikhalot* (Palaces)—This book expounds on the detailed descriptions of the Seven Palaces in the celestial Garden of Eden. These palaces can be accessed through meditation and prayer, and is the final resting place for the religiously pious after their death. It includes special prayers and the angelology associated with the seven palaces. There is also a brief exposition of the seven palaces of uncleanliness, which would represent the domains of Hell.

Despite its irregularities and peculiar writing style, the Zohar helped overall to bring the Qabalah into the mainstream of Jewish thought. This did not happen immediately, since the Zohar was fragmented for over a hundred years into various books and sections until it was reassembled and made available to Qabalists a few generations after Moses de Leon had passed away in 1305. The Zohar later became an important foundation for the work that was to come. Those who came afterwards owed a great debt to the obscure but daring writings of Moses de Leon and his great masterwork.

Moses Cordovero and Isaac Luria

When the Jews were expelled from Spain in 1492, some of them found their way to Palestine, where they built a new home. Safed in Palestine was the location where some of the greatest Qabalists from this era lived and worked. This is where Moses Cordovero and Isaac Luria lived out their lives, evolving the discipline of the Qabalah from the point where it had been developed in Spain and refining it into a modern religious system. It is here that the Tree of Life glyph was developed, and the problems of creation from nothing and the existence of evil and material imperfection were brilliantly resolved. Most of what we know about the Qabalah today has its origins in the writings of Moses Cordovero and Isaac Luria.

Moses Cordovero

Moses Cordovero (1522–70) was a lifelong resident of Safed in Palestine. Little is known about Cordovero's actual birthplace, but his family likely came from somewhere in Spain, and this is attributable to his family name. Cordovero was something of a remarkably intelligent man, having written his first monumental work when he was only 27 years old. His teachers were Joseph Caro and Solomon Alkabez, but he soon eclipsed them in his mastery of the arcane subject matter of the Qabalah. The great works of the Middle Ages wrought by the Gerona, Castile, and Toledo Qabalistic schools were brought to a whole new level of refinement and synthesis, and one of the leading minds in that work was Moses Cordovero. He wrote two major works, the *Pardes Rimmonim* (Garden of Pomegranates) and the *Elimah Rabbati* (Great Elm). These works were finally published in the 1590s in Cracow, likely promoting and preserving Cordovero's work among the Hassidic communities in Eastern Europe.[21] One can also assume that these works were read and studied by Christian scholars as well.

While Cordovero and his work are well known to scholars of Jewish history, he is little known and unappreciated by occultists. This is likely because his student, Isaac Luria, became so famous that Luria altogether eclipsed him. Luria and his teachings became so popular, in fact, that few outside of the more hardcore adherents of the classical Jewish Qabalah had ever heard of Cordovero. It is also likely, although disputed, that many of Isaac Luria's ideas were based on or taken directly from Cordovero's teachings and

---

21. Scholem, *Kabbalah*, 401–2.

writings. Whereas Luria sought to promote a sensationalized version of the Qabalah, Cordovero was more interested in quietly tackling all of the various different perspectives and speculations in the Spanish Qabalah, and then building a synthesis that united them all into a single doctrine. Cordovero was the great bridge-maker and synthesizer who brought the Qabalah from out of the medieval epoch and into the brilliance of the Renaissance. Cordovero created a speculative Qabalah that had more in common with a philosophical system than a religious creed.

Some of Cordovero's ideas include the notion that the ten Sephiroth acted as a bridge between the Deity and the world, and that the emanations came directly from the Godhead. He tackled and resolved one of the more difficult controversies in the Spanish Qabalah, which revolved around whether the Sephirah were imbued with the substance of the Godhead or were merely instruments, devoid of any of the substance of the Deity. Cordovero determined that both approaches were correct, which meant that the Sephiroth were instruments but they also were imbued with the essence of the Godhead.

He also taught that the emanations were forms of light that came directly from the source of all, the *Ein Sof*. While preserving the immutability of the Godhead, Cordovero also argued that the essence of the Godhead was in all created things, thus establishing a powerful link between the humblest aspects of creation and the Deity. It is also very likely that Cordovero determined the Three Pillar structure of the Tree of Life and the linear structure of the paths. In fact, he developed at least two different versions of the Tree of Life, and one of them, which was missing the lower paths between Malkuth and Hod, and Malkuth and Netzach, was adopted and promoted by Luria in his work.

Isaac Luria Ashkenazi

Isaac Luria Ashkenazi (1534–72), known as the "Ari," or Lion, is credited for bringing all of the various strains of the Spanish Qabalah together, synthesizing them into a powerful modern religious system. However, some would say that Luria borrowed heavily from his teacher, Cordovero. Although Luria left very little writing to posterity, the bulk of his teachings were written by his students, most notably Chayyim Vital. It was also likely that his students distilled ideas from both Luria and Cordovero but attributed them to Luria. However, many of the troubling idiosyncrasies and philosophical problems in the Qabalah were brilliantly and completely resolved exclusively by the teachings of Luria.[22]

It was the Ari who developed the concept of the Sephiroth as divine personalities, arranging them into Three Pillars (thereby creating a cosmogonic dialectic), and saw them as the dynamically changing and evolving manifestation of the will and mind of the Deity. He also developed the notion of the Four Qabalistic worlds, and resolved the issue of how the infinite unmanifest Godhead was able to create a finite material world through the mysterious artifice of contraction, concealment, and veiling, which he the-

---

22. Scholem, *Kabbalah*, 420–23.

orized as the necessary generation of a vacuum of empty space prior to creation.

Isaac Luria also developed the speculation that later became the Qliphoth, which he described as the shattering of the six Sephiroth above Malkuth. This shattering (*shevirah*) allowed for the incursion of evil into the world, and it caused the dispersal of all those points of light from the shards of the broken Sephiroth that ultimately became the souls of humanity. It was also the source of a mythic and psychological drama associated with the restoration (*tikkun*) of those spiritual sparks that had become individual human entities, now divided into four specific parts of the soul. With the dispersal of those sparks of light, a process of restoration was also determined by the Deity, made possible through the agency of a cosmic messiah.[23]

Luria's teachings had a powerful messianic quality, particularly when he predicted that the cosmic messiah was imminent, and that the event of restoration would also begin the ending of the world, as the messiah collected all of the spirits of humanity (as the myriad points of light) and delivered them up to the Deity. After his death, Luria's teachings, for a time, eclipsed all other teachings and became part of the Jewish mainstream. The messianic tensions found in his teachings, along with his various vague apocalyptic pronouncements, ultimately produced the heresies of the aborted Shabbatai Zevi messianic crusade.

---

23. Sanford Drob, *Symbols of the Kabbalah*, 14–16.

Qabalah Denudata:
Rise of the Christian Qabalah

There are many indicators that Christian intellectuals had been distilling the Jewish Qabalah since the time that it had emerged into Europe during the Middle Ages. An examination of Cornelius Agrippa's work, the three volumes of the *Occult Philosophy*, demonstrates that by 1531 the entire corpus of the practical and occult Qabalah had already been thoroughly translated and dispersed by academics throughout most of Europe. This would lead one to conclude that the various contents of the Zohar and the writings of Isaac Luria and others had been leaked or deliberately shared with sympathetic Christian scholars and occultists. We need to keep in mind that the Qabalah was an initiatic tradition that was discreetly propagated within the Jewish community. The fact that this knowledge became known to Christian circles is quite an amazing story by itself, and one that certainly needs to be told. It was also likely that various Jewish magical practices and techniques had also been appropriated by individuals in Christian circles.

How and when this actually occurred is unknown, but it was likely the impetus for the development of the Solomonic system of ceremonial magic. Frances Yates identified Pico della Mirandola as the primary teacher and promoter of the Christian Cabala in the late 15th century.[24] Mirandola greatly influenced Johann Reuchlin, who happened to be a Classical Hebrew scholar. Thus, it was Reuchlin who likely found great use for the Italian Jewish Qabalistic lit-

---

24. Frances Yates, *Giordano Bruno and the Hermetic Tradition,* 94–102.

erature of Rome available to those who could read Hebrew and Aramaic. He also published a work in 1516 entitled *De Arte Cabalistica*, which likely helped to promote the Qabalah among Christian scholars. Also in the early 16th century, Cornelius Agrippa published his *Three Books of Occult Philosophy*. What was still missing for scholars who could not read Hebrew or Aramaic were translations of the actual foundational documents of the Qabalah. That process began later in the 16th century, when the first Latin translation and commentary of the Sepher Yetzirah was written and published by Guillaume Postel of Paris.[25] More published works were to follow in the 17th century, which was to become one of the greatest periods for both the Jewish and Christian Qabalahs.

Another early published book on the Qabalah was the *Oedipus Aegypticus*, written by the brilliant Jesuit scholar Athanasi Kircher in 1652. This book was important because it contained an engraving of the Tree of Life from a previously published but obscure Cordovero source. It is also likely that this illustration of the Tree of Life was the one adopted by the Golden Dawn for its version of the Qabalah.

However, it was not until the year 1671 that Christian Knorr von Rosenroth translated and published four books of the voluminous Zohar in Latin: the *Qabalah Denudata* (Qabalah Unveiled), making it available to nearly anyone who had at least a rudimentary education. Additionally, Von Rosenroth published other translated Qabalistic writings, and these included works by Luria.[26] It is also possible

---

25. Dan, *Kabbalah: A Very Short Introduction*, 68.
26. Scholem, *Kabbalah*, 416.

that the spread of the Qabalah within the Christian community also facilitated the spread of Qabalah within the European Jewish community.

Decline of the Jewish Qabalah

The Jewish Qabalah reached its ascendancy in the century after the death of Luria, becoming the active theological arm of Judaism. However, the Jewish Qabalah began to decline after the failed messianic mission of Sabbatai Zevi, who had been declared as the Qabalistic Messiah prophesized by Isaac Luria. (We will discuss more about this event later, in chapter 6 of this book.) After this peak event, the Jewish Qabalah began to lose popularity in the 18th century, and by then it was no longer considered an authoritative theology by mainstream Jewish rabbis. It would seem that the harsh lesson of the apostate Sabbatai Zevi, and the obvious heterodoxic nature of the Qabalah, caused it to become increasingly rejected by various orthodox groups, with the exception of Hassidic Jews, among whom it continued to be practiced into the 20th century.

Mystical Qabalah of Dion Fortune: Occult Qabalah

In the mid- and late 19th century, the scholarship of Éliphas Lévi and S. L. MacGregor Mathers established the current structure of the Qabalistic Tree of Life (based on Kircher's illustration), and attributed the Tarot trumps to the 22 letters associated with the Pathways. Mathers reintroduced the discipline of the practical Qabalah and translated the works of Von Rosenroth into English. Mathers' co-chief, W. Wynn

Westcott, also produced a number of Qabalistic documents, including a translation of the Sepher Yetzirah into English. The teachings of the magical fraternity that they founded (the Golden Dawn) have influenced many subsequent students of the Qabalah.

Mathers' and Westcott's groundbreaking work was taken up and developed by other occultists, who brought it into the mainstream of occult beliefs and practices of the 20th and 21st centuries. Most notable for their contributions were Aleister Crowley, Dion Fortune, and Israel Regardie, who distilled and advanced the basic Qabalistic knowledge of the Golden Dawn so that it became more of a meta-system than a repository of Jewish Gnostic and Theosophic speculation. Like Mathers, these individuals intrinsically wedded the Qabalah to the practice of Western magic (following the precedent established by Agrippa). Aleister Crowley was the first to publish the Golden Dawn Qabalistic writings on Gematria and tables of correspondences, as well as his own writings and interpretations.

Dion Fortune blended many extensive theosophical and modern psychological speculations into the Qabalah and in 1935 wrote an important book specifically dedicated to the Qabalah, entitled *The Mystical Qabalah*. Paul Foster Case wedded the Tarot with the Qabalah so that the Tarot was defined and given its meaning solely through Qabalistic symbolism. W. E. Butler and Gareth Knight, who were both students of Dion Fortune, produced a correspondence course on the Qabalah, and Knight later wrote a very popular book, *A Practical Guide to Qabalistic Symbolism*, that many modern occultists have read and studied.

William Gray wrote a concise work, *The Ladder of Lights*, and established himself as one of the truly gifted occultists of the 20th century. He went on to write many more books about ceremonial magic and the Qabalah. Israel Regardie developed and refined the Golden Dawn teachings of the Qabalah first put forward by Mathers and Westcott. Kenneth Grant sought to develop and integrate the Qliphoth with the Sephiroth, calling it the backside of the Tree of Life. His books showed the integral relativity of both the left-hand and the right-hand occult paths. (Left-hand occultism is based on an inversion of the rightful order and lawfulness as established by status-quo spirituality, so it is often seen as a form of diabolism or demonolatry.)

Modern occultists are divided as to whether the Qabalah should be used for meditation and contemplation only, or included with the practice of ritual and ceremonial magic. Certainly Mathers and Crowley proposed the full incorporation of the Qabalah when they wrote their books, formulated their rituals and ceremonies, and taught these practices to their students; but others have moved away from the practice of magic, considering it to be too controversial and prone to heretical practices and derivations. Still, for practicing ritual magicians, the Qabalah is of critical importance.

Philip S. Berg and Z'ev ben Shimon Halevi: Jewish Resurgence

During the sixties and seventies, a noted Israeli historian and scholar named Dr. Gershom Scholem began to publish books on the Qabalah and the history of the Jewish religion. His books successfully restored the Qabalah to a specifically Jewish religious study, and he became the scholarly authority that presaged a Jewish resurgence of the Qabalah. It is likely that such a thorough historical analysis on the part of a world-renowned scholar either precipitated or augmented an already established renewed interest in the Qabalah by Jews. Dr. Scholem gave creditability and respectability to a scholarly study, and later, to a practice of the Jewish Qabalah.

Needless to say, not long afterwards, other authors and teachers began to surface from the various concentrated locations of the Jewish diaspora. One of these was Scholem's friend and protégé, Isaiah Tishby, who translated and wrote commentaries on the Zohar, along with many other books.[27] Another notable individual was Rabbi Judah Ashlag, who was one of the main religious promoters of the Qabalah. Rabbi Ashlag lived in Jerusalem during the first half of the 20th century, and was one of the foremost authorities on this obscure subject. His work became the basis for a modern Jewish interpretation of the Qabalah.

Some factions of the Jewish religious tradition, most notably the Hasidim, had never abandoned the study and practice of the Qabalah. Other Jewish religious scholars sought to redeem and reinstate a modern Jewish study of the Qabalah. While much of the source works had not yet been translated into modern languages, this renewed interest began a period of intensive translation and publishing that continues to this day. Perhaps the strongest motivation for this task of translating the source works of the Qabalah is that Jewish adherents are seeking to re-establish it in the

27. Dan, *Kabbalah: A Very Short Introduction*, 110.

shape and manner that it existed before Christians, and later, occultists, made revisions and additions to its lore.

While there are many schools and organizations that promote a Jewish version of the Qabalah, there are basically three major schools of thought that have emerged from this renewed engagement among Jewish students of the Qabalah, and these can be encapsulated by certain personalities and groups.

Dr. Philip S. Berg, who leads the Kabbalah Centre (of Madonna and the red string bracelet fame), has written numerous books and runs a very successful organization located on the West Coast of the U.S. He teaches a decidedly Jewish form of the Qabalah, but has made it available to everyone. Dr. Berg was taught by an eminent rabbi and student of the Qabalah named Yehuda Branwein, who was his father-in-law and the leader of the prestigious school "Yeshiva Kol Yehuda," located in modern Israel. Since Rabbi Branwein's death, Dr. Berg has claimed to be the head of that school, although the deceased rabbi's son has disputed his claim. Dr. Berg has also incorporated many of the writings and teachings of Rabbi Ashlag into his school.

Z'ev ben Shimon Halevi (Warren Kenton) lives in the United Kingdom and has founded his own school of the Qabalah. He has also written a number of books on the subject since the late 1980s, and travels the world teaching a course called the "Way of the Kabbalah." When I was living in Santa Fe in 1994, I attended a lecture given by Halevi, and overall I found it quite informative. Halevi teaches that only those of the Jewish faith should pursue a study of the Qabalah, which is unlike Dr. Berg, but his books and lectures are attended by people of all faiths. Halevi has merged modern Jungian psychology with a Toledo variant of the Qabalah to produce a fresh perspective. A number of artists and musicians have credited Halevi and his literary work as a source of personal inspiration.

Jewish scholars and Jewish students of the Qabalah, most notably those who are part of the academic and religious organizations in modern Israel, have harshly criticized both Dr. Berg and Halevi as New Age popularizers of what they believe is an exclusive domain of Jewish theology and mystical philosophy. Individuals and groups belonging to this faction believe that the Qabalah should only be studied by men who are practicing Jews. While scholars in this group seek to study the history and content of the Qabalah in a secular but respectful manner, the Jewish followers who practice the Qabalah believe that only properly authorized and recognized rabbis should teach this discipline to others, and then only to properly schooled Jewish men. As a group, these two factions have taken it upon themselves to be the arbiters and critics of the various teachers and authors of Jewish Qabalistic books and materials.

It remains to be seen what will come from this renewed interest and practice of the Qabalah from adherents of modern Judaism, yet the outpouring of translated source works (such as the multivolume *Pritzker Zohar*) and various other scholarly writings will greatly assist everyone who has an interest in the Qabalah, helping them to further refine and develop their understanding of that discipline.

———

I hope this brief historical analysis has assisted you in realizing that the Qabalah is an ever-evolving discipline, which has undergone considerable change and revision over the centuries. Still, the overriding theme of the Qabalah through the ages has been its continual engagement with Gnostic-inspired theosophy and practical applications of theurgy. While some adherents may divorce their tradition from these considerations, I believe that the Western occult version of the Qabalah should keep them intact.

Qabalah of the Ten Sephiroth

The core of the Qabalah consists of the ten emanations called the *Sephiroth*. Each of these Sephirah has a specific name, title, and set of correspondences. The Sephiroth represent the stages of creation, from the most abstract to the most dense and material levels of being. The names and descriptions of the ten Sephiroth were first revealed in the Sepher Yetzirah, yet, over time, each of these emanations were elaborated upon and additional attributes were added to them.

Qabalistic correspondences for each of the ten Sephiroth found here are meant as a brief synopsis of the Sephiroth in the Tree of Life, and do not represent a deep or detailed explanation of them. For a more thorough understanding, I recommend that you at least read Gareth Knight's book *A Practical Guide to Qabalistic Symbolism.* You can also look over the books listed later, in chapter 16 and in the bibliography.

1. **Kether** (the Crown), God-name: Ehieh (I am); Archangel: Metatron; Order of Angels: Chaioth he-Qadesh (Holy Living Ones); Body Part: crown of head; Symbol: swirling swastika. Description from the Sepher Yetzirah:

> *The First Path is called the Admirable or the Concealed Intelligence (The Highest Crown)—for it is the Light giving the power of comprehension of that First Principle which has no beginning, and it is the Primal Glory, for no created being can attain to its essence.*[28]

Kether is the first manifestation of being that emerged out of non-being, yet it is non-dual and whole, and it is the pure and undiluted source from which all other Sephiroth emanate. Kether is called the Crown of Creation, but it was created by the vast and unknowable (unmanifest) Deity, and so all of the ten Sephiroth are equal in their importance. The unity of Kether is within all of the emanations, thus representing the unity of the Deity itself. Where Kether is the indivisible One, the Unmanifest Godhead behind it is the indivisible *None.* Kether can therefore be seen as the confluence and manifestation of the invisible

---

28. All quotations for the Sepher Yetzirah were taken from the public-domain translation made by W. W. Westcott (1887) found on sacred-texts.com: www.sacred-texts.com/jud/yetzirah.htm (accessed February 2012). (See *The Thirty-two Paths of Wisdom, Appendix to the Sepher Yetzirah.*)

veils that wrap the Tree of Life in a perfect embrace, containing the pure essence and expression of the One True Being.

2. ***Chokmah*** (Wisdom), God-name: YHVH or Yah; Archangel: Raziel; Order of Angels: Auphanim (Wheels); Body Part: right side of head; Symbol: Zodiac. Description from the Sepher Yetzirah:

> *The Second Path is that of the Illuminating Intelligence it is the Crown of Creation, the Splendor of the Unity, equaling it, and it is exalted above every bead, and named by the Kabbalists the Second Glory.*

Chokmah is the active expression of the unity within Kether, the will to create multiplicity from unity. It is an expression of the archetypal masculine, where Kether is the union of All. Chokmah is also wisdom, the expression of the mind of the Deity as the first thought, and that expression is the impulse to apprehend that unity and reflect upon it. It is the natural process of spiritual wisdom having achieved its highest expression. Chokmah is also the vision of God (as Kether) face to face, and the direct brilliant illumination of unity that results from that vision.

3. ***Binah*** (Understanding), God-name: YHVH Elohim; Archangel: Tzaphkiel; Order of Angels: Aralim (Thrones); Body Part: left side of head/face; Symbol: Saturn. Description from the Sepher Yetzirah:

> *The Third Path is called the Sanctifying Intelligence the Foundation of Primordial Wisdom: it is also called*

the Creator of Faith, and its roots are in Amen. It is the
parent of faith, whence faith emanates.

Binah is the reception or formulation of the unity within Kether; the reception of the creative power of Chokmah into the patterns that reflect the unity of the source. Development implies limitation, and so the passive feminine power of Binah establishes the first archetypal pattern and structures, and the first laws. For Binah is the arbiter of all cause and effect, and is the judge of fate. The formulation of wisdom is found in understanding and in faith, and this is required before there can be a practical application of wisdom into the world of forms.

4. **Chesed** (Mercy), Godname: El; Archangel: Tzadkiel; Order of Angels: Chasmalim (Brilliant Ones); Body Part: right arm; Symbol: Jupiter. Description from the Sepher Yetzirah:

The Fourth Path is named Measuring, Cohesive, or
Receptacle; and is so called because it contains all the
holy powers, and from it emanate all the spiritual vir-
tues with the most exalted essences: they emanate one
from the other by the power of the primordial emana-
tion (The Highest Crown), blessed be it.

Chesed is called the receptive intelligence, since it receives the wisdom and understanding from the supernal triad, thus causing them to coalesce into conscious forms that will prepare them for the ultimate process of manifestation. Chesed is the highest level of conscious formation, so it establishes the patterns that lead to mental forms and the creation of physical matter. It is also the underlying process that begins the incarnation of beings, which are a combination of both mind and matter. Chesed represents the forces of divine love (as compassion) and also the will to exist, and these two forces join together to determine the divine destiny for all subsequent creation. This destiny is the ultimate realization of the internal spiritual source, and its call to return to the greater glory of the unity of all being (Kether). Chesed is the power that redeems, and it invests everything that passes through it with the memory of the source. This is because it is the bridge between that spiritual source and all of manifestation. Chesed is the platform that exists before a great chasm called the Greater Abyss, which also represents the process of the translation from pure archetype to the formulation of the universal mind and the source of all consciousness.

5. *Geburah* (Power), Godname: Elohim Gebor; Archangel: Khamael; Order of Angels: Seraphim (Fiery Spirits); Body Part: left arm; Symbol: Mars. Description from the Sepher Yetzirah:

> *The Fifth Path is called the Radical Intelligence, because it is itself the essence equal to the Unity, uniting itself to the Binah or Intelligence which emanates from the primordial depths of Wisdom or Chokmah.*

Geburah is power, and the disciplined will to use it wisely and justly. Geburah is the Sephirah that takes the understanding of Binah and fashions it into archetypal truths and spiritual values, purging from forms and attributes all that is an illusion or is defective. Geburah and Chesed, together, forge only the perfect images as derived from the source, and so Geburah acts as a governor to the boundless creative energy received from Chesed. The realizations of the limitation of fate found in Binah are adjudicated in Geburah, and so Mercy/Compassion (Chesed) and Severity/Judgment (Geburah) preserve the creation of pure mental forms that are redacted from spirit so that they remain balanced and integral.

6. ***Tiphareth*** (Beauty), Godname: YHVH Aloah ve-Da'ath; Archangel: Raphael; Order of Angels: Malachim (Kings); Body Part: heart; Symbol: Sun. Description from the Sepher Yetzirah:

> *The Sixth Path is called the Intelligence of the Mediating Influence, because in it are multiplied the influxes of the emanations; for it causes that affluence to flow into all the reservoirs of the Blessings, with which these themselves are united.*

Tiphareth occupies the very center of the Tree of Life and reflects the light of Kether (unity) into the plane of mind, becoming the Logos, or Word (divine directive of the Absolute). The thoughts and the actions that sustain it are joined together into a synthesis. Thus this Sephirah is called the mediating intelligence and the heart (core) of the Deity. The divine plan of the supernal triad is brought into a harmonious manifestation in Tiphareth, and so it is also called beauty, representing the perfect mental reflection of the Deity in all its grace and perfect symmetry. Tiphareth symbolizes regeneration and rebirth, as associated with the upward process of evolution, and it is the final expression of perfect unity before the fall into the lower realms of manifested being, which is the downward path of involution.

7. **Netzach** (Victory), Godname: YHVH Tzabaoth; Archangel: Haniel; Order of Angels: Elohim (Gods); Body Part: right leg; Symbol: Venus. Description from the Sepher Yetzirah:

> *The Seventh Path is the Occult Intelligence, because it is the Refulgent Splendor of all the Intellectual virtues which are perceived by the eyes of intellect, and by the contemplation of faith.*

Netzach is the source of all mysteries, being the occult intelligence and the first emergence of the lower mind or intellect, which is the creative imagination and also inspiration. Netzach consists of the balance of the force and form that drives creation, producing the vision of beauty triumphant, which is its spiritual experience. Beauty is the perfection of form and essence, and it is within the influence of this Sephirah that the archetypal mental pattern receives its ideal form—the domain of platonic ideals. Netzach is, in essence, the activation of the magic of transformation and translation; since from these two methods of reconciling spirit and matter, all physical manifestation proceeds, and the idealization of matter as art assists in the inspiration of the archetype as perceived (by humanity) within the material world.

8. **Hod** (Glory), Godname: Elohim Tzabaoth; Archangel: Michael; Order of Angels: Beni Elohim (Sons of the Gods); Body Part: left leg; Symbol: Mercury. Description from the Sepher Yetzirah:

> *The Eighth Path is called Absolute or Perfect, because it is the means of the primordial, which has no root by which it can cleave, nor rest, except in the hidden places of Gedulah Magnificence, which emanate from its own proper essence.*

Hod is where the idealized form of Netzach becomes realized in the concrete forms of mental perception. Whereas Netzach is perceived as art, Hod is science, since it concerns itself with the concrete apperception of the material universe. It is also analogous to the great complexity and symmetry of the domain of the mental world. Hod is the great lens through which one can realize that the underlying structures, principles, and laws of the greater cosmos are the same as those operating at the subatomic level. It is also the first ordering principle through which pure ideals are structured within the holistic hierarchy of ascending and descending levels of conscious being.

9. **Yesod** (The Foundation), Godname: Shaddai El Chai; Archangel: Gabriel; Order of Angels: Cherubim (Strong Ones); Body Part: genitals/anus; Symbol: Moon. Description from the Sepher Yetzirah:

> *The Ninth Path is the Pure Intelligence so called because it purifies the Numerations, it proves and corrects the designing of their representation, and disposes their unity with which they are combined without diminution or division.*

Yesod is the underlying structure that embodies the entire material universe. It can also be found in the animating vitality and dynamic qualities associated with living beings. This Sephirah represents the integrating forces that link the idealized forms and mental structures with the actual material world. This fusion of ideation and structure represents the occurrence of the laws of limitation and probability, which seek to confine the boundless potential found in the higher Sephiroth. Yesod is the great physical organizing principle, the lattice or skeletal structure upon which all manifestation depends. It is the domain that drives the activated laws that govern all physical objects in space and time. Yesod is the creative intelligence that imbeds the potential of physical evolution and superior adaptation, regulating those impulses that cause some life forms to survive, evolve, and awaken into consciousness, and others to become extinct.

10. *Malkuth* (The Kingdom), Godname: Adonai ha-Aretz; Archangel: Sandalphon; Order of Angels: Ashim (Souls of Fire); Body Part: feet; Symbol: Sphere of Elements. Description from the Sepher Yetzirah:

> *The Tenth Path is the Resplendent Intelligence, because it is exalted above every bead, and sits on the throne of Binah (the Intelligence spoken of in the Third Path). It illuminates the splendor of all lights, and causes a supply of influence to emanate from the Prince of countenances.*

Malkuth represents the physical universe and all it contains, thus it is the objective and exterior world of the senses. It is the Sephirah of both space (matter) and time (change) that locks all energy and matter into a finite representation. For all things of Malkuth are born and then decay and die, or change into other forms less complex. The principle agent or power of change is entropy (balanced by the higher agent of union called synergy), and this force reduces all things to their simplest and most inert forms. In Malkuth, evolution and involution have achieved their highest level of expression, since all of the pure essence of Spirit has been potentialized into matter, making it ready for immanent evolution and the return to the source of all Spirit.

Note: Da'ath and Paroketh are the gates of the Greater and Lesser Abysses, respectively. To complete the system associating body parts with the Sephiroth, a point is assigned to each: to Da'ath is the throat, and to Paroketh is the solar plexus.

Sephiroth Da'ath

Da'ath is not a member of the classical ten Sephiroth, and it was not mentioned in the Sepher Yetzirah. Still, it was later hinted about, and over time it became a kind of hidden or obscured Sephirah that had certain attributes which caused it to become related to the gateway of the Greater Abyss and the Qliphoth that resided on the other side of that doorway. (The nature of the Qliphoth is covered below, and the Greater Abyss is dealt with in chapter 5, regarding the 22 Pathways.)

11. ***Da'ath*** (Knowledge)—Magical Image: Head with two faces looking both forward and backward (analogous to the Roman God Janus, or any other liminal Deity); Godname: YHVH & YHVH ALYM (Yahweh Elohim); Archangel: Four Archangels of the Cardinal Directions; Angelic Choir:

Nechasim (Serpents); Body Part: throat; Symbol: Sothis/
Sirius (Dog Star). Various titles: Invisible Sephirah, hidden
or unrevealed cosmic mind, union of Chokmah and Binah,
Nominal (Negative) reflection of Kether.

Considering all of its symbology, it would seem that
Da'ath is obviously a liminal or threshold junction in the
Tree of Life, representing the union of Chokmah and Binah,
the archetypal masculine and feminine. Four archangels
would characterize the wards for this portal, and the angelic
choir of the Nechasim would symbolize the raw forces that
emanate from it. Interestingly enough, the verb root for
Nechasim is (NChSh), which means "to practice sorcery
or divination." With the addition of the Dog Star and the
pagan Deity Janus, one could see this Sephirah as functioning in a very ambiguous manner, symbolizing the qualities
of "otherness" and "alien" that have become attributes of
dark and forbidden spirituality. Such Godheads as Typhon,
Set, Samael, or even Shaitan could easily represent the divine
aspects of this Sephirah. One could also see it as symbolizing
the supernal triad as seen through a mirror darkly, revealing
all of the attributes of the negative or unconscious aspects of
the operative Deity.

Ten Qliphoth

A number of occultists have, over the last few decades, written about the *Qliphoth*, or *Qliphah* (singular), and some have
stipulated that there is a Tree of Evil or Death in addition to
the Tree of Life, acting as its reverse or negative image. This
seems to be a theme expressed by some adherents of the

left-hand path, and some have proposed a Tree of Evil, and through it assign a quasi-hierarchy for the various lists of evil spirits and devils that supposedly populate the material world. Having two such trees allows a student the duality of choosing one or the other, or perhaps going from one to the other.

According to Genesis there were two sacred trees in the Garden of Eden: one was indeed the Tree of Life, but the other wasn't its opposite. The other tree was the Tree of the Knowledge of Good and Evil. Since humankind ate from the latter and not the former, we have the power and potential of knowing truth on all levels of being, but we are not immortal. Yet the scriptures never mention a Tree of Evil, so one would have to assume that it is apocryphal or even a recent urban myth. Some of these themes are discussed more fully in chapter 6, where the origin of evil is examined. It is likely that the problem of explaining the occurrence of evil caused some of the Spanish Qabalists to conjecture on a Tree of Evil. However, there is another way of interpreting the Qliphoth and determining how they fit into the overall scheme of the Qabalah without having to propose two opposing trees.

The word *Qliphoth* or *Qliphah* comes from the Hebrew root QLPh, which means "to peel off," and the noun means "husk," "shell," or "rind." Qliphah, therefore, means in Hebrew a "shell or the outer covering of some kind of fruit or nut." When applied to the Qabalah, it has been variously interpreted as a kind of afterbirth or discarded element. It could even be defined as a previously failed attempt at creation (an abortion), but only if one doubted the perfection of the Godhead.

Still, there is another meaning to the word that would allow it to merge into the Tree of Life, but only if we can overcome the basic prejudice built up by the previous definitions. The Qliphoth could simply be the outer shell or husk of the corresponding Sephiroth, and in actuality, it would function more like a socket or the bottom foundation of a specific Sephirah. In other words, the Qliphoth are the backside or unconscious dimensions of the Sephirotic Tree of Life.

Based on this revelation, the Qliphoth are neither evil nor the negative partners to the Sephiroth in the Tree of Life. The troubling Tree of Evil or Death disappears, and in its place is the night side and light side of the one Holy Tree. Just as we human beings have a light and dark side, so, too, does the Tree of Life; but that dark side represents neither a duality nor a split between good and evil. As the glyph of the Tree of Life is outwardly defined, all of the elements contained within it are seen as a unified whole, and that includes the Sephiroth, Pathways, and even the Qliphoth.

I have found it most productive to see the Qliphoth as the arising potential for Sephiroth. They are, in a word, the unmanifest potential first laid down by the emanations of the Negative Veils. The fusion of Sephirah and Qliphah is seamless, but each represents a different kind of spiritual quality and hierarchy. One can't enter into the corresponding Qliphah from the Sephirah, since through the Sephirah, they are both perfectly united.

The backside of the Tree of Life can only be accessed through the portal of the gateway of Da'ath, which is also the gateway of the Greater Abyss. Therefore, the individual Qliphah can be acquired and realized only by someone passing through the gateway of Da'ath, otherwise their influences are nearly invisible except through the periodic subtle dark emanations coming from the abysmal gateway. (Some have called these dark emanations the heartbeat of darkness itself.)

It is my belief that the Qliphoth contain all of the unknown and invisible chthonic proto-elements of our spiritual, mental, and physical worlds. Atavisms, archaisms, and dark inner Pathways connect the backside of the Tree of Life, like the endless tunnels of the catacombs underneath Rome or Paris. The light side of the Tree of Life has only 22 Pathways, but the backside has as many possible permutations for Pathways as there are Sephiroth. Thus all of the Sephiroth are interconnected with "wormholes" below the surface and at the level of the Qliphoth. The underworld domain of the backside of the Tree of Life is populated with dead ancestors, gods and goddesses of the underworld, and the various demonic and sub-elemental spirits and powers.

Aleister Crowley, Kenneth Grant, and other occultists have taken some incomplete information from Jewish Qabalistic sources and have given names, qualities, and rulers to the ten anti-Sephiroth of the Qliphoth. I have found their work to be quite weak and incomplete, based as it is upon a decidedly Jewish monotheistic mystical bias, which I think is contrary to any practical magical workings with these forces. These anti-Sephiroth themes likely originated in the

13th century from the Castile (Isaac ha-Kohen) school of the Qabalah, which was more occultic, Gnostic, and based wholly within the art of theurgy.

I would recommend that the forces and spirits of the Qliphoth and their wormhole Pathways be examined as merely the negative source potentials for the obverse Sephiroth and glyph-determined Pathways. If they have any names or qualities, it would not be just a reversed mirror image of the surface structures of the Tree. They would be the veritable archaic sources for those structures. The backside of the Tree of Life is without morals and spiritual values, and is therefore, beyond good and evil.

See the table of correspondences of the ten Sephiroth and Da'ath on the following pages.

Table of Correspondences of the Ten Sephiroth and Da'ath

	Sephiroth	English Name	Godname	Archangel	Angelic Choir
1	Kether	Crown	AHYH	Metatron	Hiyoth Haqadesh
2	Chokmah	Wisdom	YH	Ratziel	Auphanim
3	Binah	Understanding	YHVH ALHYM	Tzaphkiel	Aralim
4	Chesed	Mercy	AL	Tzadkiel	Chasmolim
5	Geburah	Strength	ALHYM GBVR	Kamael	Tarshishim
6	Tiphareth	Beauty	YHVH ALHYM VDOTh	Raphael	Malakim
7	Netzach	Victory	YHVH TzBAVTh	Haniel	Elohim
8	Hod	Splendor	ALHYM TzBAVTh	Michael	Beni Elohim
9	Yesod	Foundation	ShDY AL ChY	Gabriel	Alim
10	Malkuth	Kingdom	ADNY MLK	Sandalphon	Eshim
11	Da'ath	Knowledge	YHVH / YHVH ALHYM	Four archangels	Nechasim

Note: * indicates my own selections or variations. Body Points are based on my own deductions.

Rest of correspondences derived from *Liber 777* and *The Complete Magician's Tables.*

Figure 5: Table of Correspondences of the Ten Sephiroth and Da'ath

Table of Correspondences of the Ten Sephiroth and Da'ath

	Sephiroth	English Name	Cosmic Attribute	Greek Gods	Roman Gods	Egyptian Gods
1	Kether	Crown	Primum Mobile	Iacchus-Dionysus	Fascinus	Ptah
2	Chokmah	Wisdom	Zodiac	Athena	Minerva	Nuit-Maat
3	Binah	Understanding	Saturn	Demeter	Ceres-Juno	Nephthys
4	Chesed	Mercy	Jupiter	Zeus	Jupiter	Amoun
5	Geburah	Strength	Mars	Ares	Mars	Horus
6	Tiphareth	Beauty	Sun	Apollo-Helios	Sol-Invictus	Ra
7	Netzach	Victory	Venus	Aphrodite	Venus	Hathor
8	Hod	Splendor	Mercury	Hermes	Mercury	Thoth
9	Yesod	Foundation	Moon	Artemis	Diana	Isis
10	Malkuth	Kingdom	Earth	Poseidon	Saturn, Lares-Penares	Osiris
11	Da'ath	Knowledge	Underworld Double Gateway	Hades-Persephone	Janus	Set-Anubis

Note: * indicates my own selections or variations. Body Points are based on my own deductions. Rest of correspondences derived from *Liber 777* and *The Complete Magician's Tables*.

Table of Correspondences of the Ten Sephiroth and Da'ath

	Sephiroth	English Name	Metals	Gems	Perfumes	Magical Weapons
1	Kether	Crown	Uranium*	Diamond	Ambergris	Swastika
2	Chokmah	Wisdom	Magnesium*	Turquoise	Musk	Lingam
3	Binah	Understanding	Lead	Sapphire	Myrrh	Yoni
4	Chesed	Mercy	Tin	Amethyst	Cedar	Wand
5	Geburah	Strength	Iron	Ruby	Dragon's Blood*	Sword
6	Tiphareth	Beauty	Gold	Topaz	Olibanum	Lamen
7	Netzach	Victory	Copper	Emerald	Rose	Lamps or Cincture
8	Hod	Splendor	Mercury-Cinnabar	Fire Opal	Storax	Pentacles or Words of Power
9	Yesod	Foundation	Silver	Pearl-Moon Stone	Jasmine, Lavender	Perfumes or Sandals
10	Malkuth	Kingdom	Antimony	Quartz-Beryl	Dittany of Crete	Magical Circle, Altar and Shrine
11	Da'ath	Knowledge	N/A	Obsidian	N/A	Triangle-Gateway

Note: * indicates my own selections or variations. Body Points are based on my own deductions.
Rest of correspondences derived from *Liber 777* and *The Complete Magician's Tables*.

Table of Correspondences of the Ten Sephiroth and Da'ath

	Sephiroth	English Name	Body Point	Colors
1	Kether	Crown	Crown of Head	White
2	Chokmah	Wisdom	Right side of Head	Gray
3	Binah	Understanding	Left side of Head	Black
4	Chesed	Mercy	Right Shoulder	Blue
5	Geburah	Strength	Left Shoulder	Scarlet
6	Tiphareth	Beauty	Heart/Solar Plexus	Yellow
7	Netzach	Victory	Right Hand	Green
8	Hod	Splendor	Left Hand	Orange
9	Yesod	Foundation	Genitals	Violet
10	Malkuth	Kingdom	Legs and Feet	Citrine, Olive, Russet, and Black
11	Da'ath	Knowledge	Throat	Colorless

Note: * indicates my own selections or variations. Body Points are based on my own deductions. Rest of correspondences derived from *Liber 777* and *The Complete Magician's Tables*.

Qabalah of the 22 Paths

We have already examined the basic elements of the Qabalah, which include the ten Sephiroth and the basic structures of the Tree of Life. We have also examined the history and some of the uses that the Qabalah has had throughout its long period of evolution. Yet the most important part of the Qabalah, in my opinion, concerns itself with the methodology of spiritual ascent, which is formulated from the symbolic correspondences and analogies of the 22 Pathways. (See figure 6.)

Ascension is the ability to use the Qabalah so that an individual might experience complete and total spiritual transformation and union with the Godhead. Knowledge

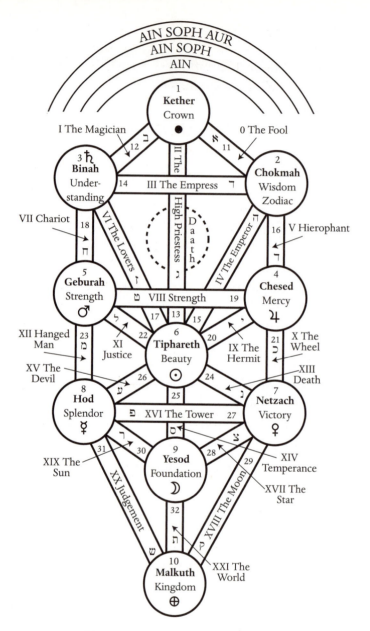

Figure 6: Comprehensive Tree of Life

of the Qabalah assumes that the occultist will seek to know and master the various higher planes, beings, and the God-head itself through direct experience. Truthfully, there are few other occult systems that incorporate so many diverse methodologies and approaches, all of which aid the student, whether mystic or magician, to achieve full spiritual mastery.

The ten Sephiroth are concerned with the cosmic processes of emanation and spiritual involution, yet the 22 Pathways are focused on the process of spiritual ascent and evolution for the individual occult seeker. It is said that the Pathways, which were responsible for the manifestation of all material things through a form of word magic, can also aid the seeker to transform and consciously evolve into the One. By reversing the sequence that caused the creation of the material world, and applying that to one's psyche, a mystic or magician may wield the power of spiritual ascension. This is done by using the special words of power and the various names of the Godhead associated with the veritable sacred letters of the alphabet of creation.

At the macrocosmic level, the process of emanation also represents a form of transformation, but only on a cosmic level. It is concerned with the ultimate and collective destiny of entire classes of beings. All individual beings partake of this process, but it is a slow and evolving one, which spans the life cycle of an entire species. For the individual being, the process of emanation is too subtle and too vast to be directly perceived, even though it is constant and dynamic. However, an individual can experience the entire destiny of his or her collective species in a single moment through the power of transformation as deployed through the Pathways. Thus, we know that the ten Sephiroth represent the cosmic cycle of emanation and involution, and the 22 Pathways characterize the individual cycle of spiritual transformation and personal evolution.

Each Pathway on the Tree of Life consists of a corridor between two Sephiroth, representing a transition from one state of emanation to the next higher (or lower). Using the structure of the Tree of Life that consists of Sephiroth and Pathways, and starting in the lowest Sephirah Malkuth, one proceeds up the two sides and central pillars of the Tree, moving from the densest spiritual aspects to the most sublime. Examining these connecting Pathways between the Sephiroth, the student will notice that not all possible connections are employed. There is an intrinsic logic associated with these Pathways, and one can especially see this occurring in the area of the Tree that is above Tiphareth. For instance, there are no Pathways connecting Binah to Chesed or Chokmah to Geburah; instead, these Sephiroth are connected through Tiphareth, which represents the center, heart, or core of the Tree. (However, these two Pathways are actually implied by a more subtle process encountered when performing the pathworking application of ascent and descent.)

There is also an order to the Pathways that is associated with the sequence of the 22 letters of the Hebrew alphabet, which is in descending order: from Aleph to Thav, from the Pathway between Kether and Chokmah to the Pathway between Yesod and Malkuth. The winding and twisting circuit by which the Pathways wend their way up and down the Tree of Life is represented by the Serpent of Knowledge, and this mythic entity offers to the aspirant the promise of both enlightenment and eternal life. This is because the Tree of 32 emanations includes both the symbolic Tree of Life and the Tree of the Knowledge of Good and Evil. It is inconceivable that one could be mastered without the other, and it would be foolish for anyone to assume that human nature has an innate monopoly on being able to choose good over evil.

In the traditions of magic, the 22 Pathways symbolize the process of personal transformative initiation. Therefore, using the methods of guided meditation or magical imagery, an individual may progress up the Tree and experience the revelation of Spirit in his or her personal sphere. This technique of ascending and descending the Pathways of the Tree is called pathworking. It represents one of the most potent visual tools in the arsenal of the ritual magician or the mystic.

Like the ten Sephiroth, the 22 Pathways have their own set of correspondences, and these correspondences are almost as endless as those of the Sephiroth. The correspondences of the paths, while based on the Hebrew letters, include the 22 trumps of the Major Arcana of the Tarot. Adding the attributes of Tarot trumps to the Pathways represents a considerable advancement for their overall meaning and significance. Other correspondences include the seven planets, the 12 signs of the zodiac, and the four elements, with Saturn sharing the attribute of the element of Earth. The zodiacal, planetary, and element attributions of the Pathways were established early in the history of the Qabalah, but the attribution of the Tarot trumps is a recent innovation. Extending the meaning of the Pathways to include the trumps gives greater depth and significance to them. It also causes them to be more like distinct and separate domains, analogous to the Sephiroth to which they connect.

Tarot trumps didn't become associated with the Pathways of the Tree until at least the middle of the 19th century, and the final form that we use today was derived toward the end of the 19th century. Influenced by the writings of Court de Gebelin in his book *Le Monde Primitif* (1781), the occult scholar and romantic Éliphas Lévi took these associations and developed them in his writings. What he ultimately came up with was unsatisfactory, due to inconsistencies and obvious erroneous associations. Mathers produced the final corrected version of the attribution of Pathways and the Tarot, and wrote them up in an order document entitled "Book T" (1887). Variations of that text have been adapted for use by the many descendants of the Golden Dawn. So the Tarot of the Golden Dawn became the prototype for most subsequent books written about the Tarot and the Qabalah, as well as being the primary influence for the symbolic depiction of many of the Tarot decks in use today. That is why it is important to explore each of the 22 Pathways in detail and to analyze their distinctive symbology, since knowledge of the Pathways will also unlock a deeper knowledge of the Tarot.

I invite you to read through these 22 brief definitions of the Qabalistic Pathways, beginning with the last path and proceeding in ascending (and reverse) order up the Tree to the first path. While performing this mental operation

I would recommend that you visually imagine your own ascent up the Tree of Life, so that you can perform a kind of preliminary pathworking.

Doing this, you will notice how the powers, attributes, and overall symbolic transitions change in the most striking and meaningful manner, beginning with the densest levels of being and on up to the most evolved and purely spiritual. After this practice ascent, you may want to visualize the attributes of the paths in reverse, beginning with the 11th path and proceeding down the Tree to the 32nd.

By the way, the first Pathway is always numbered the 11th path because the ten Sephiroth precede the 22 Pathways (in the Sepher Yetzirah). Even though the first ten paths are referred to as Sephiroth (numbers), they are also considered to be paths of wisdom (but consisting wholly of the greater emanations). Each Pathway association is self-explanatory and is followed by some strategic correspondences that will aid you in conceptualizing the ascent up or down the Tree of Life.

22 Pathways

32nd Path

(Malkuth to Yesod—Thav—Saturn/Earth): The 32nd Path is the path of entry into the domain of the unconscious mind. It also represents the threshold of inner exploration, and it is the stage where one first becomes confronted by a deeper reality, which is a hidden world that exists behind everyday experiences. This transition is like a preliminary initiation into the deeper structures of one's personality, and it is also a path of entry into the lower astral plane. The

32nd Path is often associated with underground or cavern imagery. It is also characterized by the mythic abduction of Persephone by Hades, who captured and took her from the surface world into his dark domain in the underworld— a place of mystery and death. The archangels of this path are Sandalphon (Malkuth) and Gabriel (Yesod). The Tarot trump is the Universe (World)—XXI. (Note: Tarot trumps traditionally have a Roman numeral sequence instead of an Arabic numeral.)

31st Path

(Malkuth to Hod—Shin—Fire): The 31st Path reveals the inner motivations that move and push individuals to perpetual action and reaction. These inner motivations become transparent, revealing the specific lusts, desires, passions, and needs that determine a person's present and future disposition, thereby showing not only what is, but also what will become—the future actions invested in the present. Therefore, ascending this path gives the seeker an insight into the nature of the world, stripping it of its outer opacity and revealing all of the secret inner forces that seem to be in constant conflict with each other. Everything is laid bare and nothing is hidden; this is the nature of perfect and impartial judgment. To gain true peace and peace of mind, the seeker must learn to live in strict accordance with his spiritual principles, since in the powerful light of spiritual judgment; any other course would be shown to be hypocritical. This is the trial by fire, and the trial of truth, balance, honor, and living through a spiritual discipline. What descends from this Pathway is either retribution or reward; the choice is entirely up to the individual. The archangels of this path are Sandalphon

(Malkuth) and Michael (Hod). The Tarot trump is Judgement—XX.

30th Path

(Yesod to Hod—Resh—Sun): The 30th Path is a path through which great wisdom can be attained. This is because the Sephirah Hod is the means through which one may contact the illuminated masters of spiritual evolution. These are the great teachers who are eternally employed with the guiding and teaching of humanity, and whose main sphere of influence is ultimately found in Chesed. Because there is a powerful link between Chesed and Hod (through Tiphareth), the teachings from these high spiritual sources are projected down the planes to form a pool of instruction, as it were, in Hod. The Sephirah Hod is typically referred to by Qabalists as the Water Temple because of its symbolic use as a pool in which the higher wisdom may be seen as reflected light. Because of the influence of the Moon in Yesod, and Mercury in Hod, the combination of these two Sephiroth in this Pathway produces the source of great occult wisdom, which confers complete freedom and joy in those who have received and realized its gifts. Such a confluence of occult knowledge and wisdom is like the brilliant light of the sun (Solar Logos), which illuminates everything near and far. The archangels of this path are Gabriel (Yesod) and Michael (Hod). The Tarot trump is the Sun—XIX.

29th Path

(Malkuth to Netzach—Qoph—Pisces): The 29th Path represents the biological and vital forces of all living things, including their innate basic functioning and instincts. As is true with all of the lower paths on the Tree of Life, this path has both a higher and a lower attribute. The lower attribute has much to do with the functions of living bodies, their need to survive by finding food, eating, and reproducing their numbers. The higher attribute could be compared to a simplistic but intense belief in the spiritualization of all life, as a kind of pantheism or nature mysticism, where nature itself is revered and worshiped as the source of all life. Thus the highest expression of this path is where nature is deified and idealized as being the perfect expression of the material manifestation of Spirit; in many ways, this is a great but simplistic truth.

Nature has many faces, and it can be seen as being harsh, showing itself as the rule of the strongest and the survival of the fittest, and expressing itself in the brutal cloak of bared fangs and sharp claws. Yet it can also be seen as the mother of necessity and the ever-efficient balance of life and death. Ascending this path reveals the vitality and even the beautiful wisdom of all manifested life, and descending it brings forth the power of the life force that can regenerate and heal all living things. This path can be viewed as being pitiless and cruel, showing the dark primitive aspects of human nature that society seeks to represses, but which are also an integral and undeniable part of the human animal. It is also a path that teaches caution and probation, where the seeker must face and master the dark powers that are hidden in the recesses of the human heart. The archangels of this path are Sandalphon (Malkuth) and Haniel (Netzach). The Tarot trump is the Moon—XVIII.

28th Path

(Yesod to Netzach—Tzaddi—Aquarius): The 28th Path is a conduit of inspiration and revelation, for through it the pure forces of the creative imagination pour into the unconscious mind, producing the impetus for all creative endeavors. This path is the perfect channel for all artistic inspiration, whatever its medium or manner of expression. It can also express itself as innovative discoveries in the sciences, theoretical or applied. The key to mastering this path is to learn to form a kind of reservoir with the mind, so that the glory and higher inspirational aspects of the soul will gather and accumulate in this container, where they will collectively produce great ideas, discoveries, and creative expressions. Otherwise, these inspiring forces will rapidly pass through the mind, dissipate, and then quickly be forgotten. One needs to gather these influences together and let them steep, like a cup of exquisite tea, and not be tempted to taste it prematurely.

Ascending this path is like the quest for that essential but forgotten thing—never realized until it is given form and substance, yet it awakens one to the most essential elements of creativity and invention. Descending this path unleashes the creative emanations echoing from the source of all spirit, where form and imagination magically merge to produce things of haunting beauty and astonishing ingenuity. The symbol for this special issue of creativity and discovery is the Star, which is unique yet has no intrinsic meaning, but represents all things to all people; it is, in fact a symbol of a symbol. The archangels of this path are Gabriel (Yesod) and Haniel (Netzach). The Tarot trump is the Star—XVII.

27th Path

(Hod to Netzach—Peh—Mars): The 27th Path is the main girder of the personality, linking the creative power in Netzach to the center of the concrete intellect found within Hod. Therefore, this path is concerned with the structure and the balancing of the components of the personality. These psychic components are the very ideals which act as tools for the personality to understand itself and describe the outer world. Knowing these tools, or archetypes, allows one to understand the nature of the psyche and to reveal the inner aspirations and motivations that move one to act. The foundation of one's perception of reality is revealed in this path (as ontology), and also the ability to determine inner truth from falsehood. This is also a path of converging forces, which are characterized by the eternal conflict of the sacred and the profane, faith and knowledge, magic and science. It is where all ideals and beliefs are fully tested by the greater spiritual power of the Godhead and the lesser power of material limitations. Human nature is caught in the crossfire between divine and infernal forces, although in truth, they are one and the same. The secret wisdom of this path is to find the middle point of balance, and to adhere to it despite all calamity and outrageous fortune. The archangels of this path are Michael (Hod) and Haniel (Netzach). The Tarot trump is the Tower—XVI.

Note: The three paths leading upward to Tiphareth cross a veil that is called by Qabalists, Paroketh (PRKTh—a curtain), which is known as the veil of illusion. Below this veil are the so-called illusory manifestations of physical reality and their various worldly concerns, and above this veil is the domain of the essential world, the place where the super-symbolic structures of the archetypal world reside. Between these two opposing perspectives of reality is a gulf, which is referred to as the Lesser Abyss. Crossing it is the task of the adept. This gulf is a gap, wall, or dam that hinders exchanges between the domains of the lower and Higher Self. It must be bridged in order for a true flow of spirit to be released, flooding the self and causing it to be fully integrated within spirit, mind, and body. This gulf could also be called the omega-point between the personality dominated by the mind and the Higher Self of the Spirit. On the 26th Path, the intellect can facilitate a transformation of the mind into spirit. On the 25th Path, the will, memory, and instinct associated with the lower self must be set aside before the virtues of charity, faith, and hope can become truly realized. And on the 24th Path, ego death has to be undergone before one can be reborn into a higher state of consciousness.

26th Path

(Hod to Tiphareth—Ain—Capricorn): This path, like the 27th, is a very difficult one to cross because it tests the intellect of the seeker as he goes through an intense transformative process. When the seeker passes from Hod to Tiphareth, or from self-awareness to spiritual self-illumination, his mind becomes radically changed so that he is able to briefly perceive his own spiritual source—the Higher Self. The ascent of this path is a process of personal transition, where the ego-based mind experiences the profound perception of its own godhood reflected in the Higher Self, and this causes changes of a permanent nature to occur. In descending this path, the Higher Self reveals itself to the mind, soul, and body of the seeker, and immerses itself in the dreams and illusions of the material world. The exchange between the rational intellect and the mysterious Higher Self produces a special kind of spiritual wisdom and insight, which can be used to transform the material world, and also to translate the spiritual one.

Therefore, the underlying meaning of this path is that it represents a profound challenge to the seeker's integrity. Through it, the seeker meets his internalized and personal Godhead, and that apparition emerges through the veil of his intellect, causing it to be either distorted or crystal clear. How the seeker perceives and then deals with that revelation will determine if he is able to evolve past his limitations, or succumb to self-idolatry. It will either powerfully transform him or it will ultimately destroy him. This great test is called an initiation by some, and it can either exalt the seeker with a true realization of the self as Deity, or utterly confuse him with delusion. The archangels of this path are Michael (Hod) and Raphael (Tiphareth). The Tarot trump is the Devil—XV.

25th Path

(Yesod to Tiphareth—Samek—Sagittarius): On this path, the seeker experiences the first glimmerings of the purely transcendent consciousness, the ineffable union of being, experienced fully through the emotional body. Paradoxically, this path also produces the terrible experience known as the *Dark Night of the Soul*. Symbolically, the soul engages this path as if she were traversing the endless wasteland of the desert, having left behind the fancies and delights of the material world to seek the truth in the stark but pristine world of self-denial. She walks this featureless Pathway without light, blinded by the darkness and the monotonous terrain.

The mysterious key to this path is to call upon the inner light of one's faith, that through steadfast prayer and meditation, the seeker will find the path that leads her to the blessed oasis and personal salvation. It is by faith alone, and by the will, that the soul will overturn the darkness and find its way. Even so, the passage is difficult and long, and the powerful emotions of defeat and despair are always hovering around the seeker. The ordeal of this Pathway is actually the second stage of personal transformation, but it is not the hardest, since that is to be found in the 18th Pathway. However, this path shares with the 26th and the 24th Paths the threefold ordeal of life's first major passage. Ascending this path, the seeker will find a world of apparent darkness and aridity, where her soul will aspire to the light of higher consciousness, sustained only by the power of faith and will. Descending, the seeker shall experience the downward flow of life, light, and love from the Higher and Illuminated Self, seeking to make and establish contact with its incarnated double. The archangels of this path are Gabriel (Yesod) and Raphael (Tiphareth). The Tarot trump is Temperance—XIV.

24th Path

(Netzach to Tiphareth—Nun—Scorpio): The experience of this path is one of complete physical transformation, perceived as an inexorable and unavoidable change, which is symbolized by both death and rebirth. The ascent of the 24th Path initiates a form of death or powerful transition of the lower self as the false ego, which jealously guards the self from experiencing true spiritual revelations. This "death" of the lower self can also precipitate other changes as well, including a near-death or actual-death experience. Generally, this path is characterized by the transformation of the petty ego, where the seeker experiences a radical transition that is triggered by a general collapse of the self and its many props, defense mechanisms, and illusory values. What causes this transformation is the revelation that death or change is imminent (a kind of spiritual truth), which cannot be avoided or rationalized. With the "death" of the petty ego is also experienced the rebirth and regeneration of the self assisted through an intervention of one's Higher Self, which helps the seeker to create a truthful and non-dual transcendental identity. In this type of internal death and rebirth, the seeker's outer appearances may remain unchanged, yet his inner being is completely transformed.

Often, when such an inner change becomes fully stabilized, outward changes occur as well, since the light of the Higher Self is allowed to shine forth through the lower self and the body, producing glamour and an extended charisma. A change in personal motivation and aspiration must also occur. Before this event, the seeker was very much concerned with personal ambitions and basic self-fulfillment; afterwards, he has become a servant of his greater spiritual process. No longer can he selfishly seek physical gratification and personal ambition without first fulfilling his spiritual avocation. This is because of the fact that within this path, the needs of the many do indeed outweigh the needs of the few or the one—spiritual service thereby becomes paramount. Therefore, the seeker is irreparably transformed, but in the process he loses the naivety that allowed such childlike pursuits as selfish gratification and blind ambition. The archangels of this path are Haniel (Netzach) and Raphael (Tiphareth). The Tarot trump is Death—XIII.

23rd Path

(Hod to Geburah—Mim—Water): Passage through this Pathway forces the seeker to use her mental powers to eliminate the superfluous and concentrate on what is truly important and decisive in regard to spiritual evolution. The key to this path is to become as one-pointed as possible, and to discard all extraneous beliefs and false propositions. This process is a kind of powerful mental purification, which is a necessary precursor to achieving an intellectual bond with the Godhead. This is because the Sephirah of Geburah is the testing place for all beliefs and self-definitions, and the powers that reside within it have a very low tolerance for the superficial and the irrelevant.

This path inverts all of the seeker's values and beliefs, thereby testing them, and places a great pressure on all of the components of her being. There is a sense of suspension and timelessness, and also an ending of the world that was previously known and taken for granted. It is the path of self-sacrifice, where the seeker offers up herself for the redemption of her whole being. This is the primary Mystery of the Dying God, which symbolizes the self-inflicted martyrdom of the illusory self. The activation of this mystery dispels all illusions and deceptions, making room solely for the inner truth, since it alone can assist the seeker who has dwelt in darkness until this moment. The key concept here is not to cling to falsehood, but to ardently seek the revelation of self-truth, and bravely undergo its ordeal. The archangels of this path are Michael (Hod) and Khamael (Geburah). The Tarot trump is the Hanged Man—XII.

22nd Path

(Tiphareth to Geburah—Lamed—Libra): This path is generally known as the path of balance and the adjustment of fate. This is a path where the seeker undergoes whatever is necessary to bring about equilibrium, and this becomes his ongoing and essential discipline. However, the kind of equilibrium that is suggested by the merging of the harsh forces of Geburah and the gentle sagacity of Tiphareth is one of inner strength and self-restraint. There is a need for a reduction to the basic essentials that are a necessary part of this stage of spiritual growth, and the process of refinement and reduction is well represented by this path. Yet there is healing wisdom here, and also spiritual guidance to assist and help the seeker. Through this ordeal, the seeker experiences compassion and benignity.

The seeker also understands the need for balancing the self between extremes, a process that is omitted in the previous path. Through the ordeal of this Pathway, the seeker must learn to master his more basic instincts and temper his desire to indulge and dissipate himself. Achieving this goal takes voluntarily action, so the seeker adopts the techniques of self-control and the ethics of a spiritual discipline to completely master the lower self. When the lower self is fully integrated into the Higher Self, the seeker is truly prepared for the more stressful processes of spiritual enlightenment. The archangels of this path are Raphael (Tiphareth) and Khamael (Geburah). The Tarot trump is Justice—XI.

21st Path

(Netzach to Chesed—Kaph—Jupiter): The 21st Path characterizes the potential of becoming fully actualized and, therefore, forever stepping outside of the boundaries of the capriciousness of good and bad fortune (the eternal cycle of the wheel of birth and death). The forces of the benevolent Godhead of infinite abundance and goodness bestow upon the intrepid seeker the grace and material salvation that removes, for all time, the possibility of loss and privation. The power of the Deity is so vast that it completely elevates the seeker from out of the state of constant need and want, and bestows upon her the favor of a seemingly charmed existence.

Still, this grace and abundance must be earned through a perfect and seamless connection or conduit between the seeker and the brilliant light of the Godhead; any doubt or disbelief will thwart that tenuous connection. It is only through perfect faith that the seeker is able to channel the grace of the Deity, and then, only selflessly and abundantly for all. The Sephirah into which the influences of Chesed flow via the 21st Path is Netzach, representing the creative imagination and higher emotions within the personality. Thus, the effects of this path are responsible for the ideals and aspirations that capture the imagination of humanity. Foremost of these, in the Western Mystery tradition, is the ideal for the Quest of the Holy Grail—that rare and precious restorative of perfect grace. This quest greatly affects the heart and the emotions (romance), becoming that single-most yearning for what is missing, which impels men and women to undergo the spiritual quest. Also within this path is the concept that the Quest for the Grail will forever alter and transform the seeker, and even bar those who are unworthy of its revelation. The archangels of this path are Haniel (Netzach) and Tzadkiel (Chesed). The Tarot trump is the Wheel of Fortune—X.

20th Path

(Tiphareth to Chesed—Yod—Virgo): The 20th Path symbolizes the mysterious hidden light of wisdom and the intuitive knowledge of the Deity taking root in the self, which is the inspired heart of the seeker. Therefore, this path represents the process of illumination whereby the secret knowledge of one's Higher Self is fully revealed and made conscious and knowable. Yet such a profound translation of the self requires a period of withdrawal from the material world as a form of ascetic monasticism, and by a deep, sustained, internal contemplation on the nature of one's spiritual essence. That spiritual source of the self, which is ardently and passionately sought by the seeker, is found only deep within the core of his being, and all that exists external to this source is but a poor reflection of that which is within.

It is therefore critically important for the seeker to realize the futility of any outward search for truth, and the importance of surrendering himself to that inward revelation. The Higher Self cannot be approached without spiritual love, so the seeker must first develop and realize that hallowed state. The second requirement is that the seeker must forsake all other achievements as illusory, and thereby empty himself of all expectations and premeditated beliefs—one must be completely open and without bias. All the myths about the true self must by this time be purged and abandoned, and also any ambitions or expectations that one would subsequently place upon it. The heart is purified by a renunciation of all vanity and false glamour, and by the surrendering of all the cares and concerns of the material world. The seeker has placed himself completely at the mercy of the Deity, and therein the Higher Self emerges through the refined gateway of the heart. The marriage of heart with spirit connects the seeker with the spiritual source that is pure and essential. The archangels of this path are Raphael (Tiphareth) and Tzadkiel (Chesed). The Tarot trump is the Hermit—IX.

19th Path

(Geburah to Chesed—Teth—Leo): The 19th Path is another principal girder or connecting structure for the Higher Self. As noted above, Chesed is the Sephirah associated with the compassion and spiritual love of the Higher Self and what it seeks to become in the mundane sphere. Geburah is the Sephirah associated with actions, the fate of the Higher Self, or the work that it is destined to do. The tension between these two modes of being, which is the tension of attempting to fulfill a spiritual ideal in the material world, is the essential ordeal of this path. Basically, the challenge of this path is to accept everything that has happened during the seeker's complete life cycle. The seeker must accept her fate as it exists, without any evasions or excuses. Acceptance is the key to this path, and the seeker must accept not only her true nature, but also her destiny, which is the union of the essence and the motivation of the Higher Self. The necessity of balancing Severity and Mercy within the core of oneself so as not to be dominated by either one represents a virtue of complete self-mastery. The other Pathways below this one have helped to determine the nature of the seeker's inner Deity, and now she must assume that inner Godhead and fulfill her personal destiny. It is because of the fact that this ordeal, as splendid and magnificent as it may seem, is only a precursor to the supreme ordeal, which is the crossing of the Greater Abyss. The archangels of this path are Khamael (Geburah) and Tzadkiel (Chesed). The Tarot trump is Strength—VIII.

Abysmal Crossing

All of the paths that lead to the supernal triad of Kether, Chokmah, and Binah (Paths 18 through 15, and 13) must pass over a great barrier that is known as the Greater Abyss. This chasm is similar to the Lesser Abyss or Veil of Paroketh, which was previously mentioned. The Greater Abyss is the barrier that isolates the seeker's individual conscious being from the absolute Godhead; yet this barrier isn't insurmountable, representing the fact that human nature and the nature of the Deity are more closely related than most realize. The barrier is really a wall consisting of super-consciousness and the at-one-ment of perfect conscious union, which separates the One from the many. Whichever spiritual path the seeker undertakes, whether it is the path of the mystic, the magician, or the philosopher, crossing the Greater Abyss represents the most exalted transformation, where he is wholly dissolved within the achievement of union with the One. The successful passage of the Abyss is characterized by a total awareness of the divinity that is now awakened within oneself. That the Godhead is alive and connecting all sentient beings into itself fosters the impression that the seeker as God is one with all things, and all things are one with him.

18th Path

(Geburah to Binah—Cheth—Cancer): The 18th Path is the place where the confluence of the dynamic and ever-moving spiritual powers merges into the peaceful, still, and pure intuitive wisdom of the Deity. It is where the spinning wheel of the cosmic spiral and the chalice container of the infinite source unite into a single expression—the Merka-bah or chariot, the Holy Throne and the grail as the Well of Souls. Thus, force, form, and source are joined together to produce the ineffable mystery of this Pathway, which is the embodiment and empowerment of the Feminine Archetype (Binah) as the primal creative female—the Great Goddess.

The spiritual light that ascends this Pathway reveals the primal forces of creation, where the One is refracted and distilled to become the great potential for the myriad of individual souls. Conversely, the descent of this supernal light is the creation of the souls of the living. The seeker who follows this path discovers that essential key to all mysteries, which reveals the primal motive for her individual creation and the creation of all beings, occurring beyond all time and space. The 18th Path, as all the paths associated with the supernal triad, represents a mystery of being, and as the feminine polarity of the Tree of Life, it is the feminine mystery of creation and formation. The archangels of this path are Khamael (Geburah) and Tzadkiel (Tiphareth). The Tarot trump is the Chariot—VII.

17th Path

(Tiphareth to Binah—Zayin—Gemini): The 17th Path is the mysterious corridor that fosters the union between the Higher Self and the ultimate aspect of the Godhead, who are known as the mysterious twins (Dioscuri)—one mortal, and the other immortal. The mystery of this Pathway is found in the alchemical wedding between the lower self, the Higher Self and the Deity, where dual aspects of the self are merged into a perfect union through the Mediation of Absolute Spirit. Perfect union has many attributes, but is represented in alchemy as the manifestation of the philosopher's stone and the universal medicine. The conduit between Binah and Tiphareth symbolizes the power to create, regenerate, and exalt all living things, which represents the very end and beginning of all spiritual and magical accomplishment. This path represents the mystery of the Marriage of the Holy Spirit, which occurs through the joining of the Archetypal Feminine with the Divine Son as Mediator. The archangels of this path are Raphael (Tiphareth) and Tzaphkiel (Binah). The Tarot trump is the Lovers—VI.

16th Path

(Chesed to Chokmah—Vav—Taurus): The 16th Path is where wisdom and grace join to formulate the perfect illuminating power of the active Godhead, manifesting its beauty and charisma into the world through the mediation of the avatar, which is the physical representative of the Godhead among all sentient beings. This Pathway, as the masculine refection of the 18th Path, is a fulcrum of creation and love, wisdom and compassion, emanating perfectly from the Greater Wisdom of the Godhead so that it shines both above and below, illuminating everything with its brilliant light. Emanating in a descending arc, this illuminating light becomes the enlightened mastery of the messiah achieving the Great Work, and it is the inspired word of the Deity. Ascending upwards, it is the words of power as sacred invocations that cause the light of the Godhead to be realized in the mind of human beings and to reverberate through the material world. The descent is symbolized by the Horn of Plenty, the manifestation of all grace.

The key to this Pathway is that through the divine word, or Logos, all things are created in both heaven and earth, and that the avatar or messiah holds the key to unleashing and using the divine word. This path represents the integration of the cosmogonic cycle with that of the individual cycle of initiation, thus seamlessly blending the individual into the infinite. The archangels of this path are Tzadkiel (Chesed) and Raziel (Chokmah). The Tarot trump is the Hierophant—V.

15th Path

(Tiphareth to Chokmah—Heh—Aries): The 15th Path symbolizes the incarnation of the holy anointed leader as the temporal representative of the Deity in the mundane world, who is guided by the wisdom and foresight of the Higher Self. This Pathway is the conduit of divine kingship, where through a mortal mediator the powers and wisdom of the Godhead are brought into harmonious union with the earth. Thus all things are balanced and made perfect through the harmonious interaction of heaven and earth.

The key to this Pathway is that the mediator as divine leader must be a perfect channel for the expression of divine wisdom and power, and he or she must be completely unbiased and without prejudice, since any interference with the Deity will destroy the delicate balance of heaven and earth. Such a divine leader is given the power and authority of the Deity to use with justice, wisdom and compassion, since what is given can easily be taken away. Wisdom flows down from Chokmah to assemble in the heart of the Higher Self in Tiphareth, and in order to channel this wisdom, the seeker must mediate selflessly and without any interference. Only in this manner is the will of the Deity brought into perfect alignment with the will of the leader, and in perfect harmony with the kingdom. The archangels of this path are Raphael (Tiphareth) and Raziel (Chokmah). The Tarot trump is the Emperor—IV.

14th Path

(Binah to Chokmah—Daleth—Venus): The 14th Path is the cross-path or girder for the triad of Spirit, as the 27th Path is to the personality and the 19th Path is to the Higher Self. The 14th Path is the first path that is completely within the supernal triad, so it exists within the world of ideas without form. It is the gateway or doorway that guards the domain of the Absolute Spirit, signifying that individual consciousness may not pass through this point. This path unites the archetypal masculine (Chokmah) with the archetypal feminine (Binah), so that the full light of perfect illumination is joined with the receptive and formative intuition, thus becoming the first cause of the manifestation and creation of all things. Within this unified field of consciousness, the thoughts of the One seek to formulate the perfected state of being in all its glory and simplicity. The archangels of this path are Tzaphkiel (Binah) and Raziel (Chokmah). The Tarot trump is the Empress—III.

13th Path

(Tiphareth to Kether—Gimel—Moon): The 13th Path is the Pathway of the Mystic, where the brilliant and pure light of the Deity is directly and perfectly received in all its terrible majesty. The mystic seeks not the redemption of himself or the world, but only the pure and unadulterated revelation of the Godhead. The mystic performs this action selflessly, grounded in humility and wholly absorbed, since he only seeks to behold it. The method of spiritual achievement through this path is the slow and painful elimination of all that might act as a barrier between oneself and the Deity. The first stage is the revelation of the Deity within oneself, and the second is the realization of the unity of everything within the Godhead. The world and its concerns, including the needs and the wants of the self, have long been eliminated, so that nothing interferes with the simplicity and purity of the experience of blissful spiritual union. The final stage is achieved through the annihilation of the self as container and the total identification of the self with the Deity, so that there is no part of the seeker that is not a part of that Unity. The archangels of this path are Raphael (Tiphareth) and Metatron (Kether). The Tarot trump is the High Priestess—II.

12th Path

(Binah to Kether—Beit—Mercury): The 12th Path is called the Occult Intelligence (Prophecy), because it represents the revelation of all things (archetypal forms) as they truly are, but seen as if in a vision. All veils are cast aside and the Pure Light of the Absolute Spirit is allowed to be perceived by the intuition instead of the mind, so the nature of divine prophecy is revealed. Divine prophecy is defined as the illuminating vision that reveals the manifestation of the ultimate inner mechanism of divine fate, showing everything that ever was and will ever be as a single suspended moment. It is also true that the seeker may find herself fully conscious in that vision, directing the manifestation of the universe through her being and acting as a cosmic channel. Through the power of this path the seeker is able to comprehend and work through the Godhead, investing all time and space with the essence of herself, and therein creating a universe. The experience of the Godhead is softened by dreams and visions. The manifestation of the feminine archetype personifying the Absolute Spirit represents the activation of the powers of creation, and also the qualities of compassion and preservation. In this manner the love and wisdom of the Deity is expressed for all created things, and this symbolizes the perfection of all magic. The archangels of this path are Tzaphkiel (Binah) and Metatron (Kether). The Tarot trump is the Magician—I.

11th Path

(Chokmah to Kether—Aleph—Air): The 11th Path is the corridor where one receives the vision of the Absolute Spirit, face to face, as co-equals. The power of the Absolute Spirit engenders itself; therefore it gives birth to the First Principle that is its reflection. In this fashion was Spirit made manifest as an ideal, thereby causing its own dissemination. Yet the Light that comes from the Primal Source is blinding and when one is exposed to it, the singular sense of being-ness becomes an illuminating self-knowledge that annihilates all else. It's like a circular mirror reflecting the light of the Deity in all directions at once. A devotee of this Pathway is one who is divinely mad, denoting that the expression of pure genius is without regard to form or process. The key to this path is that it represents the introduction of a singular paradox into the unified domain of the One. It is the mystery of the self and the reflected not-self. That paradox is also found within the nature of the Divine Fool, who is simultaneously wise and giddily foolish. The Fool is the one who expresses wisdom in its most essential and simplistic form, but who cannot speak anything but nonsense. The pure expression of Spirit causes the Fool to become ecstatic and wild, where he is released from all concerns and limitations, and so is truly free and whole. The archangels of this path are Raziel (Chokmah) and Metatron (Kether). The Tarot trump is the Fool—0.

Pathway Patterns and Considerations

There are several different patterns when examining the structures that the Pathways produce in the diagram of the Tree of Life. While there are the obvious and subtle geometric patterns found in the Tree—such as a pentagram, heptagram, crosses, triangles, and a hexagram—these I will leave to others who are more interested in the details of sacred geometry. Sacred geometry, and a detailed analysis of the patterns in regard to the structures that the Pathways produce, could easily fill a book, so we will concern ourselves instead with just a few of the more important patterns and leave the esoteric anatomy of the body of the Godhead to those more inclined to occult minutiae. The Tree of Life in its classical illustration has three horizontal paths, seven vertical paths, and 12 diagonal paths, which is similar to the division of the 22 letters of the Hebrew alphabet. Still, there are just four major patterns that should occupy the essential Qabalist, and these are the lightning flash, Three Pillars, Four Worlds, and the Serpent's Ascent.

As a side note, Moses Cordovero included an illustration of his Tree of Life design in the book *Pardes Rimonim* (Garden of Pomegranates) and that became the classical design most recognized today; but another version (without the two lower Pathways) was illustrated in the same work. So, at least two versions were promoted by Cordovero. The second version without the lower Pathways became the version lionized by Isaac Luria, and is now the version used by many Jewish Qabalists.

Lightning Flash

This is an emblem of the process of emanation and involution, where the unmanifest and unknowable Godhead created the first Sephirah, and from that foundation-point in the manifested universe, it created the other Sephiroth. The Pathway of emanation and involution follows what Qabalists have called the *lightning flash*, since the process of creation was instantaneous and proceeded from the highest level to the lowest. In fact, because the process of emanation is not something that occurred just once, but is an ongoing and continuous process, the lightning flash is a pattern that is also continuously occurring, although less dramatically than the very first time it occurred. The lightning flash is a zigzag pattern that moves down and to the right, connecting all ten of the Sephiroth. Many of the conduits of this flash coincide with Pathways on the Tree of Life, except for one, which is a noted hypothetical Pathway but where no actual path exists. That hypothetical Pathway is from Binah to Chesed, where the lightning flash must pass if it is to follow the most direct path from Sephirah to Sephirah. The other points of the angular path of the lightning bolt cover specific Pathways in the Tree of Life, marking them as uniquely associated with the direct emanation of the Godhead.

A curious thing about the implied Pathway from Binah to Chesed is that there were once thought to be two crossing Pathways, which included yet another implied Pathway, and this one was from Chokmah to Geburah. So there are actually two implied Pathways that cross in the area of the Greater Abyss, although in the modern Qabalah, these Pathways don't really exist. In an 18th-century diagram of the Tree of Life (an example can be found in Gershom Scholem's book *Kabbalah*, page 146), the crossed Pathways that directly connect Binah with Chesed, and Chokmah with Geburah, are plainly shown; but the two Pathways connecting Malkuth with Hod and Netzach are missing. This diagram of the Tree of Life was known as the Sephed Tree, and as previously stated, was originally designed by Cordovero.

There can only be 22 Pathways because there are only 22 Hebrew letters, so some possible Pathway connections must be omitted for the sake of establishing others. What we can assume by this small revelation is that the implied Pathway associated with the emanating flash of Lightning is one of perhaps a few other implied Pathways. However, the cross-paths from the supernal triad that are missing and only implied do have a subtle importance, and should be the subject for further meditation and investigation.

Pathways associated with the lightning flash are: 11, 14, Binah to Chesed (implied), 19, 22, 24, 27, 30, and 32. There are nine paths associated with this pattern, but only eight are actual Pathways out of a total of 22. These Pathways are uniquely qualified as being on the direct route of the divine emanations, and when meditating on the 22 paths, this should be an important point to consider. (See figure 7.)

Three Pillars

Isaac Luria was the master scholar who first organized the Tree of Life into a dialectic arrangement (thesis, antithesis, synthesis) between Three Pillars: that of Mercy, Severity, and the Middle Pillar. One could also consider the left hand (Severity) to be feminine, and the right hand to be masculine (Mercy), with the Middle Pillar representing the synthesis of the two polarized extremes—a place of Mediation. The differentiation between left hand and right hand can also be interpreted as the difference between the left-hand and right-hand spiritual paths. Thus the Sephiroth

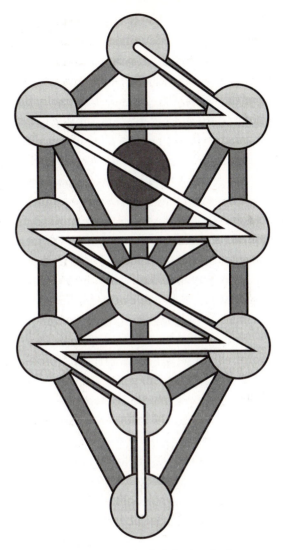

Figure 7: Tree of Life lightning flash

Binah, Geburah, and Hod make up the Pillar of Severity, and Chokmah, Chesed, and Netzach make up the Pillar of Mercy, while the Sephiroth of Kether, Tiphareth, Yesod, and Malkuth make up the Middle Pillar.

Additionally, there are three groups of Pathways in this configuration: those that make up the Three Pillars and those that cross-connect the pillars. By far, the cross-connecting Pathways make up the larger share of overall Pathways, showing that the Tree of Life is mostly concerned with the synthesis and mitigation of the polarities of Severity and Mercy, thereby ensuring overall harmony and balance within the framework of the Tree.

Pathways of the Pillar of Severity: 23 and 18.

Pathways of the Pillar of Mercy: 21 and 16.

Pathways of the Middle Pillar: 32, 25, and 13.

Cross-connecting Pathways: 31, 29, 30, 28, 27, 26, 24, 22, 20, 19, 17, 15, 14, 12, 11. (Of these fourteen paths, which cross-connect the Three Pillars, only three actually connect the Pillars of Severity directly with Mercy, and are considered the main girders of the structure of the Tree. These are Paths 27, 19, and 14; the rest bind the middle with the two outlying pillars.)

When analyzing the qualities of the Pathways, special consideration should be given to those Pathways that are part of the Three Pillars, and those that cross-connect the Three Pillars (especially those that join Severity with Mercy), thereby resolving and harmonizing the evident polarities. (See figure 8.)

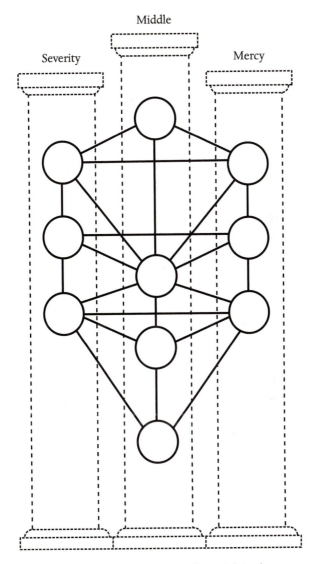

Figure 8: Tree of Life as Three Pillars with Pathways

Four Worlds

The Qabalistic Four Worlds structure is often considered a separate way of examining the process of creation through emanation and involution. In fact, Qabalistic scholars have shown that each of the ten Sephiroth can be shown to contain each of the Four Worlds, as is aptly demonstrated in William G. Gray's ingenious book *The Ladder of Lights*. Thus, using this paradigm, one could conceivably show a complete Tree of Life structure encapsulated by one of the Four Worlds, therefore making a total of 40 Sephiroth and 88 Pathways, which would make most Qabalistic speculation quite complicated to say the least. Still, there is another way of comparing the Tree of Life with the Four Worlds[29] to produce a method of dividing the Tree into these specific domains.

The highest world is Atziluth, which represents the archetypal world of pure ideals, which are unchanging and immutable, but dynamic rather than static. This world would be the exclusive domain of the Sephirah Kether.

Briah is next highest world, which represents the ideals or archetypes in motion, thus representing the impulse of creation, where form and ideation come together into a synthesis. This world would be the domain of the two Sephiroth Chokmah and Binah.

Below the supernal triad is the Qabalistic world of Yetzirah, the formative world, where the aspects of personality and individuality merge to formulate individual entities, which are spirits and souls. Despite the formulation

---

29. See chapter 7 for a complete discussion of the Four Qabalistic Worlds.

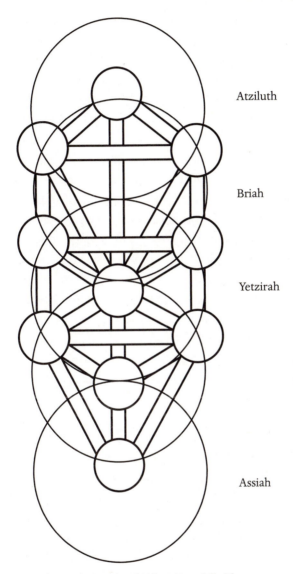

Figure 9: Tree of Life as Four Worlds

Atziluth

Briah

Yetzirah

Assiah

of individuals and the establishment of limitations, all of the entities of this world are still consciously connected to the one. This world would be the domain of six Sephiroth: Chesed, Geburah, Tiphareth, Netzach, Hod, and Yesod.

Assiah is the lowest world, where souls merge with material bodies to populate the physical world and to animate it with life. This world would be the exclusive domain of Malkuth.

Pathways that cross between the Four Worlds can be considered the important conduits of creation and illumination. They should be given that special consideration when they are examined. Therefore, the paths that connect Assiah to Yetzirah would be 32, 31, and 29; the paths that connect Yetzirah to Briah would be 18, 17, 16, 15, and 13; and the paths that connect Briah to Atziluth would be 12 and 11. These bridging Pathways could be considered the veritable portals between worlds. (See figure 9.) (Another variation would be where Kether and Chokmah would be Atziluth, and Binah, alone, would be Briah, such as depicted in Crowley's Naples arrangement.)

Serpent's Ascent

This pattern of Pathways represents the slow and meticulous ascent up the Tree of Life, where the guiding rule is to always proceed from left to right, and from lower to higher, so that the paths of the lower Sephirah are considered before the paths of a higher Sephirah. The Ascent also follows the opposite direction used when reading Hebrew (left to right instead of right to left). This cyclic pattern is useful for performing pathworkings, which is a topic that we will examine in chapter 10.

The Pathway pattern for the Serpent's Ascent consists of the following paths in the following sequential order: 32, 31, 29, 30, 28, 25, 27, 26, 23, 24, 21, 22, 20, 17, 13, 15, 18, 16, 14, 12, 11. (See figure 10.)

Crossing Paths

One of the most interesting things about the Pathways on the Tree of Life are the specific points where they cross. For whatever reason, there is nothing mentioned about it in any of the books that I have read. While this phenomenon does not commonly occur, pathworkings, as well as analyzing the qualities of a specific path, are performed in isolation of any other path that might cross the one being considered. In order to determine the nature of a specific Pathway, we must, of course, examine the two Sephiroth that it connects, but nothing is ever said of the Pathways that it intersects. Certainly, if two paths cross each other, then it would seem obvious that this incidence should have some kind of effect. Curiously, I have seen some diagrams of the Tree of Life where the crossing Pathways are shown to actually pass over and under each other, so that they never actually meet.

At some point, a Qabalist can discover some additional insights when considering those Pathways that cross each other. It is my belief that this junction of two paths is particularly significant, symbolizing that the confluence of Pathway correspondences meet and briefly merge at this point. Crossing paths make a sign of the cross in the structure of the Tree, so I believe that we should examine the nature of the paths and where they cross.

Curiously, there are five points where paths cross each other, and these occur at the three bridging Pathways that

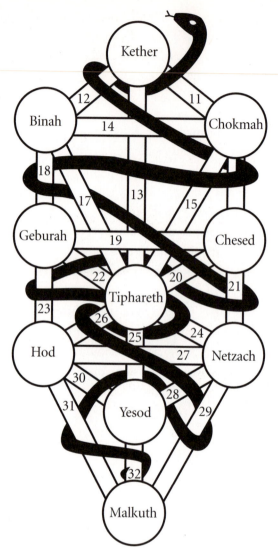

Figure 10: Tree of Life and Ascending Pathway Serpent

join the Pillars of Mercy and Severity. There is one cross-path between Tiphareth, Yesod, Hod, and Netzach, which occurs with the Paths 25 (Samek—Temperance) and 27 (Peh—The Tower). This cross-path would seem to symbolize an aspect of the crossing of the Lesser Abyss and the realization of initiatic adepthood.

The other four cross points occur at the threshold of the Greater Abyss. Path 19 (Tet—Strength), which is the girder of personality (and the Higher Self) is crossed by three paths, which are Paths 17 (Zayin—Lovers), 13 (Gimel—High Priestess), and 15 (Heh—Emperor). These three paths represent the three points of transition from Tiphareth to the supernal triad, which would symbolize a series of profound transformations, where the individual becomes one with aspects of the Godhead. Additionally, Path 13 (Gimel—High Priestess) also crosses Path 14 (Daleth—Empress), signifying that the final perfect mystical union of the seeker and the Godhead occurs through the aegis of feminine mediators, since Path 13 penetrates not only the Greater Abyss, but the supernal triad itself.

These strategic points where paths cross and connect could also be considered *nexus* points, since they are also important stages of transition and transformation for the seeker. At any rate, a lot more thought and consideration can be applied to these mystical points. Certainly, through meditation and magical envisioning, additional subtle insights might also be revealed. I have found in my own inquiries and discoveries that the cross points actually indicate hidden additional Sephiroth, which are not part of the canonical considerations of the classical Qabalah.

Crowley and the
"Tzaddi Is Not the Star" Controversy

If you continue your studies of the Tarot and the Qabalah, at some point you will notice differences between the sequential numbering between Tarot decks and their associated placement on the Pathways of the Tree of Life. To deal with these differences, and the fact that they are sometimes not explained, I decided to address a couple of the discrepancies here.

The first difference has to do with the placement and sequential associations with the cards/paths of Strength and Justice. I have decided to maintain the traditional sequence and placement of the Tarot cards to the paths as set down and used by the Golden Dawn, and these become readily apparent when examining the Tarot Roman numerals used for Strength (trump VIII—path 19) and Justice (trump XI—path 22). The path numbering is easily derived by adding 11 to the Roman numeral. A cursory examination of the Rider-Waite-Colman Tarot will verify the sequence of these cards. However, other decks, such as Crowley's Thoth Tarot, use the Roman numerals XI for Strength (Lust) and VIII for Justice (Adjustment), but their placement on the Tree of Life is preserved. This difference could cause some confusion for the beginner.

Whatever the sequence of Roman numerals used in either Crowley's Tarot or in the traditional Golden Dawn, the position of these two cards on the Tree of Life is identical. Yet Crowley's choice of numerals for Justice and Strength are not uniquely his own invention. They are the same as the Tarot of Marseilles, which has been dated back to the late 15th century. So there would appear to be more than one traditional sequence to the Tarot. Perhaps it would be more significant if the associated paths were changed, but, in fact, the placement of paths is the same between the two systems. This has the effect of making the differences less strategic (and important) than they might otherwise be.

Not to be outdone, Aleister Crowley has also determined another change in the attributes of the Tarot trumps. I am referring to the controversy over the attributions of the Tarot trumps of the Star and the Emperor. He has written that the Hebrew letter *Tzaddi* is not to be associated with the Tarot trump the Star (XVII), and it would also mean that the Tarot trump the Emperor, which is its zodiacal opposite, would exchange its association with the letter Heh, with that of the Star card, Tzaddi.

What this means is that the Tarot trumps associated with the paths are swapped, but the path associations and their corresponding Hebrew letters would remain the same. So, the letter Tzaddi would become associated with the Emperor Tarot trump and the 28th Path (Yesod to Netzach), and Heh would become associated with the Star Tarot trump and the 15th Path (Tiphareth to Chokmah). The astrological signs would remain the same and so would the sequence of the letters, but the two Tarot card associations with the two paths would change. I believe that this alteration would have quite a dramatic effect on the way in which the Tarot cards might be depicted, which is a reasonable assumption.

Crowley's defense for making this switch was based on the famous Double Loop in the zodiac, where the signs of the zodiac are associated with specific Tarot trumps. As already noted, Crowley had previously changed the numbering of the Tarot trumps Strength (XI—Leo) and Justice (VIII—Libra) also based on the Double Loop, and these changes have been pretty much accepted by many occultists.

Still, even Crowley's Tarot deck, the Thoth Tarot, didn't seem to really incorporate this change to the Emperor and Star cards, which still appear to have the old associations. One would think that these two cards would also radically change in how they were depicted if they indeed became associated with a different Hebrew letter and relative position in the Tree of Life.

The inspiration for this change occurred in the transmission of Crowley's *Book of the Law*, which Thelemites accept as the truly channeled and inspired pronouncements of the Godhead of the New Aeon as revealed by Crowley's higher self, Awaiz. It would seem that this alteration has not been universally adopted by others who don't share the beliefs of Thelema. So for this reason I have chosen to present the 22 Pathways using their traditional correspondences and associations, even though I find myself tentatively agreeing with Crowley in this matter. I might even go further and seek to change the associated astrological signs, which was something that Crowley and his fellow Thelemites didn't do.

However, what would the Tarot trump, the Emperor or the Star, look like if they used a different Hebrew letter and associated astrological sign, not to mention their place in the structure of the Tree of Life? I have given this a lot of thought and consideration over the years and have come up with some ideas that might help this new variation become more accepted.

If the Emperor Tarot trump was changed to the 28th Path (Yesod to Netzach) and associated with the Hebrew letter Tzaddi, and the astrological sign of Aquarius (which I believe goes with the letter Tzaddi—a fish hook), then what we would get would be something more akin to the Fisher King of the Grail Myth instead of the imperial and majestic power associated with the 15th Path.

Likewise, the Star Tarot trump, if it was changed to the 15th Path (Tiphareth to Chokmah) and associated with the Hebrew letter Heh, and the astrological sign of Aries, then we would get something akin to the star of doomsday, which would show that the Fire of the Godhead was preparing to descend upon the world and engulf it in a final conflagration. That same star could represent a sign of the immanent appearance of the avatar as son of the Godhead (like the Star of Bethlehem).

Of course all of this is speculation, and Crowley did leave the astrological signs in place on the Pathways, so the change wouldn't be quite as dramatic. Crowley does talk about the Fisher King in regard to the Emperor trump, but employs a rendition of Nuit as the Seven-starred Goddess who is engaged in drawing forth and pouring fluids from one cup into another, which is analogous to the Aquarius theme, but with the difference of channeling the majesty of

Chokmah into the domain of Tiphareth. I will leave making any kind of determination one way or the other to you, my readers, depending on whether you accept the teachings and inspirations of Aleister Crowley or not.

Table of Correspondences of the 22 Pathways

Path No.	Hebrew Letter	Meaning	Attribute	Tarot Trump	Queen Scale Colors	Path Positions—Sephirah to Sephirah
11	Aleph	Ox	Air	0: Fool	Sky Blue	Kether—Chokmah
12	Beth	House	Mercury	I: Magician	Purple	Kether—Binah
13	Gimel	Camel	Moon	II: High Priestess	Silver	Kether—Tiphareth
14	Daleth	Door	Venus	III: Empress	Emerald Green*	Chokmah—Binah
15	He	Window	Ares	IV: Emperor	Red	Chokmah—Tiphareth
16	Vav	Nail	Taurus	V: Hierophant	Deep Indigo	Chokmah—Chesed
17	Zayin	Sword	Gemini	VI: Lovers	Pale Mauve	Binah—Tiphareth
18	Cheth	Fence	Cancer	VII: Chariot	Maroon	Binah—Geburah
19	Teth	Serpent	Leo	XI: Strength/Lust	Deep Purple	Chesed—Geburah
20	Yod	Hand	Virgo	IX: Hermit	Slate Gray	Chesed—Tiphareth
21	Kaph	Palm of Hand	Jupiter	X: Wheel of Fortune	Violet*	Chesed—Netzach
22	Lamed	Ox Goad	Libra	VIII: Justice/Adjustment	Blue	Geburah—Tiphareth

Figure 11: Table of Correspondences of the 22 Pathways

Table of Correspondences of the 22 Pathways

Path No.	Hebrew Letter	Meaning	Attribute	Tarot Trump	Queen Scale Colors	Path Positions—Sephirah to Sephirah
23	Mim	Water	Water	XII: Hanged Man	Sea-green	Geburah—Hod
24	Nun	Fish	Scorpio	XIII: Death	Dull Brown	Tiphareth—Netzach
25	Samek	Prop	Sagittarius	XIV: Temperance/Art	Yellow	Tiphareth—Yesod
26	Ayin	Eye	Capricorn	XV: Devil	Black (Flat)	Tiphareth—Hod
27	Peh	Mouth	Mars	XVI: Tower	Scarlet*	Netzach—Hod
28	Tzaddi	Fish Hook	Aquarius	XVII: Star	Azure*	Netzach—Yesod
29	Qoph	Back of Head	Pisces	XVIII: Moon	Ultra Violet*	Netzach—Malkuth
30	Resh	Head	Sun	XIX: Sun	Gold-yellow	Hod—Yesod
31	Shin	Tooth	Fire/Spirit	XX: Last Judgement/Aeon	Vermillion/Deep Purple	Hod—Malkuth
32	Tav	Tau Cross	Saturn/Earth	XXI: World/Universe	Jet Black/Amber	Path joins Yesod - Malkuth

Note: * Indicates that the color was adapted from the King Scale or other selection to ensure uniqueness of color

Selections are taken from Traditional Golden Dawn Correspondences via *Liber 777* and *The Complete Magician's Tables*.

six

Creation, Unmanifest Godhead, and the Nature of Evil

In the beginning God created the heavens and the earth. Now the earth was a formless void, there was darkness over the deep, and God's spirit hovered over the water. God said, 'Let there be light,' and there was light. God saw that light was good, and God divided light from darkness. God called light 'day,' and darkness he called 'night.' Evening came and morning came: the first day. —Book of Genesis, ch. 1, v. 1–5 [30]

Jewish theology proposed that God created the world and all it contains in six stages (called *days*), and at the end

---

30. *The Jerusalem Bible* (Doubleday, 1968).

(the seventh stage), he rested, marking this point as the cosmic Sabbath. Christianity and Islam have both adopted this creation myth, so it has powerfully impacted our culture and the thoughts and imagination even of modern people. Some will perceive this as a myth; others, as the literal truth.

Whether one believes in physical evolution or divine creation, the story of the creation of the world is generally taken as an allegory by most rabbinic scholars and religious academics. This is because they believe that the allegory veils the greater truth, which can't ever be known. In my opinion, more can be learned by seeing this story as an allegory than attempting to somehow explain the actual creation of the physical universe using mythic themes and symbols, rather than scientifically provable theories. This is where taking a literal approach to biblical interpretation can lead one terribly astray; the Bible should be accepted as the written wisdom, myth, and folklore of a specific people, adapted and extended to become the sacred scriptures of three world religions. This is also where the occultist has a particular advantage, since the Bible is then seen as containing many layers of myth and meaning, with an added hidden inner layer of spiritual significance, obscured and veiled by the obvious plot and story.

The basic assumption found in the biblical creation myth is that a limitless, unknowable, infinite, and unmanifested Deity was the sole author of everything that has a material form, mind, and conscious being (soul and spirit). In other words, an infinite God created a finite world out of nothing. The Qabalah deals with this allegory by explaining how a being that is infinite and unmanifest could create a material world that is finite and bounded by limitations.

Our perception of the Godhead is through the *lens* of our material existence, so we can never truly know or understand a being that is not part of our material nature. The barrier is nearly insurmountable between what is manifest and what is unmanifest, but still the unmanifest Godhead exists as an entity. Yet despite this handicap, Qabalists have been able to describe not only the nature of that Deity, but also how it was able to create a finite material universe using itself as a model and a conduit for creation. So they sought to describe and talk about what existed before the first act of creation, when light was commanded to be, and then it was used to separate the darkness into day and night.

Let us also keep in mind that not everyone will believe that the world was created by a Being that was completely separate from its own creation, particularly since many Pagans believe in exactly the opposite—that Deity and creation are inseparable. They also won't accept that the barrier between Deity and humanity is insurmountable, and in fact, to them, the Deity is immanent in all spiritual, mental, and material things, even inanimate objects. Yet despite these points of disagreement, the Qabalistic perspective has a great deal of relevance to those who are of a Pagan persuasion. I will try to explain why I think this is true.

The Qabalah clearly shows that due to the Sephiroth and Pathways of the Tree of Life, the attributes of the Deity are included in all manifested reality as well as the unmanifest. Also, these attributes represent an aspect of Deity that is finite, and it is only from the standpoint of the One that

Deity becomes transcendental. Therefore, the Qabalah, perhaps unlike pure monotheism, demonstrates that the Deity is engaged in and very much a part of creation. So, the beliefs of the modern Pagan are not that far removed from either the Qabalist or, for that matter, the Neoplatonist of antiquity. The key for the Pagan is to come to the conclusion that the Deity is not something that can be strictly defined as this god, goddess, or animal spirit, without also looking at it as being possibly inclusive of all aspects of Godhead. This is a paradox, and one that is sometimes difficult to completely embrace, but I found that after much deliberation, many Pagans can admit that this is a true condition.

Once this truth can be realized, then all of these different groups can see the Deity as being an expression of the greater union of the One, and that the One was the original author and source of the spiritual and mental dimensions of all sentience. This is the point where all three of these different perspectives can come together and meet, and it is also why some aspects of the Qabalah are troubling to the true adherents of monotheism. To the Pagan mind, the Sephiroth Godhead attributes are like separate and distinct deities, like a pantheon, and I suspect that many monotheists see the same thing and reject it.

Some of the questions that the Qabalists sought to answer, which could not be answered from the wisdom found in the Torah, Midrash, or Talmud, are:

- What is the nature of the Deity, specifically the unmanifest and unknowable Being that existed before creation? How is that Being related in some manner to what became created?

• How did an infinite Deity create a finite world out of nothing? What were the stages of that creation and how did it proceed?

• If the Deity created the world and everything in it, then how did evil occur?

• Why is the material world imperfect and inherently defective if the Deity who created it is perfect and incapable of error?

As you can see, these are very perplexing questions. They are not only difficult to answer, but the answers themselves stretch the very fabric of coherency and rational thought. Yet the Qabalah, over time, managed to answer these questions, though only in a mystical, and at times, very theosophical manner. This represents the one great truth about the Qabalah: that it consists of many speculations, intuitions, and veiled insights because it is a product of the rational mind attempting to know what is essentially trans-rational and unknowable.

Nature of the *Ein Sof* (AIN SOPh)

Early Qabalists of Provence and Gerona[31] (particularly Isaac the Blind and Azriel, in the 12th century) coined a term that succinctly expressed the infinite nature of the unknowable and unmanifest Godhead, and that term consisted of the Hebrew words *Ein Sof* (without end or limitless nothing), which taken together means "infinite." This phrase became an expression of the unknowable Godhead itself, even though it was used as a technical term divorced from

31. Scholem, *Kabbalah*, 88–90.

the actual name or quality of the Deity, a being that had no real name or identity. Thus Ein Sof became the identifying name and quality of the unknown Deity, describing the manner that it existed before anything was created. Yet this quality of the infinite had within it the nature of a kind of emptiness that was without end, even though the nothingness was, in actuality, a kind of *something*.

This may seem a little confusing, but what it actually refers to is an attempt to explain a phenomenon that is indefinable and indescribable through the use of double negatives, such as "endless nothing." These kinds of paradoxical concepts are common in many forms of mysticism, from the Jewish Qabalah to Vedanta, Taoism, Zen Buddhism, and many others. It is an attempt to arrive at a concept by creating an anti-concept, like the famous Zen koan of the "sound of one hand clapping." By coining a term that negates itself, the mind is momentarily freed of misconceptions and prejudices, seeing, through intuition, the true nature of a thing. Therefore, we should see the Ein Sof as clouds or veils of negative existence that hide the unknowable and pre-existent unmanifest Deity. It is a kind of absolute reality that is unreal and unimaginable, at least to anything that is the product of creation and imbued with the *stuff* of the material world.

Ein Sof can also be seen as a progression that occurred just before creation. The *Ein* is the *void* that the Spirit of the Creator passed over, and the *Ein Sof* is the *Spirit* of that Deity, passing over that void. The final part is called the "Ein Sof Aur" (Limitless Light), where the Deity, through an act of will, caused there to be *light*, thus separating the darkness. Even so, the material world has not yet been created, since these three words constitute what is called the *three veils of negative existence.* Even so, the limitless light might be perceived by the spiritual eye of humankind in the deepest state of contemplation. Interestingly enough, these three words contain three letters each, making nine letters total (AIN SOPh AUR). The letters of these three words are broken up into the stages of the pre-creative formulation, and these are arrayed in the following pattern:

AIN

AIN SOPh

AIN SOPh AUR

The numbers for this progression are 3, 6, and 9, and these three words can be placed on a flower arrangement with three petals in the center, then six surrounding the three, and then nine surrounding the six, creating a device consisting of three concentric circles.[32] (See figure 12.)

This device is used in other Qabalistic structures, most notably in the division of the Hebrew, Greek, and Latin/English alphabets (for the creation of sigils), but it also symbolizes the prototype design of creation. The Ein Sof Aur is conceived of as a circle consisting of an endless line that is self-contained, without beginning or ending, timeless, without dimensions or space. It is, in a word, all of the potential to be and nothing more. It reminds one immediately of the definition of the Deity as pronounced by Empedocles (the Greek philosopher who first spoke of the

---

32. Gareth Knight, *A Practical Guide to Qabalistic Symbolism*, 55.

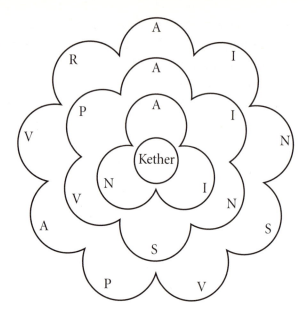

Figure 12: Ein Sof Aur flower

four elements): "God is a circle whose center is everywhere and whose circumference is nowhere."[33]

So, if the Godhead is something that is nothing, then how did creation proceed? How was everything in the material world created from nothing? That would almost seem like an absurd notion, known generally to philosophers as *creatio ex nihilo*, or "creation from nothing." From a logical perspective, you can only create nothing from nothing. So it would seem that the act of creation was a phenomenon

---

33. This quotation has been variously attributed to Voltaire, St. Augustine, and others, but rightfully belongs to Empedocles. See "God Is a Circle," ThinkExist.com (accessed November 12, 2011), http://en.thinkexist.com/quotation/the_nature _of_god_is_a_circle_of_which_the_center/173078.html.

that focused on something material—in other words, creating something out of something else, which seems to be what the Genesis account of creation in the Bible is actually discussing. In other words, the Deity creates the material world from within itself (*creatio ex materia*, where that material is some kind of pre-existing matter), by acting on an inner aspect of itself, since in the beginning there was nothing but God. The nihilistic naming conventions of the Deity as the Ein Sof is nothing more than a device to ensure that the Godhead is indefinable and unknowable—a complete and unfathomable mystery.

Therefore, creation ensues from the Ein Sof Aur, where the Deity withdraws into itself, then creates through a combination of will, thought, absolute nothingness (as a pre-existing matter or chaos), and the inner radiation of the supernal lights of the Negative Veils, called "splendors" (*tzachtzachot*), which are higher than any emanation.[34] That the Godhead manifests itself in the Sephiroth (in a sequential manner) completely within itself shows that the Deity is both the Ein Sof and a manifested Being within the emanations of the Sephiroth. Both of these perspectives are paradoxically true, depending on one's point of view. So this would represent that the Godhead is both a manifested part and the original source of the manifested world. All things are a part of God, but God is both a part of manifestation and also beyond it.

This paradox is the manner in which the modern Pagan, Neoplatonist, and Jewish Qabalist can feasibly arrive at the same point or perspective. Through the knowable

---

34. Scholem, *Kabbalah*, 91.

and manifested aspect of the One, a person can know the unknowable and unmanifested Deity (the None); therefore, there exists a powerful bridge between all aspects of the Godhead and humanity, which is what we would expect from a practical Qabalah.

Thus, the Three Negative Veils, through an act of thought and will, and acting upon the proto-matter of chaotic nothingness, condense into the manifested form of the One, as the first Sephirah, Kether, the Crown of Creation. The three invisible lights of the Ein Sof Aur become the single stellar light of the manifested "I Am" (*Ehieh*), which represents the beginning and the first expression of the manifested Deity as the primal spirit, or Ruach—the breath of the Living God. Once the One became manifest, it initiated a process of emanation that caused the branching creation of the Many. We can integrate the sequence of creation as it is depicted in the Sepher Yetzirah, which only now makes complete sense.[35]

Emerging from the first Sephirah, Kether, came forth, through emanation, the three primal elements as the three Sephiroth, which are Chokmah, Binah, and Chesed. In this manner, Spirit (as Kether) gave birth to Air (the primary element as Chokmah), which in turn created the spheres of Water (Binah) and Fire (Chesed). In the Hebrew metaphysical system, there are three elements and not four, and the element of Air is considered more refined than Fire or Water, since it is less dense and does not rely on any material substance. From Air was created the 22 divine Hebrew letters, out of Water was formed the greater cosmos, and through Fire was the Throne of Glory and all of the hosts of angelic

---

35. Scholem, *Kabbalah*, 24.

spirits created. One interesting point to consider is that the angels were created out of fire, but demons were derived from the winds, so perhaps they might be different in regard to their origins. Then you have the fallen angels, and references to the infernal lords, so fire and air are both attributes of the angelic and demonic spirits.

The final five Sephiroth (minus Malkuth), were precipitated out of the first four Sephiroth, perhaps being produced through the artifice of the lightning flash that exploded from Kether and proceeded downward into more dense material formulations. There is a great deal of speculation about whether Malkuth was created, made as a mirror image of Kether, or whether it was precipitated out of the supposed fall, which is a topic we will attempt to expound upon later. One can see that the first four Sephiroth (Kether, Chokmah, Binah, and Chesed) were perfect in their formulation, and that the lower six were less perfect, and therefore subject to error and deviation from the divine plan.

Still, the ten Sephiroth established the modes of existence and the 22 Pathways established the experience of consciousness, from the level of the divine to the level of individual material sentience. The Three Pillars (Mercy, Severity, and Mediation) represent the possibilities of manifestation, with their root firmly entrenched within the Three Negative Veils and the lights shining from within them. From the vantage point of created beings, the totality of the Tree of Life seems perfect and complete. However, this does not explain the fact that the material world is imperfect and that evil not only exists but also is allowed to freely corrupt and destroy all things within the lowest world of Assiah. In order to fully understand the worldview of the Qabalah, we should seek out the answers to the other questions in our list.

Origin of Evil in the Qabalah

We come now to the difficult considerations about how and why evil exists in the world, and why we need ethics and morality to determine good from evil. How did this state come to be when the guiding architect for the creation of the world was inherently perfect and incapable of error? This issue is referred to by philosophers as *theodicy*, which is the justification of the goodness of the Deity in the midst of obvious evil and human suffering. It has been one of the main controversies since the days of the ancient Greek philosophers, and has continued in Christian and Jewish theological discussions. (Of course, if the Deity is perceived as being finite and fallible, then the whole issue is readily resolved.)

What this question brings to light is that either evil was created by the One as part of its overall plan, or that evil somehow crept into the creation of the world and infected it. The former consideration would seem to indicate that the Deity is capable of fomenting evil, since it had designed it into the creation of the world. The latter consideration would show the Deity as being incompetent or capable of committing an error. Either of these considerations would be troubling, since the operant theory of the One (as far as Neoplatonists and Qabalists were concerned) is that it represents all that is perfect and good. The real solution to this conundrum will be a truly fascinating dance between a belief in a sinister Deity, or one that is defective (finite).

The earliest considerations associated with this thorny issue occurred during the advent of the Spanish Qabalah, and those who followed it focused on the nature of the first Sephirah that emerged outside of the four that were part of the initial and perfect creation, and that was Geburah. The word *Geburah* comes from the root (GBR), which means "to become strong or mighty," and with the addition of a feminine noun ending it is translated as "strength," "power," "force," "courage," or "victory." The martial qualities of this Sephirah are easily seen in an examination of its name. However, there is also a negative connotation associated with it, and that is found in the concept of excessive force, such as violence, murder, and wanton destruction.

So, for this reason, the Sephirah of Geburah was called the "left hand of the Holy One,"[36] representing the forces of extreme judgment. In time, this quality became a separately manifested attribute, known as the *sitra achra*, or the *other side*, which could be considered a euphemism for the left-hand path. The phenomenon that caused Geburah to become the source of evil was believed to have occurred in the latent power and then rapid growth of judgment (*din*) divorced from its opposite, which is Mercy and compassion. Therefore, harsh and extreme judgments, even if they were considered just, were associated with evil if they were not equally balanced by compassion.

According to this idea, evil was the result of unbalanced and aggressive judgment, as that which emerged from the

---

36. Scholem, *Kabbalah*, 122–23.

Sephirah Geburah. Since this Sephirah was the first of the six, and ruled the left side or pillar of the Tree underneath the supernal triad, it became the *seed* of the left, giving sustenance to all that was unbalanced and destructive (evil) in manifestation. The flow from this current went down and away from the divine qualities of Geburah, following its true nature, and collected in the lower realms, where it became a counter-force to the forces of creation and good. From this dark current and counter-force was born a negative hierarchy, resulting in the demons and evil forces that plague all those who reside in the material world.

Another theory, which came from the Zohar, stipulated that evil arose from the leftover residue of worlds that were destroyed in an earlier attempt at creation.[37] Another theory (from the same source) defines evil as originating in and being analogous to the outer covering or the shed bark of a tree—in this case, the Tree of Life, thus functioning as a discarded outer husk or covering (shell), so it was called the *Qliphoth*.[38] This covering was also called the *ha-ilan ha-chitzon*, or the "outer tree," and it was also called the "mystery of the Tree of Knowledge." According to one legend, the Tree of Life and the Tree of Knowledge were once bound together into a single organism, and they weren't distinct until Adam came and forcibly separated them, thereby giving substance to evil, which materialized at that moment as the "instinct to do evil" (*yetzer ha-ra*).

All of these theories about the origin and nature of evil would seem to indicate that it occurred due to an imbal-

---

37. Scholem, *Kabbalah*, 124.
38. Ibid., 125.

ance of judgment, as the aftereffects of creation (residue), or because of the actions of humanity (precipitation of the fall from grace and the expulsion from paradise). Yet evil is neither a part of the superior architecture of the Godhead nor is it due to any flaws in that process of creation. It could be seen as an unavoidable derivative of the imperfections of the material world, or it was due to the negligence and flaws inherent in human nature. What this means is that evil is a temporary manifestation or a fluke in the process of creation, which will be eliminated as that process moves inexorably to its ultimate conclusion—the redemption of the material world.

Lurianic Doctrine of Creation

Isaac Luria's contributions to the Safed Qabalistic community were both profound and far-reaching, even though he lived in Safed for only two of the last years of his life. Among his many teachings and ideas (as written by his disciples), his approach to solving some of the most puzzling questions about the nature of creation and the manifestation of evil were eminently brilliant. Many of these ideas were later incorporated into the occult variation of the Qabalah of the 19th and 20th centuries without either questioning their significance or citing the sources where they were found. However, after examining some of Luria's ideas and thoughts about these questions here, it will be fairly obvious that the scholars of the later occult version of the Qabalah took many of their ideas from his teachings.

Much of this speculation has to do with the mythic concept of the fall of humankind, and the overall impact that event had on the spiritual and material nature of the world. This is not a new concept or one particular to Judaism and Christianity. Many ancient cultures believed in a previous Golden Age that occurred not long after the origin of the world, and that subsequent ages have resulted in a kind of devolution, particularly in the disposition of the human race and the manifestation of the material world. This is a major part of the "mind before matter" metaphysical theory of creation. (As you recall, science takes the opposite view, seeing physical evolution as an upward progression and overall advancement of humanity.) The Golden Age was idyllic and perfect compared to life today. In the Golden Age there was no sickness or death, and humanity lived in a kind of peaceful stasis with all creatures and the Godhead itself. This was the fabled Garden of Eden, from which place humanity, as Adam and Eve, were expelled, ending the time of idyllic perfection and beginning the time of suffering, trials, sickness, and death.

Even Greek myth had such a devaluation of ages: from gold, to silver, to bronze, and then to iron, which is our current and much-devalued age. At each stage of devaluation, the world became less perfect and humanity became less ennobled and idealized. This process continued until human nature had been completely debased in nature as to be indistinguishable from it. Mythic worldviews from most cultures talk about the fall of humanity from a greater estate. This fall also produced a chasm between humanity and the various Deities, and allowed for the inclusion of many disharmonious elements, such as sickness, death, evil, and worldly catastrophes, all of which didn't happen when humanity was in its original sublime state. One need only consult the myth of Pandora's box to see how the Greeks perceived the intrusion of darkness into the world, as well as its redemption through "hope."

Perhaps one way to imagine this epochal devaluation is to see it as an intrinsic attribute of the process of emanation, where the continual copying of less perfect copies ultimately produced images that were degraded and corrupted. This would be analogous to making Xerox copies using each copy to make another copy instead of the original. Eventually, the imperfections will become so greatly amplified as to completely obscure the original image.

Humanity's fall from grace would then seem to be a way of explaining how the world became imperfect, and why suffering, sickness, and death appears to be the fate of all living things. Yet another way of looking at this progression is to see it as the natural process of incarnation within a world where Spirit and Mind existed before matter, and that the fall was actually the process by which humanity acquired a physical existence. Life has both its positive and its negative aspects, such as the pleasures and joys of living, experiencing, growing, acquiring wisdom, and ultimately rejoining with the Deity at the end of life. The negatives, of course, would be the pain, suffering, disease, misfortune, and the unavoidable event of death.

One of the first problems that Luria tackled was the one associated with the act of creation performed by the Godhead. If the Deity was all that existed, even though it was in a state where it was unmanifest, how could it create anything if there was not any space for that creation to occur? Before one can create something, there has to be empty space for that something to occupy.

Luria proposed that the Ein Sof contracted (*tzimtzum*) into itself, and therefore produced an empty space (a kind of vacuum), which made room for creation.[39] Another issue involved how an infinite Deity could be capable of creating a limited and finite material world. This was resolved through a process in which the Deity imposed upon itself a kind of self-limitation. A third issue was the fact that the act of creation would reveal the Deity in all of its mystery and splendor, which would be impossible for an unmanifest and unknowable Godhead. Luria proposed that the act of creation was done through a cloak of deliberate concealment, so that the unknown and unmanifested Deity would remain invisible and unknowable. Thus, according to Luria, the Deity contracted, established boundaries, and cloaked itself in order to create the universe and not violate its own integrity.

The Deity's will to create generated and transmitted the letter *Yod*, as a formulation of power and organization, imprinted with Divine Mercy, which created the first manifestation. It should be recalled that Yod is the first letter of the *Tetragrammaton*, which is the secret name of the Deity. What was first created was a manifested expression of the Deity itself, which was the proto-man known as *Adam Kadmon*.[40] This proto-man as God was a necessary first step,

---

39. Drob, *Symbols of the Kabbalah*, 120–21.
40. Scholem, *Kabbalah*, 130.

since humanity later was created in the image of the Deity according to scriptures; therefore, the Godhead must have an image. Another attribute for this proto-man was called the *Glory of the Godhead*, who was the driver that sat upon the Throne of Glory in the Divine Chariot, or *Merkabah*.

This primary phase of creation produced a geometric world consisting of concentric circles, but also simultaneously one that had a linear structure, which formulated the outer skeleton of Adam Kadmon. The combination of these two processes (circles and lines, inner light and outer light, substance and vessels, direct light and reflected light) produced the dialectic process whereby all creation was made manifest, bringing forth the Tree of Life through the Three Pillars of Mercy, Severity, and Mediation.[41] Thus lines and circles joined together to fashion the Tree as we know it. The lines were defined as emanations of the divine Ruach, and the circles were emanations from the divine Nephesh, and combined they produced the body and soul of the proto-man, Adam Kadmon. The three lights of the Ein Sof Aur would have functioned as the *Yechidah* part of the soul for this macrocosmic being. (We will cover this in more detail in the next chapter, where we will discuss the four parts of the human soul.)

Breaking and Restoration of the Vessels

Luria's Qabalistic speculation answered questions associated with how an infinite and unmanifest Deity was able to create a limited and manifested world, but he also

---

41. Scholem, *Kabbalah*, 131.

attempted to explain the nature of evil—how imperfection caused a catastrophe to occur and how the Deity sought to redeem and rectify that cosmic disaster afterwards.

Luria explained how the great fall from grace occurred, what happened afterwards, and how everything that was affected by it was supposed to be redeemed. Luria not only discussed the nature of that redemption, but he also talked about when it might occur and who would be its agent in the material world. That agent would be the Messiah, yet it would not be a military or political leader who would liberate the Jewish people, but a cosmic spiritual agency that would redeem all of humanity—beginning, of course, with the Chosen People.

Luria taught that the fall from grace was not the fault of humanity, but an inherent weakness in the creation of the lower vessels (*kelim*) or Sephiroth. This inherent weakness was fostered in the subtle effects of what was called "reshimu," or residual remnants of creation, particularly, the leftover judgment (from Geburah) and the imperfectly reflected or refracted lights from the Ein Sof. This produced what Gershom Scholem called, using a Gnostic term, a kind of "hylic" substance, or matter divorced from Spirit.[42] That hylic substance had left behind trace elements in the lower six Sephiroth, thus weakening them. The residual matter, and the periodic leaking transmission of negativity from Geburah, as the *sitra achra*, joined at the lowest levels of manifested being, where it formed a kind of pool—inchoate and completely inert. Therefore, there was imperfection in

---

42. Scholem, *Kabbalah*, 130.

the Sephirotic vessels and a chaotic potential building in the nether realms below the Sephirah Malkuth.

The outer form of the Sephiroth were perceived as acting like vessels, which, like a cosmic chalice, could contain the flowing form of a liquid light cascading down from the Ein Sof, and these were formed out of the circles and lines that made up the body of the Adam Kadmon. The light that filled these vessels had its origin in the light of the Negative Veils, so it was a pure emanation of the Ein Sof that continuously flowed through them. However, because of the inherent flaw in the vessel of the Sephirah Geburah (due to the potential excess of judgment), the flowing of light down from the Ein Sof caused the vessel to shatter, creating a cascading event that proceeded down the Tree of Life, all the way to Malkuth. Another theory was that the light was too great for the lesser Sephirah to hold, and so, due to their inherent flaws and the stresses that were overwhelming, they shattered.

All six of the lower Sephirah shattered (*shevirah*), but the lowest, Malkuth, wasn't broken into pieces and cast down into the nether realms below as were the rest. Instead, it was broken, cracked, but still managed to function. Some of the light was deflected and returned to its source, but the rest fell down to where the shards of the vessels had fallen and was trapped there. These shards became known as the Qliphoth, the dark forms of the *sitra achra* that held the lost light in captivity. Yet the supernal triad of Will, Wisdom, and Understanding alone remained intact.[43]

---

43. Drob, *Symbols of the Kabbalah*, 297.

This catastrophe profoundly affected the world, from Chesed (which was also impacted by the flaw in Geburah, even though it was slightly above it) down to Malkuth (with the epicenter of the catastrophe in Geburah), and allowed for the generation of evil forces to infect all of the lower Sephiroth. Humanity did not bring forth this calamity, since it was due instead to forces and designs that were far greater. Yet the release of evil into the world that this event caused had many ramifications, including the expulsion of humankind from the Garden of Eden and the release of evil into the lower worlds. It was the fall of a greater portion of the macrocosm and the creation of a great chasm between the Godhead and much of the manifested world that changed everything—and this chasm would be called the Greater Abyss. The event of shevirah was even said to be the ultimate cause of the destruction of the Temple and the dispersal of Jews around the world.

Despite this terrible calamity, the core of the Adam Kadmon wasn't touched by it; only the lower outer vessels were affected. Therefore, the proto-man, as Adam Kadmon, took steps to redeem what had been broken and to restore what had been lost: namely, the lost light of the emanations. This restoration of the world, which was called *Tikkun ha-Olam*, first emerged as a light shining from the forehead of Adam Kadmon. That light was the medium through which the chaos that had been unleashed would be calmed and reorganized, and the shattered vessels replaced by a new formulation. The attributes of the affected Sephiroth would be merged with the power and majesty of the Adam Kadmon, and new, inviolable vessels would thus be created, and these were called "faces" (*parzufim*).[44] Therefore, through this intercession, the lower six vessels were replaced or repaired, and the light from the Ein Sof continued to flow uninterrupted from level to level. However, the final restorative task was to be the most difficult, for that entailed gathering up all of the points of light that had fallen to the lowest level and been held captive by the Qliphoth.

The task of collecting the various points of light was made more complex because they had also found their way into the souls of individual human beings and other entities as well. This was not a task that the Adam Kadmon could perform, but instead was a role for the Messiah. Such a being was supposed to be a special incarnation created in the likeness of Adam Kadmon, but it would also be a mortal man living in the world. Therefore, as a godlike messianic figure, he would gather together all of those lost points of light until none were left in the material world. Then, having absorbed these points of light into himself, he would ascend again to the greater Adam Kadmon, and there return these lights to their source. When this happens, of course, the life of the material world will become bereft of the lights of emanation, thus marking an end to the race of man and the ensouled world through a process called *gilgul*, which is the reincarnation of the divine thought as the Primordial Man. Thus the cycle ends where it begins.[45]

---

44. Scholem, *Kabbalah*, 140–41.

45. Drob, *Symbols of the Kabbalah*, 393–95.

A cosmic Messiah has the central role in the Lurian Qabalah, and when he manifests in the world, it will represent that the end times have arrived. The Lurian Qabalah merged both messianic aspirations along with a belief in an apocalypse, and this was a very intoxicating combination, particularly since Luria believed those end times were imminent.[46] It was only a matter of time before someone would claim this role as cosmic Messiah, and that someone was Sabbatai Zevi (1626–76). Not only did he not turn out to be the Messiah, but he likely helped to invalidate the Qabalah as a serious form of Jewish theology. His apostasy (conversion to Islam after being threatened by the Turkish sultan) signaled the beginning of the end of the Qabalah, which had all but disappeared from mainstream Judaism by the advent of the 19th century.

Final Considerations

We have examined the tenets of the Spanish and Safed Qabalah with regard to the nature of creation and the occurrence of evil and the imperfections found in the natural world. There are a number of different directions that one can mentally travel with these many speculations. The question is how the modern occult Qabalist will use these different perspectives, and that depends on whether one is a Christian, Jew, or Pagan.

Those who are Christians, Jews, and Muslims can rely on their own theologies and spiritual teachings to determine the nature of creation and the occurrence of evil and

---

46. Scholem, *Kabbalah*, 245.

imperfection in the world. However, from the standpoint of the Pagan, these considerations are more difficult to resolve. Because most Pagans reject the concept of a Devil, or that the world is a battleground between the forces of good and evil, one of the few ways to explain these things is to consider that the nature of evil and imperfection in the natural world, although real and quite compelling, is in fact ultimately an illusion.

Another perspective is that the natural world is perfect, and that evil is just the way that humans relate to things they object to or find threatening. Certainly, animals don't appear to subscribe to a concept of good and evil, so it would seem to be an attribute wholly within the human sphere. The reason why evil and imperfection could be considered illusory is because whatever becomes a living part of the One is wholly vested in that which is intrinsically good and perfect. Whatever is evil or imperfect is actually divided against itself, so it is also diminished and not part of the One. Thus, that which is evil has no absolute reality since it is fleeting and temporary.

Qabalah teaches us through the Lurian concepts of *shevirah* (shattering) and *tikkun* (restoration) that evil is a form of imperfection that pervades all things. That it is found even in the Deity and resides at the core of all things. This imperfection can't be morally judged since it is just a natural part of the material and spiritual world. The universe is temporarily shifted into a polarized duality for the ultimate sake of union; thus evil is a precursor to the final and perfect restoration.

This is another way of saying that something that is negative and dualistic, and therefore evil, only exists in the moment and will perish as all physical things perish. Evil has an innate tendency toward complete self-destruction; whereas good draws all things to it, forming a greater union in emulation of the One. As time is allowed to take its natural course, eventually evil will cease to exist and only good will survive. However, once that happens, then good will cease to exist as well, and all that will be left is the One. I think that is a good general approximation of what the Qabalists were attempting to teach from the standpoint and perspective of a Pagan.

Adopting this perspective will in no way diminish or put aside the many concerns that self-aware beings have living in this world. There are a multitude of problems to solve, and they will not solve themselves if we ignore them or pretend that they don't exist because they are somehow "illusory" in the long term. The Qabalah teaches us that the material world in which we reside is important and sacred. This is because Kether is reflected in Malkuth, and vice versa. What that means is that we have a responsibility to our spiritual selves as well as our bodies and the world that we live in. Life and the material world are precious gifts given to us, and how we treat them will ultimately demonstrate our true worth as human beings.

Therefore, based on these considerations, we could further state that an enlightened person would be more sensitive to the needs of every living being, the environment through which they exist and the world itself. A person who is closed off and completely self-absorbed is the opposite of what would be considered a fully and spiritually awakened person. To be aware of the moment and everything that is contained in that moment, from the most sublime to the most mundane, is to be truly awakened and engaged with the One.

seven

Four Worlds
and the Four Subtle Bodies

The Four Qabalistic Worlds represent the four basic planes of being that exist within the domain of the Tree of Life and the continuous process of emanation and creation. If we wanted to somehow use the structure of the Tree of Life to define these Four Worlds, we could draw a line around the highest Sephirah of Kether, and then another just below the pair of Sephiroth of Chokmah and Binah. The last line would divide the lowest Sephirah of Malkuth from the rest of the Sephiroth. These divisions could be considered analogous to the Four Worlds, representing an absolute plane of origination, a plane of creation, one of formulation, and finally, one of materialization. These Four Worlds would be called by their Hebrew names:

Atziluth (Origination)—World of Archetypes, source of all material and spiritual reality—ideation of Godhead (Deity); Godhead element letter: Yod; Name: ALHYM (Elohim)

Briah (Creation)—World of Creation, where archetypes join with meaning, relationship and signification—activation of Spirit (archangels); Godhead element letter: Heh; Name: AL (El)

Yetzirah (Formation)—World of Formation, where meaningful ideation is structured and given form and duration—building up of networking structures and the establishment of boundaries and limitations (angels); Godhead element letter: Vav; Name: YHVH (Yahweh)

Assiah (Expression)—World of Materialization, where archetype, significance, and structure join together to formulate the material reality (vital force, chakras, and elements); Godhead element letter: Heh-final; Name: ADNI H-ARTz (Adonai ha-Aretz—Lord of Earth)

As you can see, I have additionally applied the four Godhead element letters and the four Godnames to the Four Worlds. In this configuration, these worlds characterize a kind of element attribute and division of the universe. This configuration also links the four archetypal elements with the four letters of the *Tetragrammaton*, where the Yod = Fire, Heh = Water, Vav = Air, and Heh-final = Earth. The term *Tetragrammaton* is a Greek word meaning a four-letter word, used to describe the name of the Hebrew Deity that is not pronounced (YHVH).

I would also propose that the Four Worlds consist of the word concepts of Godhead, Spirit, Mind, and Body, representing the cosmic being of the great Adam Kadmon, the archetypal man as the manifested expression of the unmanifest and unknowable Godhead (Ein Sof). Since human beings were created in the *image* of the manifested Deity, then these four levels also apply to each and every person.

The Four Worlds can be compared to the seven planes in the Eastern and theosophical systems, where those seven planes are grouped together to form just four. The seven planes are known in English as the Absolute, Spirit, Mind, Higher and Lower Astral, Etheric, and Physical planes. The Astral, Etheric, and Physical planes would correspond to the World of Assiah, and the rest would correspond one to one with the higher three Worlds. So the following list could be created to show how these two systems relate to each other:

- Atziluth—Absolute plane
- Briah—Spirit plane
- Yetzirah—Mental plane
- Assiah—Astral (Higher and Lower), Etheric, and Physical planes

We should keep in mind that these comparisons are useful analogies, and that they can show some interesting additional information otherwise not easily seen. For instance, the world of Briah is associated with the Spirit plane, but spiritual entities can and do function in the lower world of

Yetzirah, even though it is associated with the Mental plane. This would represent that there is a soft boundary between these two planes, and that mental structures can also function as autonomous spiritual beings, and vice versa.

Additionally, the Mental plane houses a greater cosmic intellect, which is called the Universal Mind. This construct would seem to be better placed in the world of Briah, and in fact it resides in both worlds, with its roots in the absolute plane in Atziluth. Another thing to consider is that all of the elements in the top three worlds and planes exist within a unified field of spiritual consciousness that has its source in the absolute plane. This is not the case with the lower three planes and their associated world, Assiah, where there is division, uniqueness, and individuation operating within the domain of matter.

The dream worlds of the Higher Astral plane, and the emotional tides and storms of the Lower Astral, are both associated with the physical body, but can blend into the Mental plane, although there is a strict barrier between the Spirit and the Etheric/Physical planes.

You can imagine this model of the planes and worlds being represented by a rainbow, where the divisions in the colors can be only be seen and compared between distinct areas, but the borders consist of a gradual blending.

I believe that this combined structure shows the difference between the physical, mental, spiritual, and Godhead levels of being, all of which exist in the same space. However, the higher planes are not so restricted by space and time as the lower, so they often seem timeless and fluid when one experiences them. Also, the planes above the Mental could be considered the domain of the Inner Planes, but the upper reaches of the Mental Plane might be perceived as occupying that area as well. As you can see, the boundaries between planes and worlds are not dramatic but blend into each other, and aspects of one can also be emergent into another that is higher, so our use of boundaries is limited to uniquely defining and understanding them.

Four Bodies of the Individual Human Being

As these Four Qabalistic Worlds represent the worlds in which all things reside, they are also found within the division of different bodies within human beings.[47] These different bodies are concurrent, but they represent the qualities of the physical body, mind, and spirit. Since there is an absolute plane associated with the totality of all being, then there is, paradoxically, an absolute plane in each human being. This would be comparable to what is known in Indian metaphysics as the *Atman*. Indian sages differentiate between the One that is God, as associated with the cosmic Brahman, and the individual One that resides within a person, which is called Atman. The Atman is the Godhead within an individual person, and that Godhead is actually undifferentiated from the greater Godhead, Brahman, but only appears to be unique from the standpoint of individual human beings.

This Godhead within a person would be analogous to the absolute plane or the world of Atziluth. The Qabalists call

47. Israel Regardie, *A Garden of Pomegranates*, 92–105.

this aspect of the self the *Yechidah*, which is the individual Monad or Atman within a person. Below the Yechidah is the individual spirit, which would be analogous to the world of Briah, and it is called the *Neschamah*, or intuitive self. Below the Yechidah and the Neschamah are the *Ruach* and the *Nephesh*, which are the levels of intellect (mind) and the emotional body (animal soul), respectively. These two lower levels would be associated with the worlds of Yetzirah and Assiah. Some authors, such as Israel Regardie, have stipulated that there is a physical body aspect, called the *Guph* (body), but that level or attribute would normally be seamlessly joined to the Nephesh.

We could easily create a table that shows how these four levels of the integral human being exist and interact. (We should keep in mind that these comparisons are analogies that are used to help make these basic definitions more informative.)

- Yechidah—Monad—Absolute plane (Atziluth)
- Neschamah—Intuitive Self—Spirit plane (Briah)
- Ruach—Intellect—Mental plane (Yetzirah)
- Nephesh—Animal Soul—Astral/Etheric/Physical plane (Assiah)

In addition to the Yechidah, there is also an element called the *Chiah* (life force), which represents the active element that functions as the *power* of the Monadic self. Another element is called the *Zureh*, which is the conduit that exists between the Yechidah and the Neschamah. These two additional elements are joined to the Yechidah and are typically not seen as distinct bodies.

Ruach, which functions as the empirical ego, actually consists of five dimensions that make up the active intellect of a person. These five dimensions are Memory, Will, Imagination, Desire, and Reason, and they are ordered from the highest expression of the mind to the lowest. This sequence of qualities also seems to be related to the five Sephiroth, from Chesed (memory), Geburah (will), Tiphareth (imagination), Netzach (desire), and Hod (reason).

Part Two

Practical Qabalah:
Qabalistic Magic Simplified

Overview and Cosmological Framework

The most basic and essential elements of the practical Qabalah are that the various tables of correspondences and the Tree of Life structure consist of symbols. Symbols are the foundation of the Qabalah, but these symbols are very much alive. We have already covered this in the second chapter, where I wrote:

"Symbols are conscious markers for deep-level psychic processes that are transcendental and transpersonal, and, I might add, usually mysterious to most people. Focusing on symbols can give one access to deeper layers of meaning and collective significance. Sources of symbols are numinous, archaic, and inexplicable."

Accessing the symbols of the Qabalah is the primary exercise of the practical Qabalah, since it is through accessing them that they become alive and reveal their greater significance and power. Minutely examining these symbols and forming various tables of correspondences or variations on the Tree of Life glyph will have a profound effect on the consciousness of the operator. It could even be said that merely attempting to organize the symbols of any religious or occult system will produce corresponding visions and insights, as if the symbols as a whole were capable of sentient communication. Many occultists have reported this phenomenon, but in my opinion the ultimate visionary structure of all mystical and magical systems is the Qabalah itself.

When I first approached studying the Qabalah, it was only when it became alive and sensible to me that I truly discovered its power and ability to directly affect my inner self and my outer world. If an occultist does not have a unifying structure and system like the Qabalah, then working with the symbology of an occult system will likely produce one at some point.

All of this hinges, of course, on the greatest power that any spiritual seeker has at his or her fingertips, and that is the power of the imagination. It is the imagination that makes the symbology of the Qabalah come alive. It also allows the seeker to discover new perspectives and insights through the power of analogy. Analogy is the ability to play the "as if" game with your mind; it allows for the creation of new frames of reference, which in turn produces new insights and realizations. This process of analogy is the foundation of Qabalistic speculation. It is the basis for all practical work in the Qabalah. The imagination fuels the other methodologies of practical work, such as meditation, contemplation, pathworking, and theurgy.

The power of analogy allows us to group, configure, and compare various disassociated religious symbology to create a unified field where everything is connected to everything else. Creating connections in this manner causes symbols to become triggered, activating them so that they reveal their importance and meaning. In the art of magic, causality is believed to be absolute, which means that everything is linked. Therefore, by creating or realizing existing connections within tables of correspondences or by reconfiguring the Tree of Life, one is working a form of powerful magic that directly affects the mind and soul of the seeker.

This line of thought leads me to a rather humorous story. Years ago, I was experimenting with putting together different variations on the Tree of Life, attempting to see if I could discover a new way of encoding the 32 elements of the Qabalah. I was talking to a friend of mine about what I was doing while we were both visiting the local occult bookstore, when an old man with a white beard overheard what I was saying. He turned to look at me and gave me one of those disapproving looks, mixed with a certain amount of shock and disbelief. Then he came over and interrupted my conversation, sternly rebuking me while shaking a gnarled finger in my face, saying emphatically that manipulating the Tree of Life was not only very impious but also downright dangerous. I could screw up the whole universe by mucking around as I was supposedly doing. (Who in the heck did I think I was, after all?)

Of course, my friend and I smiled at this rude interruption, and we just nodded to the old codger, as if to acknowledge that we heard him, but offered no comment. He turned around and stormed away while muttering to himself, and we collectively shook our heads and sighed, then continued with our discussion as if nothing had happened. To this day, I can't remember the guy's name or even exactly when and where this scene occurred, but I remembered it as being quite silly.

However, now that I have come up with this very fascinating and even startling perspective on the nature of occult symbols and how they function in the Qabalah, I not only remembered this conversation, but it also doesn't seem so absurd as it did many years ago. If organizing and shaping the structure of the tables of correspondences or formulating a glyph which contains them will have some kind of impact on the one doing it, then that old codger wasn't really too far off.

Will the world end if I turn the Tree of Life upside down? No, of course not! But it might have some impact on how I see and perceive things within my own magical and spiritual perspective. The impact is individual and very subtle, but it does exist—the very nature of magic makes it so. Making such topical and graphical changes has an even greater effect when they are accepted by other practitioners.

Ironically, that old guy was right, but perhaps if he had explained himself instead of acting like a cranky old fart, I might have learned something then that I have only realized now. Then again, maybe he was as clueless as I had first thought he was back then.

———

Strategically regrouping, restructuring, and reconfiguring the various symbology of the Qabalah produces four different categories that are very important domains where the practical work is to be performed. These four groupings are: Tables of Correspondences, Maps of the Inner Planes, Maps of the Sacred Body, and Realizing the Great Cycle. Let us examine each of these four domains.

Tables of Correspondences

Not all symbologies are important or relevant to the work of the Qabalist. At some point, he or she needs to choose which symbols are important and focus solely on them. How a Qabalist chooses is based on the spiritual discipline that he or she employs as the foundation of the work. If the Qabalist is a Pagan or Wiccan, then some symbols will be relevant and others will not, such as a table containing the Greek, Roman, Egyptian, and Celtic gods and goddesses instead of theological aspects of Christianity or Buddhism. Once these various tables of symbols are selected, they are joined together to become attributes of a larger overall structure that represents the specific spiritual discipline of the Qabalist. Organizing such a selected and relevant list of tables would also cause the religious symbology of that practicing Qabalist to become enlivened and powerfully awakened.

Maps of the Inner Planes

These maps would consist of specialized tabular structures (matrices) or even glyphs, using various groupings of symbols. Inner Plane maps consist of symbolically defined domains that contain a specific set of spiritual entities. Knowing the qualities and the defining elements of these matrix cells would greatly aid the Qabalist in gaining access to the domain and the spirits contained within it. An example of such a map would be found in tables of the four elements, Four Qabalistic Worlds, seven planets, 12 zodiacal signs, 16 elementals, 28 Mansions of the Moon, 36 zodiacal decans (10 degree segments), 72 zodiacal quinians (5 degree segments), etc. The number of lists is endless.

Maps of the Sacred Body

This is where the macrocosmic symbology of the Tree of Life is applied to the microcosmic archetypal human body. As you can see, this is a typical use of the power of analogy, and it creates a potent bridge between the material and spiritual worlds as centered on the human anatomy. It is also where the Four Qabalistic Worlds are mapped to the body to facilitate control of the spiritualized body-mind.

Realizing the Great Cycle

The two great cycles found in the doctrine of the Qabalah consist of involution and evolution. Involution is where the manifested One creates, though emanation, the various elements of the greater cosmic Spirit, Mind, Soul, and Body. Involution causes the imbedding of Spirit within the elements of matter for the purpose of its conscious awakening and self-realization. However, the other half of this cycle is where the consciously awakened individual proceeds through the long process of spiritual awakening, illumination (awareness of the God/dess Within), and the ultimate spiritual union with the One. The Qabalah assists the seeker in understanding the latent legacy within all living things, and then it aids him or her in mastering the art of spiritual ascension to the One.

These four groupings of the symbology of the Qabalah represent the foundation for the practical work of the Qabalah. This practical work is achieved through the use of the basic toolkit, which consists of eight essential skills. These eight skills are: study, analysis, contemplation, meditation, pathworking, theurgy, adopting a basic discipline, and performing bodywork. These eight skills cover the entire spectrum of practical Qabalistic work, from the highest forms of mystical speculation to essential forms of bodily exercises, posture, and diet. This is why the Qabalah is considered a comprehensive spiritual and magical discipline.

In addition to these eight skills, there are also some basic practices that the aspiring Qabalist will need to consider. These additional practices are: empowered faith, where one's spiritual faith is empowered by one's emotions and feelings; performing acts of spiritual devotion; engaging in active forms of prayer; and spiritual service. There is a need to follow a spiritual path in order to divest the self of worldly concerns and personal (ego-based) self-importance. Also, a faithful engagement with one's personal and public religious practices (as a form of piety) is important.

Overall, these practices might seem a bit alien to the typical Pagan or Witch, especially prayer. Yet prayer is nothing more than developing an internal dialogue with one's Deity, which is certainly not something that is exclusive to monotheistic religious traditions. Prayers can also consist of reciting to oneself any inspirational or spiritual writing that is personally significant and meaningful. Christians and Jews recite psalms, but Pagans and Witches can find other important material to use in a similar fashion, such as the Homeric or Orphic hymns, for example.

- **Study**—Examine all of the symbolic elements of the Qabalah. This is accomplished through exhaustive research and also by deeply scrutinizing these symbols while meditating. Look at them in isolation and also how they relate to other classes of symbols. Because everything is by analogy joined to everything else, then how different symbols interrelate is part of the greater mystery of the Qabalah. Master the five essential elements of the Qabalah (covered in chapters 2 through 7 of the first part of this book) but also expand this research to include other materials and books.

- **Analysis**—Actively build up analogies, comparisons, and groupings, and then use them to create new structures. Creative analogy is the most important key to making the Qabalah come alive in one's mind. The key to creative analogy is the use of divergent and convergent thinking skills. Divergent thinking is where the student maps various associations by making notes and pictures on paper, allowing for a stream of consciousness to be documented. Then these notes and pictures are examined, grouped into patterns, and then compared with actual research, and the end result is that a new body of lore is developed. Included in these skills would be various systems of arithmology, which we will cover later on in chapter 15.

- **Contemplation**—Using the techniques of discursive meditation, intently focus and reflect on various Qabalistic materials, such as a concept, short paragraph, or symbolic emblem. Observe any and all thoughts and sensations regarding that focused subject matter. Once this is accomplished, use a form of effective prayer to rejoice in this revelation and to thank one's Godhead for it.

- **Meditation**—Emptying the mind of any thoughts or concerns and focusing on being in the moment of one's spiritual element. This is where the meditation session is completed by its opposite state, which is relieving the self of all thoughts and just absorbing the beauty and majesty of the Godhead. (Emptying the mind is done passively by just letting go, and is not actively enforced by the will.)

- **Pathworking**—Using the power of visualization, the Qabalist creates an inner experience of the Sephiroth and Pathways of the Tree of Life. This technique is called "Walking the Tree of Life."

- **Theurgy**—Performing rituals that invoke the spiritual hierarchy of the Godhead as associated with the various elements of the Qabalah. This often includes forms of Godname-vibrating and even Godhead assumption.

- **Basic discipline**—Performing daily and weekly practices and exercises. These exercises would include bodywork (posture, breath control, prayer, and meditation), study and analysis, and special theurgic workings, as well as engaging in one's exoteric religious celebrations.

- **Bodywork**—This involves the basic six methods of mind control (posture, breath control, meditation, contemplation, concentration, assumption of ecstatic trance) as well as other foundational practices, such as diet, cleanliness, and maintaining a spiritual environment, both within the mind and in one's home. (I will defer to the individual tastes and needs of the seeker rather than impose my own expectations in regard to these practices.)

These eight practices are dealt with and elaborated on in the following chapters. However, I have sought to include and incorporate them in a more traditional format, associated with the sacred workings of theurgy and ritual/ceremonial magic. From my perspective, magic and occult speculation, as well as religious based practices, are the foundation for the practical Qabalah. Let us now examine how the second part of this book will be configured so that we might learn to adopt what has been expounded on in the first part into a spiritual and magical discipline.

Basis of Practical Work

Having covered the basic information about the Sephiroth and Pathways in the first part of this book, I will now present the practical uses of the Qabalah that will aid you in mastering ceremonial or ritual magic. This particular discipline is known as the Practical Qabalah (*Qabalah Ma'asit*), and is thought to be associated with the esoteric practices of theurgy that the Jewish Qabalists had derived from a rich source of Middle Eastern mystical, Gnostic, and magical beliefs and practices, as well as Greek philosophical practices.

Qabalistic magic was born long ago in obscurity. It was developed over a long period of time, and it evolved to become a monumental system of occultism. It was passed down from teacher to student, but obviously only to those chosen few who saw its importance and merit. Those individuals copied and added new ideas to this lore, causing it to grow and expand, so that by the time of the Age of Enlightenment, it had become quite vast and all-encompassing. The Qabalah revolutionized the practice of magic. It assisted Jews and Christians in experimenting with contacting and channeling the wisdom and power of the Deity through its various surrogates (spirits) for the purpose of directing and implementing divine change in the world. The magical formulas that were used to create words of power and the revelation of the secret names of the Deity were derived from specific Qabalistic techniques, and these formulas and words of power were even used to create ritual patterns, saturating the liturgical structures of ceremonial magic with the authorities and insignia of the Godhead.

The later derived structure of the Tree of Life assisted Qabalists in mapping the Inner Planes and the Pathways, providing a system of guided imagery. The associated correspondences between the Sephiroth and Pathways helped

Qabalists to build a meticulous categorization of the various characteristics of the spirits. The Pathways, as represented by the Hebrew alphabet, also established a direct relationship between numbers and words, creating various numerological systems that assisted in the generation of formula-words and semantic linkages between the generated magical powers and the defined target, using a system of operant links. This relationship between numbers and letters also allowed for the formation of magical sigils or signatures, which assisted the magician in uniquely identifying a spirit for the purpose of conjuration. It also produced specialized words of power that helped to empower magical rituals.

Therefore, it can be seen that the practical Qabalah can be defined as representing the following ten techniques (based on the eightfold toolkit discussed above):

- Cosmological framework for the Inner Planes
- Mind control and the experiential Qabalah
- Pathworking
- Godnames and their use
- Spiritual hierarchies
- Theurgy and Invocation
- Systems of correspondences establishing the relationships between various different spiritual entities and qualities
- Systems of word manipulation consisting of a letter numerology that associates words with numerical values

- Building of word formulas as acronyms
- Creation of sigils from names and word formulas

These ten different methodologies represent the core discipline and applied lore of the Qabalah, and are essential for the practice of Qabalistic or high magic. However, it is important to keep in mind that all of these exercises are empty of meaning, power, and significance if the symbols of the Qabalah remain opaque and dormant for the seeker. They must be made to come alive in the mind and soul of the operator by using the powers of the imagination and analogy.

We will now proceed to discuss each topic in much greater detail and elaborate upon them. The practical Qabalah consists of the most important set of methodologies, beliefs, and techniques that the spiritual seeker could possibly wield, even if he or she were to employ nothing else in their regimen.

Cosmological Framework

We have already discussed the Sephiroth and Pathways of the Tree of Life as representing a glyph for the Inner Planes. The system of pathworking establishes Inner Plane connections, which are important to one's personal and spiritual evolution. Pathworking, where the initiate traverses either up or down the Tree of Life or intensely focuses on just one of the paths, represents an integral practice in magic that assists the aspirant in spiritually transforming and consciously evolving.

The symbology of each path powerfully impacts the mind, body, and spirit of the magician. The magician, by practicing pathworking, directly encounters the Deity and experiences the vision and the power of that Godhead affecting the material world. This vision reveals the essential truth that a magician may represent and act as a surrogate for that Deity.

The structure of the Tree of Life when viewed through the multiple occurrences of the Four Qabalistic Worlds becomes analogous to the structures associated with the magician's magic circle and the domain of the four Watchtowers of the elements. Each Watchtower is the ward for a host of spirits and forces whose correspondences are described by the Tree of Life. Furthermore, the Four Worlds each have a Tree of Life structure within them, and so the ultimate organization and structure of the Watchtowers are formed around each Tree. (See figure 13.)

This multiple Tree of Life scheme represents one of the more important structures of the Inner Planes, which the magician can make accessible to her mind through the artifice of creating a visual model. This model is also represented by the 40 Pip (*Naib*) cards of the Lesser Arcana of the Tarot (Ace through 10 of the four suits), and also by the mechanism of the 36 Decans (ten degree segments) of the zodiac and their associated spiritual hierarchies. Using these models, the magician constructs ritual structures that allow for the manipulation and expression of these forces and intelligences, which through the corresponding association of the Inner Planes to the earth plane, allows the magician to directly cause changes within her mind and in

Figure 13: Diagram of the four Trees of Life with a common root

the physical world, according to her will and intent. This is one plausible definition of how magic might be performed utilizing the Tree of Life.

Techniques of Mind Control

Because we have previously discussed the Four Worlds and the Four Bodies, I can now present some simple techniques that will help you to acquire the necessary altered states of consciousness to do Qabalistic work. These techniques will help you to fully experience the symbolic correspondences and the allegorical domains of the Inner Planes, and the mental and spiritual dimensions of the various levels and models of the operant Qabalah. As I stated previously, it is very important that you gain direct access to the various descriptions and symbolic expressions of the Tree of Life and the Four Worlds, particularly the higher mental, spiritual, and Monadic levels. Entering into the Inner Plane domains of the Qabalah will help you cross the boundaries of the microcosm and enter into the macrocosm, allowing you to realize the symbology from a personal and cosmic level simultaneously.

The techniques available to the Qabalist are meditation, contemplation, visualization, and simple forms of ceremony. He may fashion and make a wand and a dagger, as well as acquire an unadorned white robe. He might also collect various Qabalistic diagrams and posters and hang these at an easily viewable height in a room that can be used primarily for meditation and study. Salt water is useful for ablutions and blessings, and so are special pure extracts of perfumes and the herbal gums of burnable incense. A simple incense burner that can accommodate burning charcoal will easily be able to dispense a scented aura of sacredness whenever required.

Sessions that involve meditation and contemplation should be formalized with a special bath, anointing with perfume, donning a clean white robe, and then sequestering oneself in the designated room, with incense burning and the dim illumination of oil lamps. The foundation for all Qabalistic work should be simple, efficient, and easily within one's means. There isn't any need for assembling all of the paraphernalia associated with high ceremonial magic, since the Qabalist relies more on the power of Qabalistic symbolism and associated Godhead attributes. Therefore, the operator should keep things simple, easy to remember, and, more importantly, modest.

There are five essential operations that a Qabalist will perform in order to make her discipline one that is experiential. These five operations are the *basic meditation session, contemplation session, pathworking, ceremonial invocation,* and *Godhead assumption*. There are also five basic states of alignment employed as simple ritual expressions, which are used in these five operations. These are S*elf-Crossing* (Mantle of Glory), the *Middle Pillar exercise, Opening of the Self, Closing of the Self,* and *Grounding the Self*. We will discuss each of the five operations below, but first I would like to discuss the five basic states of alignment.

A *state of alignment* refers to the disposition of the operator's bodily energy field and its associated state of consciousness. Each of these simple rituals works with several points on the body, which is analogous to the same points on the Tree of Life. Just imagine the Tree of Life as if it were superimposed over the body. Therefore, the following 11 points of the body would represent the ten Sephiroth of the Tree of Life and Da'ath, and their corresponding word and/or Godname (see figure 14):

- Kether—crown of head (Atah [unto thou]—Ehieh)
- Chokmah—right side of head
- Binah—left side of head
- Da'ath—throat (Yahweh Elohim)
- Chesed—right shoulder (ve-Gedulah (and Mercy)— El)
- Geburah—left shoulder (ve-Geburah (and strength) —Elohim Gebor)
- Tiphareth—heart (le-Olaham Ve-eid (forever)—Yahweh Aloah ve-Da'ath)
- Netzach—right hand

- Hod—left hand
- Yesod—genitals (Shaddai El-Chai)
- Malkuth—feet (Malkuth (Kingdom)—Adonai ha-Aretz)

Arms and hands are typically not used as power centers in most systems of body points, and they are not used as such in these five simple rites of alignment. They are utilized instead to direct or focus the energy. These five simple alignment exercises use the head, throat, shoulders, heart/solar plexus, genitals, and feet as representations of the six Sephiroth applied to the body to energize points of power, or, as the Eastern tradition calls them, *chakras*. The operator touches the power point with the right hand, vibrating the word or name, and then feels an energy pass into that point while breathing in the force and imagining it as the specific Sephirah blazing forth on an imaginary body of light, which is superimposed over one's own.

Four of these bodily power points can be used to connect to the four parts of the human soul. The crown of the head, which is also associated with Kether, is the point where the practitioner may connect to the highest aspect of the self—the Yechidah (self as Godhead). The heart, attributed with Tiphareth, would be associated with the Ruach (rational mind), and the genitals, attributed with Yesod, would be associated with the Nephesh (emotional body). The Neschamah, which is the individual spirit, would be defined as a combination of Chokmah (right side of head) and Binah (left side of head); therefore, it would be centered at what the Eastern traditions call the third eye. Since the Yechidah is typically inaccessible to the practitioner, it

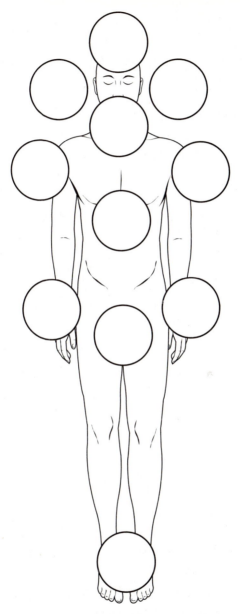

Figure 14: Tree of Life as human body

can be accessed only through the third-eye power point, invoking the part of soul associated with the Neschamah. The practitioner would contact the Neschamah through an intense period of meditation, where the Godnames for Chokmah and Binah would be alternately vibrated and the focus of the practice would be on the third eye. This technique is not part of the basic regimen for the practicing Qabalist, but could easily be added to any of the exercises below.

The following exercises show how these power points are used to create specific states of bodily alignment:

1. **Self-Crossing or Mantle of Glory** (similar to Qabalistic Cross)—Used for self-empowerment and protection. Operator can be seated or standing, using the right hand, or clasping the dagger by the hilt (forming a cross). He then touches the forehead (with the butt end of the dagger, if used), and vibrates "Atah," pauses, then visualizes the energy going down through the genitals to the feet, touches genitals and vibrates "Malkuth," pauses, then touches the left shoulder, vibrates "ve-Geburah," pauses, touches the right shoulder, vibrates "ve-Gedulah," pauses, and then touches the heart, vibrates "le-Olaham ve-Eid. Amen." Operator should visualize an illuminated cross aligning the power points of the body and creating an impregnable shield over it, while thinking the words "Unto thee (is) the Kingdom, the Power, and the Glory, Forever. Amen."

   This exercise may be similar to the Qabalistic Cross, but the right shoulder is aligned to Chesed, and the left, to Geburah. This is different from what is practiced in the Golden Dawn. I always felt that it was important for these two Sephiroth to line up with the proper right and left shoulders of the body, instead of how they are traditionally aligned. Also, *le-Olaham* by itself is incomplete, so I added the *ve-Eid* so that it would be a complete, meaningful sentence (it is Hebrew for "forever").

2. **Middle Pillar exercise**—Used for centering. Operator can be seated or standing, using the right hand to charge the power points where possible. Start with eyes closed, visualizing the qualities of the Sephirah as it is fully activated on the body, and then perform a cycle of slow and continuous breathing. To begin, the operator circles the head with her hand and then touches the crown, vibrating the Godname "Ehieh," pausing for a short period, then proceeding down to the next point, which is the throat. She then vibrates the Godname "Yahweh Elohim," pauses, then proceeds down to the next point, which is the heart. At this point, she vibrates the Godname "Yahweh Aloah ve-Da'ath," pauses, then proceeds down to the next point, which is the genitals. Lightly touching the genitals, she vibrates the Godname "Shadai El-Chai," pauses, then focuses on the energy as it is pushed down to the feet. At the last point, she vibrates the Godname "Adonai ha-Aretz." She then remains in her position for a short period of time, feeling all of the energy flowing from the crown of the head to the

feet, producing a feeling of complete relaxation and mental regeneration.

3. **Opening of the Self**—Used in order to be more receptive and open to spiritual impressions and sensations. Operator is typically seated in the restful but alert posture (using a chair, or on a pillow, legs crossed, back straight), and engages in a short period of breath control. Then taking his right hand, he touches his forehead and vibrates the Godname "Ehieh," pauses, touches the left shoulder, vibrates the Godname "Elohim Gebor," pauses, touches the right shoulder, vibrates the Godname "El," and then touches the forehead for a second time to complete the circuit, but doesn't vibrate the Godname. He then crosses his arms over his breast (with hands held in a fist), pauses for a moment, uncrosses them, then brings them forward so that they form right angles to the body and with the palms facing up and open. This is the posture of receiving. While the operator is doing this alignment, he should imagine that a gateway has opened in his heart for anything that is positive and spiritual to enter. (Note: This action should not be performed until after the self-crossing has been done.) To give greater emphasis to this exercise, the operator can also use the wand to touch the points of the body, and also to draw an invoking spiral before him. (Invoking spiral: clockwise, outer to inner.)

4. **Closing of the Self**—Used in order to break off any connections and to close the self from all impres-

sions and sensations. Operator begins with the posture of the Opening of the Self, with arms at right angles to the body and the palms up and open. Then with the right hand, she touches the right shoulder and vibrates the Godname "El," pauses, touches the left shoulder and vibrates the Godname "Elohim Gebor," pauses, touches the genitals and vibrates the Godname "Shadai El-Chai," pauses, and then touches the right shoulder for a second time to complete the circuit, but doesn't vibrate the Godname. She then repositions her arms in the receiving posture, but then moves her arms so that they are crossed over her breast (with hands held in a fist). While the operator is doing this alignment, she should imagine that a gateway has been closed in her heart which will protect it from anything attempting to enter. To give greater emphasis to this exercise, the operator can also use the wand to touch the points of the body, and also to draw a banishing spiral before her. (Banishing spiral: counterclockwise, inner to outer.)

5. **Grounding the Self**—Used in order to project any energy held in the body into the earth. Operator begins in the closed-self posture, then uncrosses his arms and extends them forward with the palms open and facing down. Then he touches the floor in front of him with the palms pressed to the floor while vibrating the Godname "Adonai ha-Aretz," and imagines all of the excess energy flowing from his body into the earth. (It is also a good idea to extend the grounding by getting something to eat and drink,

and also taking a complete break from whatever activity required the grounding.)

We have now gone over the five simple alignment exercises, and these should be committed to memory so that they can be performed automatically whenever needed. Do not be too concerned if some of the actions that are supposed to be done in these five alignment exercises are either a bit vague or haven't yet been defined (like the breathing techniques). These will be covered in greater detail in the text that outlines the five basic operations, which we will be covering next.

———

Meditation Session

The operator begins with a comfortable but wakeful posture, sitting with the back straight, and begins the meditation session with a period of controlled breathing. This is a simple process of just counting the breaths and making certain that they conform to a specific count. For instance, I typically use what I call the four-fold breath counting technique, where I count to four while inhaling, then hold for a count of four, exhale for a count of four, and then hold my lungs empty for a count of four.

In another breathing technique, the operator will relax and slow down his breathing until the period of inhalation is exactly the same as the period of exhalation, and the transition between them is almost nonexistent; in other words, the breathing is continuous, which is why it is called continuous breathing. These are the only two breathing techniques that you will need to put yourself into a splendid altered state of consciousness. It is a state of mind that is deeply relaxed and yet also completely awake.

Once a period of controlled breathing has been accomplished, the operator can add either a vibrated or intoned prayer or choose instead to stare fixedly at a picture, poster, or diagram.

To use the intoned prayer technique, the operator must first choose a set of words that are significant or meaningful. This can be a phrase or even a single word, or it might be one of the special Godnames or other such symbolic terms as are found in the Qabalah. This word or phrase is slowly and verbally pronounced, hummed, and vibrated in the nasal passages with the mouth closed until it almost seems to have a ringing quality. The operator performs this vibrating and intoning over and over again for many minutes until the sound just appears to drone in the mind and the actual meaning of the word seems to disappear. The key is that operator must focus on the sound of his voice and not allow any other thoughts or impressions to invade his mind.

The same is also true for staring fixedly at a poster or picture. While continuing the controlled breathing cycles, the operator will stare and seek to eliminate everything from her mind except for the image that she is seeing. The image might waver or become distorted; the eyes might water, perhaps even burn a little; but the operator continues to stare fixedly as long as possible, pausing to briefly blink, as little as possible.

The meditation session should always be performed for a fixed period of time, and once that period is over the exercise should be closed. I would also recommend that the operator perform this meditation session at around the same time during the day or night and, when possible, to do it every day without fail. The operator can vary the routine, but the time for meditation is most important, and like a critical event, it should be performed without fail. To perform any operation for a fixed time period, the operator can use any kind of timing device with an alarm, as long as the alarm itself is neither loud nor jarring.

Contemplation Session

The operator begins the contemplation session by performing a short but intense meditation session, and then once within that optimum state of mind, she can then begin the contemplation session. While the objective of the meditative session is to empty the mind of all extraneous thoughts until a state is produced where there are no thoughts occupying one's mind, a contemplation session is used to focus the quiescent mind upon a single topical concept, word, or idea—and nothing more. This single thought then occupies the mind fully and completely, and the operator dispassionately notes all that transpires within her mind during the period of contemplation. However, any extraneous thoughts, sensations, or intruding emotions that are not directly attached or associated with the contemplative target will be dispassionately suppressed.

The operator should be able to identify a relevant chain of thought associated with the target word from one that is irrelevant or extraneous. I would recommend that the period of contemplation be rather short at first, perhaps ten minutes, and then lengthened as the operator gets used to doing this for longer periods. After this period is completed, then the operator should reflect on what was received and perform an inner kind of thanksgiving to the Godhead.

I am using the term *contemplation* as it is used in a modern context. I define contemplation in a manner that was previously used to define what was called *discursive meditation*, or meditation on a specific subject, paragraph of words, or symbolic emblem. Often, the period of discursive contemplation would be followed with an affective prayer, which would be a spontaneous reaction in response to the reflections received during meditation (think of it as a kind of internalized thanksgiving). Contemplation, as it is classically defined, is where the mind is emptied of all thoughts and impressions to create a state of inner quiescence. Since Eastern systems of yoga and meditation have become popular, meditation has come to mean emptying the mind, and contemplation is where a specific topic is intensely focused on for a period of time. You can use either definition or approach, just as long as what is done is represented by the above techniques applied in a consistent manner.

Pathworking

I will be covering pathworking in the next chapter, in which it will be thoroughly explained. However, I would advise that the operator should begin this operation with a deep meditation session, to be followed with the mantle of glory (self-crossing), and then the Opening of the Self exercise. Once the pathworking is completed, the operator can perform the Closing of the Self exercise, followed by the Grounding the Self exercise.

Invocation

This operation is covered in chapter 13, so there is no need for me to expound upon it here. Still, two key activities that should be performed in this operation are the exercise of the Mantle of Glory (to protect oneself), and the operation of Godhead assumption, which we are going to cover next.

Godhead Assumption

This operation is similar to the contemplation operation, except that the target is one of the specific Godnames as found associated with the ten Sephiroth. The operator should spend some time elaborating on that Godhead, associating it with Pagan gods or goddesses, heroes, or avatars if he is Pagan, or specific Christian or Jewish themes if he is a follower of one of those traditions. The more information that he gathers about the target Godhead, the better the assumption will be. Additionally, the operator should approach this Godhead with love, devotion, and service. I would recommend that he actually assemble a small shrine to that Deity and make offerings of flowers, incense, and anything else that would seem appropriate. This period of devotion should last a while (a couple of weeks), making the target Godhead into an object of the operator's aspirations and spiritual desires. Then, when that Being seems to come alive in the imagination of the operator, the time for assuming the Godhead has arrived. The operator performs the following steps to acquire a type of Godhead assumption within a Qabalistic framework:

1. Begin with a long and extended meditation session with the shrine of the Godhead as the focus of the meditation.

2. Perform the Middle Pillar exercise.

3. Perform the Opening of the Self exercise. The operator should feel himself completely filled with love and desire for the Godhead. (This is a necessary precursor to the assumption.)

4. Perform a contemplation session while in the Opening of the Self posture. The focus should be only on the Godhead, with the object to make full contact with that entity. Once contact is made, draw it into oneself slowly but completely, perhaps by breathing it in or feeling it enter into the heart. Touching and focusing on the heart power point during this exercise would also be very helpful. Allow the Godhead to completely occupy the self and to reside there for a brief time. (This can be facilitated by vibrating the Godname as a kind of mantra.)

5. Perform the Closing of the Self exercise. The operator should feel a necessary regret at being parted from the Deity, knowing that there will be other opportunities for assumption and union at a later time.

6. Perform the Grounding the Self exercise.

7. Spend some time immediately afterwards writing down all that was experienced during the assumption.

We have now covered all of the exercises and operations that you will need to fully activate your studies of the Qabalah. This section should guide and assist you in being able to tangibly experience all of the theoretical, occultic, and philosophical notions as found in the study of Qabalah.

The Art of Pathworking

Now that we have discussed in detail the various elements of the 22 Pathways (and the ten Sephiroth), we should discuss how the student could go about assembling these components together to formulate what is known as the Art of Qabalistic Pathworking. This methodology is a rather recent innovation, particularly since the Tarot trumps were only recently associated with the paths, giving them a greater depth of symbolism than what they would otherwise possess. The purpose of this technique is to emulate the process of ascent, using the combination of the ten Sephiroth and 22 Pathways to aid the seeker in creating as real a transformative experience as possible. What this means is that Qabalistic pathworking is not just a form of simple guided visualization or dry meditation. It is instead a system of magical envisioning, where the various symbols are used to build up in the imagination the actual inner domain of the Sephirah and its associated Pathways.

The basic components for a pathworking exercise are the two Sephiroth and the associated Pathway that connects them, which would also include all of their relevant correspondences. Typically, the operator will perform just one pathworking exercise at a time, seeking to reveal unique insights and psychic occurrences to be followed with later meditations on those specific revelations. The technique employed to facilitate pathworking is called *astral clairvoyance,* but that actually consists of using one's creative imagination with or without an accompanying partial trance state. Pathworkings are often performed over a period of weeks or months, where the operator will incrementally ascend up the Tree of Life. He or she will use the Serpent's Ascent sequence of paths, following them up the Tree of Life to its summit. It is important that the operator ensures that the entire Tree of Life is explored in this manner consistently over a period of time, and it is even better if each of these pathworking sessions are scheduled in advance and given a specific time limit.

It is also a good idea for the session to be performed in a temple or a place where the operator will be undisturbed for the allotted time. Purification exercises, ablutions, anointing, donning vestments, and then stretching the body and emptying the mind are all excellent preparations for the pathworking session—so is establishing sacred space and setting a magic circle. In fact, in the Order of the Gnostic Star[48] we have a specific magical ritual that can be used to perform a ritualized pathworking, deploying a double gateway and an underworld crossroads for this purpose. Needless to say, the more that one puts into this working, the more dramatic and profound the results. Of course, the operator should also keep this working focused and brief so it does not become so elaborate that it is too cumbersome to perform. I would also advise the operator that such a pathworking exercise must ultimately accommodate 22 distinct sessions over a given period of time. An overly elaborate pathworking exercise would become unendurable over the long run, and this could cause one to quit before all the paths had been explored.

To begin this working, the operator may want to use special incense, colored candles, and some kind of colored banner or altar cloth associated with the correspondences of the starting Sephiroth, creating, as it were, a kind of simple inner temple based on those attributes. The operator can envision or perhaps even portray in his temple a facsimile of the base temple, such as having a central altar adorned with an oil lamp, and some kind of twin pillars (right—white, left—black) on either side. *Most of the effort of pathworking is done in the mind of the operator.*

At the end of the imagined Sephirah temple is a doorway or gateway that has a veil before it, which represents the access threshold into the target path. To fully establish the Sephirah temple, the operator will intone and visualize the associated Godname and archangel. He may even assume

---

48. See www.gnosticstar.org.

an associated Godhead into himself for this domain, as well as visualize any other pertinent symbols and correspondences for the base Sephirah. Once this is done, then he will mentally advance to the gateway, open the threshold, and enter into the Pathway using the associated Tarot card as a symbolic key. Once immersed within the path, the operator may intone or visualize any Godnames, archangels, color schemes, or other relevant symbolic attributes. The Hebrew letter should be intoned, and the symbolic aspect (element, planet, or astrological sign) should also be visualized. The operator will keep his mind completely open and seek to see, sense, and perceive things within the Pathway domain.

Beyond the path will be the next Sephirah, warded by another veiled gateway, and the operator may open the threshold and enter into this domain (or not), and intone the Godname and archangel to complete the transition. Some writers have stated that the pathworking should only progress to the point just before the destination Sephirah, but I believe that a complete transit to the destination should be envisioned. Then the operator can retrace her steps back again to the base Sephirah where she started, performing a closing exercise and completing the pathworking.

While the operator is undergoing this process, she should note down everything that is seen, sensed, or perceived in the vision. These notes will be used for additional contemplation sessions that will aid her in fully comprehending the nature of the symbols and their internal meaning and significance.

An electronic voice recorder might be a very handy tool to use in this work. Keeping a record of what happens will greatly assist the operator in fully internalizing and thereby realizing the Qabalah in a very literal and psychic manner, giving it life and dynamically empowering it within herself.

A more elaborate system of pathworking would group together those paths that are associated with a single base Sephirah, actually visualizing them as veiled gateways at the points where they occur in the actual Sephirah. For instance, the Sephirah of Yesod would have one veiled gateway to the back or rear of the temple (Path 32), and then three in the front, positioned so that one would be on the left-hand side (Path 30), one in the center (Path 25), and the other on the right-hand side (Path 28), just as they are in the actual Tree of Life diagram.

Using this methodology, the session might be made longer so as to allow for three contiguous pathworkings, or the magician might start in the base Sephirah three times, one for each Pathway. This methodology of using an imagined temple for a specific Sephirah with all of its paths represented within it is similar to the initiation temples of the different grades of the Golden Dawn. An enterprising student could use this approach and perform a kind of complete transformative initiation cycle, since the symbols and spiritual hierarchy associated with the Sephirah and the Pathways are powerful enough to trigger internal transformations.

Additionally, the magician can use some of the other patterns for selecting and experiencing the Pathways, such as the Serpent's Descent (exact opposite of the Serpent's

Ascent), the lightning flash, or other patterns. Each of these directions and methodologies would teach something unique and direct to the operator, helping her to completely master the Tree of Life in all of its intricacies.

eleven

Godnames:
Explanation and Use

One of the most important keys to the Qabalah is associated with the various Godnames attributed to the ten Sephiroth. These Godnames are used to unlock the ten attributes of the Deity, and to either commune with or harness them for occult purposes. In addition to the ten Godnames, there are also other names, aspects, and attributes for the unknown, unmanifest, and nameless Deity that is responsible for the fusion of the worlds of Spirit, Mind, and Matter. In order to understand these various names, we need to examine them in detail and determine their source. Doing so will show us that the Qabalah appears to espouse a theological system that is polytheistic rather than monotheistic. For the sake of clarity, I will make a few points about monotheism just to ensure that we are all on the same page.

Monotheism is a very recent adaptation, and it is an important part of the doctrines of Judaism, Christianity, and Islam. However, Christianity is only loosely regulated by a monotheistic doctrine, since it proposes a trinity as the foundation for the One (as Father, Son, and Holy Ghost), and it allows (in Catholicism and Orthodox Christianity) the display of icons depicting a myriad of saints, angels, disciples, the Virgin Mary, and even Jesus Christ himself. In contrast, Judaism and Islam allow no human images or icons to represent any aspect of their religious creed. So it would seem that while Judaism and Islam are strict monotheistic religions, Christianity is more representative of a synthetic mixture of Hellenic paganism and Judaism, thus allowing for the use of idols, icons, relics, and many other tropes that are patently pagan in origin. However, the supposed supremacy of monotheism in Judaism hides and represses a very recent pagan past.

Much of the Old Testament is a battle royal between the singular Deity, Yahweh, and his proponents, and the indigenous Hebrew people, who were depicted as continuously falling into the habits of idolatry and pagan superstition.[49] In fact, all of the tragedies inflicted on the Chosen People occurred solely because of their unfaithful intransigence. The followers of Yahweh were the victors in this war; therefore, they got to write the history, which later became the stories of the Bible. All of the proponents of the many different and

---

49. Raphael Patai, *The Hebrew Goddess*, 30–31.

alternative pagan gods and goddesses indigenous to ancient Palestine were either completely subsumed or shown to be false, hollow, and empty deities. There are echoes of these many gods to be found in the writings of the scriptures, and from them we can gain an idea of what actually happened over 3,000 years ago. Archaeologists have also uncovered the clay tablets of other indigenous people who were not part of the monotheistic tradition (or the Chosen People), and whose translated voices, until recently, were silent and unheard.

Many scholars have determined that monotheism was actually the result of a desire for political uniformity and social identity, instead of being based solely on a theological or religious revelation.[50] The temple of King Solomon had representations of many gods and goddesses invested within its holy of holies, and later kings appeared to celebrate more than just the single insular god known as Yahweh. The kings of Israel and Judea represented a large conglomeration of peoples, some of whom had been living in Palestine long before the Hebrews arrived, such as the Canaanites. Therefore, it would seem only prudent that the royal temple housed all of the gods and goddesses of these people. It was only much later that the king and elite members of the kingdom decided to eradicate polytheism in favor of the one god, which they believed to be their ancestral Deity. This probably began to occur during the reign of King Josiah in the seventh century BCE, but was radically

---

50. See Niditch, *Ancient Israelite Religion*, 27–32, where she describes the background of the Hebrew Bibles, its writers, stories, and bias.

hastened during the first exilic period and immediately afterwards (when the books of the Tenakh were formally assembled). Some of the old Godnames survived, to be alternative names of the Deity, and others were suppressed, stamped out, and declared as false gods.

This process of political coercion met with mixed success, so other supports were brought into place, such as the feigned discovery of the lost book of Deuteronomy (which had only recently been written, according to some historians), and the assembling of the Torah into a book of strict laws and practices. The Hebrew religion was in this manner remade into a monotheism, but prior to that time, it was a loose polytheistic religion. Because of that fact, the monotheism of the Old Testament was tenuous and only skin-deep, hiding and obscuring polytheistic habits, while whitewashing the brutal immorality and savage behavior of an archaic tribal Deity.

When the Qabalah was invented many centuries later, the habits and ingrained natural tendencies of polytheism began to emerge. This had the effect of subtly influencing the attribution of the One Deity into ten different aspects, which didn't at first include the behind-the-scenes entity who was the invisible and unknowable source of everything. Whereas Judaism sought to keep the lid on any re-emerging pagan tendencies, the Qabalah seemed to encourage them. Everything was allowed in the ensuing speculation, and the sole God of Judaism seemed to spawn many attributes and aspects, some of them barely recognizable as coming from Yahweh.

This problem with polytheism becomes obvious with the ten Godnames of the ten Sephiroth. A pious interpretation would be that the ten Sephiroth are just emanations of the One; however, the hypostatization of these attributes unwittingly made them into separate but linked deities. The names of the ten god aspects actually consist of the roots of a handful of archaic and simpler Deity names, and we should first attempt to examine these roots before seeking to define how they were incorporated into the Godnames for the Sephiroth.

Two basic names of the God of Israel that are found in the scriptures are the names *Yahweh* (YHVH) and *Elohim* (ALHYM). Scholars believe that these two names once represented two different gods, and in fact Elohim, which is a plural proper noun (supposedly indicating a kind of "pluralis majestatis" or majestic plural), is from *Eloah* (ALVH) and *El* (AL). So it would seem that the original Godnames were *Yahweh* and *El*.

From *El* we get *Eloah* (ALVH—a God) and Elohim (ALHYM—Gods), and the name *El* is preserved in the name *Shaddai El Chai* (ShDY AL ChY—Almighty Living God). In ancient Canaanite mythology, El is the singular father of the gods, analogous to Zeus, but more remote to the average worshiper. Other gods and goddesses were much more active in that pantheon: most notably, Baal Hadad (Zebul), or Lord of Heaven—a storm god. El's wife was Asherah, the mother of the gods, and Baal's sister was Anath, a virgin warrior goddess. Since the god Baal stood in direct competition with the tribal god, Yahweh, who was also a storm and fire god, he was eventually supplanted and

shown to be a false Deity in the scriptures. Asherah continued to be worshiped for a long time until the advent of the
great reform, when she was also dropped. What eventually
remained in this diminishing pantheon was Yahweh and
the god El, and both of them became conflated, becoming
the combined name YHVH ALHYM, or Yahweh Elohim,
which is often found in the Hebrew scriptures.

One of the oddities of the name Elohim is that it was
written in a plural form in which the name literally means
"gods." Yet this, as I have said, was supposed to be understood as being a form of the majestic plural, such as when
a king or queen uses the phrase "we" to indicate a seamless bond between the subjects of a nation and the ruler.
Jews do not consider this word to be interpreted as a plural noun, and it is treated as an alternate name for their
God; but such an interpretation is obviously contrived. It
is one of many indications that Judaism was grounded in
polytheism despite the protestations of the scriptures and
believers alike.

Yahweh was an obscure storm-and-fire Deity who was
worshiped, among others, when the Hebrew people were
a group of loosely organized desert nomadic tribes.[51] It is
likely that this god aspect was an ancient relic of the original
sparse pantheon of these desert people. While other deities
were supplanted by the more sophisticated Canaanite deities,
the storm/fire god Yahweh maintained a certain currency
among some of the elite tribal families. Centuries later, when
the Jews were well established in ancient Palestine, this Deity

---

51. See Niditch, *Ancient Israelite Religion*, page 37, for a description of Yahweh.

hearkened back to an earlier and pristine mythic time when the ancient Hebrews were desert wanderers.

Thus Yahweh came to represent a political movement that sought to unite a people who were actually fragmented and only loosely allied. All of the oral legends and stories, as well as the laws of the people, were written down and assembled into the Holy Scriptures, thereby rewriting history and erasing all mention of the earliest members of that pantheon, except the storm god named Yahweh, who now assumed sole power and authority. A new religion was invented and a new Godhead was developed. The many deities and their myths were appropriated and associated exclusively with the Godhead known as Yahweh, and in this manner was the first true monotheistic religion born. (As a side note, I don't count the occurrence of the Egyptian god *Aten*, as established by Akhenaton, as a true monotheism, but that is whole different matter for discussion.)

To further hide the origins of this Godhead, it was forbidden to verbalize his name, and all characteristics and qualities of this archaic Deity were eliminated—since it was determined that he had neither an image nor a likeness, being invisible and unknowable to everyone except the priesthood. Yahweh, the ancient storm-and-fire god, who likely had an image that was made into an idol and who had characteristics and a known personality, became a distant and absolute Godhead who no longer had any characteristics or qualities.

In my opinion, and based on scholarly theories and speculation, this is how I think the Jewish Godhead was developed. Even as an invisible and unknowable God with an unpronounceable name, some polytheistic elements survived, since Yahweh was a jealous god, masculine, fearless, angry, vengeful, and at times completely ruthless (which is what you would expect of a storm/fire god). He was a Deity who must be obeyed unconditionally, or one would suffer the consequences. All of these themes describe a Deity that is very human-like taken from an obvious pagan pantheon, yet most of the other elements associated with such a pagan god were erased.

Jewish theologians and Qabalists would declare that the apparent characteristics of their Godhead had more to do with the human habit of animating metaphors and giving human qualities to a Being that is beyond all manifested qualities and characteristics. However, since monotheism and the various mythology of the One God was something that was brilliantly contrived, the various pagan themes were evident, although subtle and at times nearly invisible. The fact that this Godhead had two different names (and possibly two different personalities), and that it maintained the name El, a god of the previous pagan pantheon, clearly demonstrates that monotheism was not the original condition of the ancient Hebrew religion.

Another important attribute of the One God was the spiritual entity known as the *Shekinah* (ShKYNH), which means "dwelling" or "setting," so it came to be known as the indwelling Spirit of the Godhead when it was resident in the temple Holy of Holies. However, the Shekinah had definite qualities that seemed feminine in contra-distinction to the One God, and would come to represent the subtle manifesting spiritual presence or invisible face of that Being.

Possibly, the Shekinah took on qualities that had once been represented by the goddess Asherah, and whose elimination created a void that had to be filled with something. As time went on, the Shekinah became more of a distinct entity or being, particularly after the destruction of the temple in Jerusalem. It also became more associated with the missing feminine side or attribute of the Godhead. To the Qabalist, the Shekinah became the muse or spiritual mistress of the One God. She was also called the Sabbath's Bride, and symbolized the tangible spiritual manifestation of God in the world. A Qabalist would prepare himself and his meditation space for the manifestation of the Shekinah as if he were preparing for a wedding, in which he would marry himself to the Spirit of God and become her devotee and disciple.

Other attributes of the One God were to be found in the personification of the name Chokmah, or Divine Wisdom. This name, which became associated with the supernal triad of the emanations of the One God, represented another feminine spiritual form that was attached to the Qabalistic attributes of the Deity. Divine Wisdom, or Gnosis, could have originally been inspired from the Gnostics and their veneration of a Deity aspect named Sophia. Even so, Chokmah soon became synonymous with the state of enlightenment associated with achieving a kind of union with the Godhead, a merging that was poetically written as a suitor courting and seeking his bride, in which the Chosen People were that bride, and the One God, the suitor. Other attribute names of the ten emanations seemed to continue the process of qualifying the Godhead, making it more accessible to the purified and elected seeker.

Ten Qabalistic Godnames

We will now explore the ten Qabalistic Godnames associated with the One, realizing that these aspects can be perceived as being separate finite attributes of Deity, acting as a polytheistic pantheon. We can compare them to attributes of known pagan deities and understand the holy names to be associated with the Qabalistic mechanism used in that pantheon. From this perspective, the One God is actually the hypostasis of the One, the Good, and the Union of All, as defined in Neoplatonism. Each of these ten names and their meanings are sequentially equivalent to the ten Sephiroth of the Tree of Life.

1. AHYH—Ehieh, "I Am." This phrase, lionized as one of the names and attributes of the One God, was uttered by the entity when asked to identify itself to Moses. This famous event occurred when he was up on the mountain heights of Sinai ready to receive the Law. The Godhead replied, "Ehieh Asher Ehieh," which in Hebrew means, "I am [present imperfect] who I am [present imperfect]." There is a future tense implied by this statement, which would make it, "I will be whom I will be." The Godhead aspect of "I Am" is the Identity of the manifested One, the unity that unites everything into itself, but it is also above and beyond that unity. The truth behind this title is that a synergetic union is always greater than the sum of its parts, and this would be a useful approximate definition of

this Godhead aspect. The One is also perceived as entirely good, so that the source and final destination, the Alpha and Omega, of all of the emanations was expressed through the essence of that goodness. Idealized perfection, balanced harmony, grace, love, bliss, compassion, and the essence of life are all attributes of this entity. Thus, the One is both within us and without us, and represents the beginning and final disposition of all of the Gods and humanity.

In a Pagan pantheon the One is often disguised as the Son who will replace the Father, such as Horus (Egyptian) or Dionysus (Greek).

2. YH—Yah. This name represents a shortened version of the Tetragrammaton (YHVH), consisting of the masculine Yod and the feminine Heh, which could be seen as both the first and final Heh in the name of the Godhead. Yod is fire and spirit (also, phallic), and Heh could therefore be both water and earth, symbolizing the ground upon which the fiery force of the Godhead imprinted its willful desire for creation. These two letters combined also symbolizes the joining of the archetypal masculine and archetypal feminine, which produces the perfect emulation of the One. Knowledge of this process is the wisdom that leads to enlightenment and personal perfection.

This is the All-Father God in Pagan pantheons, the progenitor of all the other gods and humanity, though often he is seen as the leader of the gods instead of their creator.

3. YHVH ALHYM—Adonai (Yahweh) Elohim. Combing the two names of the Godhead of the scriptures into a single word symbolizes the joining of the two factions of

the Hebrew people into a single, unified populace. From a purely occult perspective, the Tetragrammaton, which is not pronounced, is called Adonai, or Lord, representing the primal creation of the material world through the Four Qabalistic worlds. Therefore, Yod is Fire (Atziluth); Heh (Briah) is Water; Vav (Yetzirah) is Air; and Heh (Assiah) is Earth, thereby representing the creation of the universe through the unified four-fold expression of the Godhead. Elohim symbolizes that the many gods are unified to become the One, and through the four elements (YHVH), all things are made manifest, in terms of the Gods, humanity, and the many domains in which they reside. Therefore, this attribute of the Godhead demonstrates that through the One are the many represented, which not only validates a polytheistic perspective but also shows how the many blend back into the One.

The attribute of the divine feminine is the Pagan aspect of this Godhead, so it is represented by a mother goddess. This Deity can be either the partner of the Father in creation and realization or she can be conceived of as being the sole creator of all things, having accomplished this act merely through an extension of herself. (This is very similar to how Qabalists saw the creation of the world by the Deity.)

4. AL—El. The root name of the Godhead is *El*, who was once the Father of the Gods in the Canaanite pantheon. As the source of compassion, happiness, and well-being, this aspect of the Godhead can be seen as the most positive attribute of the God of Plenty, often portrayed as a quality of justice (compensation) and mercy (compassion). Pagan deities that are associated with justice, mercy, and abundance could be considered attributes of this Godhead.

5. ALHYM GBVR—Elohim Gebor, "Mighty God." *Gebor* is a word that signifies warrior or hero, so as a God-name it represents the Deity as a fighter or powerful warrior who is able to help win battles and overcome enemies. This characterizes the distinctly martial aspect of the Godhead, which would seem to exemplify many of the attributes of the ancient storm god Yahweh. Also, because this Godhead stands in the feminine Pillar of Severity, it could be characterized by a feminine archetype, a warrior goddess protecting home and hearth.

6. YHVH ALVH VDOTh—Adonai (Yahweh) Aloah ve-Da'ath, "Lord God of/and Knowledge." The word *Da'ath* means "knowledge," and with a conjunctive Vav, it would have to indicate God (Aloah) and Knowledge (Da'ath). This is the aspect of the Deity that is the great illuminator who heals and makes right through harmony, balance, and knowledge of all things. Analogous Pagan deities would be various solar gods and goddesses.

7. YHVH TzBAVTh—Adonai (Yahweh) Tzabaoth, "Lord of Hosts." The word *Tzabaoth* means "hosts," "armies," or "troops," but in this context it would mean the hosts of angels and stars that accompany the Godhead. This Godname is similar to the one for the next lateral Sephirah, which is Hod. In this situation, the difference is with the use of Yahweh or Elohim, perhaps representing that these Deities had a different host to accompany them. Another way of looking at this name and its difference is that in the case of Yahweh, it represents that the hosts are unified into a single essence to ensure victory, and in the case of Elohim, it is broken out and

multiplied to characterize an attribute of the Deity that is a glorified multitude.

From the perspective of a Pagan pantheon, the hidden significance of this Sephirah is that it is linked with the planet Venus. It can be characterized as both a warrior and a love-goddess aspect, despite the fact that it occupies the masculine Pillar of Mercy. Such a Semitic goddess would be Astarte, Ishtar, and Anath, but in the West she would become purely a love goddess, such as Aphrodite or Venus.

8. ALHYM TzBAVTh—Elohim Tzabaoth, "God of Hosts." I have already discussed the distinction of this Godname compared to the lateral Sephirah, Netzach. This Godname would be characterized in a Pagan pantheon with a Deity of knowledge, such as those that are associated with the planet Mercury. Gods of writing and civilization would characterize this Sephirah and Godname.

9. ShDY AL ChY—Shaddai El Chai, "Almighty God of Life." This Godname symbolizes the powerful qualities of the God that gives Life to all living things—the creator, nourisher, and even healer. This is the attribute of the One that has formulated the vital force in its essence, and who has directed the actual physical formulation of all living and ensouled things. From the perspective of a Pagan pantheon, this would be the Mother Goddess in her attribute as the giver of life to all creatures, including humanity. Such a goddess would characterize the Moon and its power in the world, as reflector and refractor of the pure light of the

Sun and beyond. So, a lunar mother goddesses would be the perfect analogue of this Godname.

10. ADNY MLK—Adonai Melek, "Lord King." The lord of the material world and all it contains is the attribute of this Godname. Here, the Deity is the eternal shepherd king of all that lives on the earth. By transposition, one could also consider this Godname to represent what is below the earth as well, as a kind of underworld master of wealth and the continuance of life.

The ten Sephiroth and their Godnames can be readily compared to other Pagan-based pantheons and perceived as attributes of the One. Using this kind of approach to the ten Godnames, you can see how the Qabalah is readily used by both Pagans and adherents of monotheism. They will not agree how these attributes of the One should be characterized and used, but both can approach them through their own spiritual perspective. This shows how broad and powerful the Qabalah is, and why some monotheists have condemned it and banned its use. However, for occultists, the Qabalah has the ability to be flexible and adaptable to many different spiritual definitions. One could say that there are many qabalahs, and that there is more than one way to define and work with the aspects of Deity that lie at its core.

Other Godnames
and the Mysterious Grammatons

Qabalah incorporates words that are characterized by the grouping of letters; some of them are significant and meaningful, but not all of them. I had discovered this possibility when thinking about and modeling various four-letter words (such as AGLA), as based on the Tetragrammaton, YHVH. Extending these groups to include other letter combinations led me to determine a whole cast of various lettered sacred words. I later discovered that a number of other Qabalists had come to the same conclusion.

These sacred words are intuitively known by terms such as *monogrammata* (single letter), *digrammata* (two letters), *tetragrammata* (four letters), and then other exotic constructs, such as the *octagrammata* (eight letters), *decagrammata* (10 letters), *duodecagrammata* (12 letters), and then on to the 14, 22, 33, 42, and finally the great 72-letter name (known as the *Shem ha-Mephorash*). The "a" ending is the plural form of the word (example: *tetragrammaton*—singular; *tetragrammata*—plural).

We can briefly look over these different constructs, since they can be interesting and useful, especially in the work of magic.

Monogrammata are single letters that represent singular attributes of the name of the Godhead; most are based on the Tetragrammaton, which is YHVH. Therefore, such letters as Yod or Heh can represent a singular power of the Godhead, but also the first letter Aleph, which can be shown to be the combination of two Yod characters on either side of a diagonal Vav character, which produces the word *YVY*. This specially derived word is numerically equal through Gematria to the Tetragrammaton (both are equal to 26). Many other designs and structures can be determined using this methodology.

Digrammata are two-letter words of God that have a singular meaning and power. Examples of this kind of two-letter word would be YH (Yah), AL (El), and ChY (Chai). The ChY combination is very popular among modern Jews and it is often worn as a gold pendant on women's necklaces. We have already covered the significance of YH and AL.

Tetragrammata are four-letter words, typically YHVH, which is the primary unpronounceable name of the Hebrew God. There are many other four-letter words, such as A.G.L.A. (Ateh Gibor Le-olam Adonai—*Thou art mighty forever, Lord*) and I.N.R.I., and all of them are considered different interpretations of the unified expression of the four elements in creation. Many of these four-letter words are derived by using Notariqon, which is a mystical word system of expanding and contracting acronyms.

Octagrammata are eight-letter words. One of the examples of this magical name of God is to interleave and combine the letters of the four-letter names ADNY and YHVH, creating a hybrid word YAHDVNHY (Yahdunahai). Of course, this is a magical and mystical name of God, so it doesn't have any specific meaning by itself. Combining two four-letter names will produce an eight-letter name, but the trick is interleaving them (using the first letter of one, then the other, then the second, etc.).

Decagrammata are ten-letter words. This word can be created by sequentially adding the letters of the names of first three Sephiroth of the Tree of Life. The ten-letter word KThRChKMBYNH is produced if one drops the intermedial Heh belonging to the word Chokmah (otherwise, it becomes an 11-letter word).

Duodecagrammata are 12-letter words. Like previous letter formulations, this one is based on a composite of words, such as YHVH spelled out three times, or by using the first letter of each of the 12 tribes of Israel.

The largest and most arcane of these numbered letter words are the 72 names of God (or 216 lettered names of God), which are known as the *Shem ha-Mephorash*. This word construct is derived from three verses in the biblical book of Exodus, chapter 14, verses 19 through 21.

From these three verses are extracted letters that are formed to produce 72 words consisting of three letters each. The method of extraction is to take the first letter from each word in the first verse, then the last letter from each word in the second verse, and then the first letter again from the words of the third verse. To these three-letter words are added either YH or AL to generate the names of 72 angels, known as the angels of the Ha-Shem. Other Qabalists have used the 72 tri-literate words as special names of God, but these words, in my opinion, are greatly enhanced and empowered when they are used as the names of angels.

As you can see, there are a lot of various formulated words of spiritual power that can be derived using important and strategic words as found in the sacred texts. I have only listed a small sample that shows how these words can be structured and used, but I think that you are now able to understand their significance and importance. I suspect that some of these special words would have more meaning to a practicing occultist who happened to be Jewish, but in learning the technique, other formulations can be made to represent words of significance and power to other religionists, such as Christians and Pagans.

Using the Power of the Godnames

Now that we have reviewed the various Godnames and mysterious grammata, and shown how they can be compared to Pagan pantheons, we can review the use of these names in a kind of magical system devoid of ritual or ceremony. This is an internalized kind of theurgy, so it would be more like a form of Hermetic magic, such as that espoused by the likes of Giordano Bruno. Yet this system of magic, however simplistic and direct, requires a far greater connection to the Godhead than any other system, because it is performed through the Godhead and calls on the specific channels of emanation.

The basic premise for this magical system is that the vibration of the various Godnames can produce a powerful effect if done periodically for a specific mundane purpose. That purpose would, of course, have to be completely ethical and unselfish. Performing this kind of magic for purely selfish and unethical means could either foment a terrible backlash or cause the student to damage or destroy his all-important alignment to the One. Either situation would be catastrophic for the student, representing a profound setback of months or even years of patient work. As it is understood in most folklore, even the greatest sage does not take up the name of the Deity in vain, but only does so with the purest intent and for the greater good.

Most systems of magic that summon spirits rely on the use and intercession of intermediaries. Calling directly on a Deity to perform some work is mostly a religious or liturgical operation, often performed by a trained priest. A Qabalist intimately knows the various aspects and attributes of the Godhead, so she is perfectly capable of using that divine bond to force certain kinds of things to manifest. By pulling the levers of the Sephiroth at the highest point of the represented Godhead, the Qabalist can powerfully determine the outcome of many of life's struggles. This ability and privilege must not be abused or overused. Still, any true Qabalist must engage her community and perform good works, and that would include using her knowledge and ability to heal, seek justice, and give bounty, compassion, and light wherever it is needed. In a greater sense, such a practical Qabalist is helping to do the work of the Deity in the material world.

The ten Sephiroth and their associated Godnames and qualities represent the kinds of positive changes and life-altering work that the Qabalist may employ on behalf of the Deity that he serves. These actions must be completely warranted and properly associated with the correct Sephiroth in order to be truly effective in the material plane. Since this is a deliberate use of the Qabalah to make near miraculous changes in the world, it cannot be considered solely an act of the Deity, but one that is mediated and channeled by the Qabalist. It is therefore to be considered as nothing less than magic and, in some circles, would be considered highly impious. Regardless, the font of good that the Qabalist may bestow upon the world can be summed up in the following ten categories (to be sequentially compared to the ten Sephiroth):

1. Blessings of the One
2. Wisdom and insight
3. Realization and acceptance
4. Compassion, spiritual healing, spiritual love
5. Justice and judgment
6. Removal of sin, guilt, and self-deceit, spiritual awakening
7. Physical healing and emotional redemption
8. Knowledge and personal freedom
9. Freedom from fear, emotional and psychic security and integrity
10. Charity, hope, divine grace, regeneration, and healing

As you can see, these powers represent strategic positive changes that can be made to occur in those whose need is truly great. These are selfless powers that benefit the many much more than the one, and it would be difficult to use them to advance the greed and avarice of the individual. The ten Sephiroth and their associated powers do not aid the greedy or the slothful, so they would be useless to anyone who is seeking their own self-aggrandizement. However, in times of great need, such powers as those listed above can make a tremendous difference for individuals or groups of people.

So how does the Qabalist go about activating one of these Sephiroth for the benefit of someone who is in need? First of all, I must assume that the practicing Qabalist has a steadfast, advanced, and regular spiritual discipline that consists of a mastery of the five operations, which are meditation, contemplation, pathworking, invocation, and Godhead assumption. The experienced Qabalist has gone up and down the Tree of Life, exposing himself to many of the more powerful and holy angelic spirits. He has explored the deeper symbolic structures of the Qabalah and developed a very personal and intimate relationship with the ten Godhead attributes of the ten Sephiroth. A person with this degree of knowledge, experience, and spiritual discipline could readily use the power of the Sephirah Godhead to intercede and change the fate of an individual or even the population of a town. The manner that this could be done is found in the following four steps:

1. Perform a series of contemplation sessions to explore the ramifications of a given material request. (The request is refined, left as is, or abandoned due to a greater realization.)

2. Determine the proper outcome or response, and connect with the Godhead to discover if the request can be properly given and received through divine mediation.

3. Assume the specific Godhead of the Sephirah and seek to engage that aspect of Deity with the task. Whatever the Deity requests or requires of the Qabalist should be done as an offering and a demonstration of good will.

4. Perform periodic and continuous meditation sessions with the Godname and a simple prayer being repeated as a mantric chant.

For a more simplistic and direct effect, the Qabalist can just perform step 4, although this would be employed to merely seek a blessing and the manifestation of a quality of goodness. Simply doing step 4 would be the way that the Qabalist would request or seek something for herself, and often it would produce a powerful vision or a true realization.

This simple but highly powerful and direct manner of transforming the world, either for the solace of the individual or a group of people, is probably one of the greatest tools of the practicing Qabalist. Yet the Qabalist must be experienced, disciplined, and deeply engaged with her practice in order for such a magical methodology to work. Certainly, performing ritual or ceremonial magic is much less demanding, but the end result of a true Qabalistic working would be far more stupendous and amazing.

Spiritual Hierarchies

Spiritual hierarchies are important for one single reason: they give important information to ceremonial magicians and Qabalists so that they might summon spirits within them. The Tree of Life is overpopulated with spirits, so summoning and establishing relationships with them is a profoundly important event. These kinds of operations are not beyond even the most inexperienced practitioner, especially when armed with the necessary knowledge and experience that the Qabalah can provide. The tools for performing invocations become available to you through examining these hierarchies and combining them with their associated correspondences in the Tree of Life. This is why I feel that we need to discuss these spiritual hierarchies and determine an optimal set that any reader of this book could summon and fully experience for herself or himself. I consider invocation to be just as important as pathworking, contemplation, and vibrating Godnames; but before one can think about how to perform an invocation, one also needs to know exactly whom to invoke.

Hierarchies of spirits have long been associated with the Qabalah, and in fact it is very likely that the Qabalah helped to facilitate the access and invocation of these various entities. The most subtle relationship between the Qabalah and spiritual hierarchies is their common relationship to various tables of correspondences. It is in these tables of correspondences that a multitude of diverse elements can be compared and related throughout the symbology and meaning of that occult system. It is specifically through the ten Sephiroth and the 22 Pathways that all of these elements have their common connection.

Spirits associated with the Qabalah consist of various levels and denominations of angels, but could also include Goetic demons, Olympian spirits, Enochian spirits, Islamic jinn, demigods, nature spirits—the list is nearly endless. Because this is a book for beginners, we should pare down this list to just the essentials. This will not, however, water down what we are seeking to accomplish.

Normally, the typical system of Qabalistic correspondences would consist of the four elements, seven planets, and 12 zodiacal signs. For the sake of simplicity, we will only concern ourselves with the four elements and the seven planets—this will keep our focus on just the Sephiroth of the Tree of Life. The four elements can stand alone and be used as a rudimentary set of correspondences with a wealth of attributes. Examine any book on magic (or perform a search on the Internet), and you will find quite a few different sets of comparative correspondences for the four elements. However, based on what we have covered previously, the Sephiroth of Chokmah (Air), Binah (Water), Chesed (Fire), and Malkuth (Earth) could also be used as representations of the four elements on the Tree of Life. The only problem with this attribution is that Chesed would function as both the element of Fire and the planet Jupiter.

The seven planets are represented by seven of the Sephiroth of the Tree of Life, and include all of the various correspondences associated with them. We saw this in the previous chapter on the ten Sephiroth. However, in regard to determining a hierarchy of spirits, we will use another way of dividing spirits into groups, and that will be the Four Qabalistic Worlds. The key is to break up the four elements and the ten Sephiroth into groups of spirits, each relating to the Four Qabalistic Worlds.

Using the Four Qabalistic Worlds gives us the basic structure of a spiritual hierarchy, and this hierarchy can be established in the following manner. The spirits associated with each level of the Four Worlds are divided by the levels of *Godhead*, *Archangel*, *Angel*, and *Spirits of the Earth*. The following example will show how various spirits might be grouped within these four levels:

- Atziluth—Absolute plane—Abstract Godhead and associated attributes (or attendants)

- Briah—Spirit Plane—Individual Pagan Deities, archangels, demigods, avatars
- Yetzirah—Mental Plane—angels, planetary and zodiacal spirits, spirit servitors, angelic choirs, various Enochian spirits, Goetic demons
- Assiah—ancestor spirits, nature spirits, spiritualized natural forces (elder gods), spirits of place or location, heroes, some demonic (infernal) spirits, ghosts, mythic creatures, and household and doorway gods/spirits

As you can see, this is quite a large list, and it certainly is not exhaustive. Compiling a list of all of these spirits and filling in their characteristics and attributes would fill a book by itself. A pared-down approach, which is what I have recommended here, would use just the worlds of Atziluth, Brian, and Yetzirah, omitting Assiah. The reason why I would omit Assiah is that these kinds of spirits are particular to a specific belief system and are not universal, since they can be associated with a specific geographic location. Looking over the list of spirits associated with Assiah, you can see how this is true. This logic should be applied to both the ten Sephiroth and the four elements. What we will concern ourselves with are the Godhead aspects, the archangels, and angelic choirs, and this will give us more than enough spirits to invoke and interact with.

You will also notice that I have included Goetic demons in the plane of Yetzirah, and I need to mention that this is not universally accepted as being true. Since we are not going to be discussing the nature of these spirits, I will leave the argument as to why I have made this assumption for another time.

One further issue before we get to the actual spirit lists is to discuss the problem of projecting the four elements through the Four Qabalistic Worlds. There is no problem with projecting the Four Worlds through the Sephiroth, but it gets more complicated when attempting to do the same thing through the four elements. Dividing up a spiritual hierarchy using the Four Worlds and elements does not work very well in practice once the element Godheads are defined. This is because in some occult organizations, archangels were assigned to the elements to establish the level of Briah (Spirit Plane), and this was very likely a modern adaptation. Once we get to the level of Yetzirah (Mental Plane), the system breaks down because there isn't much usable traditional lore to determine the four angels or choir of angels for the elements on this level.

To begin our analysis, let us look at the traditional assignment of the four archangels to the four elements:

- Fire—Michael
- Water—Gabriel
- Air—Raphael
- Earth—Uriel

The first thing that occurs to anyone who has some experience when looking at this list is to notice that three of these elemental archangels are re-used from the correspondences of the ten Sephiroth; the exception is Uriel. It would also seem that the assignment of the archangels to the ten Sephiroth makes more sense than the artificial re-assignment to the four elements, especially since three of these four were originally associated with planets instead of elements.[52]

Michael is associated with the Sephirah of Hod (Mercury); Gabriel, with Yesod (Moon); and Raphael, Tiphareth (Sun). It is hard to reconcile Michael to Fire when it is assigned to Mercury; or Raphael to Air, when it is assigned to the Sun. Uriel has no Sephirah base association, but is often considered to be one of the Seraphim and associated with Fire and Earth. The only association that would make any sense is for Gabriel, if by some chance we can equate the Moon with Water. Anyway, the more we ponder over these associations, the more problematic they become. If you find these attributions of element to archangel acceptable, then you can use them without any further considerations. If, on the other hand, you would like something that doesn't duplicate or change (without any reason) the attribution of these archangels, then an alternative list can be proposed.

The clue for how to proceed is that Uriel is associated with Earth, and he is considered one of the fiery Seraphim, which are angels directly associated with the throne of the Deity, as opposed to being more distant intermediaries. Examining the book *A Dictionary of Angels* by Gustav Davidson, we find 13 different lists for the *Orders of the Celestial Hierarchy*, from St. Ambrose to Francis Barrett, and there is a lot of variance between them.[53] If you don't have a copy of this book, you can take my word for it. When we look at the various traditional lists of the angelic hierar-

52. Gustav Davidson, *A Dictionary of Angels*, 338–39.
53. Ibid., 336–37.

chy, one thing that many seem to agree on is that the Seraphim and the Cherubim were at or near the top of these lists, and that the archangels and angels were at the bottom. What this means is that there were groupings of angels who were considered closer to the Godhead level than the archangels, and that the Seraphim and Cherubim groups could be used to fill out an element angelic list for the elements adjacent to the element Godnames instead of using the four archangels.

Then there is another important table in Davidson's book, called "The Ruling Princes of the Nine Celestial Orders," which lists the angel names associated with each of the different orders.[54] If you examine all of these different lists, looking at the different groups and at the proposed list of angels in each group, you will see a lot of duplicate names and differences in the ordering of the hierarchy of groups. Sometimes, one or two will be omitted or there might even be new ones added. For instance, the Archangel Michael appears in at least three of these groups simultaneously, Gabriel appears in five, Raphael appears in two, and Satan used to belong to four of them before he was cast out. However, for the sake of simplicity, we can consolidate all of the groupings for the Cherubim, Seraphim, Thrones, Dominions, Powers, and Virtues (and also Principalities) into two sets of four angels who would, as direct links to the Godhead, express all of these variations at once. We can do this because the different celestial orders seem redundant and repetitive from a functional standpoint.

---

54. Ibid., 339.

If simplicity and uniqueness are the driving factors, then the Seraphim and the Cherubim have famous names and represent distinct angelic personalities. We could assign to these two sets of angels, which I call *super archangels*, a distinct functional grouping. The Seraphim, whose fiery nature is defined as a combination of inspiration and ardor, would represent those angelic beings that would channel the direct powers of the Deity, representing the light, power, and dominion of that Deity (Powers and Dominions). The Cherubim, who are obviously temple or throne guardians, would ward the Deity and act as intermediaries (Thrones, Principalities, and Virtues), determining the worthiness of a supplicant (as guardians) and also acting as teachers or translators (guides).

The Seraphim would represent the inner circle of four super archangels closest to the Godhead, and the Cherubim would represent the outer ring of the four super archangels. Together, they would effectively channel the emanations of the element Godhead and act as guardians, filtering those who would approach the Deity for grace and favor. The Seraphim and the Cherubim combined would represent the top-tier world of the Godhead (Atziluth) and would function as attendants to the Deity, and the archangels and angels would attend and serve the super archangels, representing the lower two worlds of Briah and Yetzirah, just above Assiah, but associated with the ten Sephiroth. We could also use the archangels and angelic choirs of the four element Sephiroth as determiners for the lower spirits.

Therefore, for the four elements we could start with the Qabalistic Godnames and add to that list the four Sera-

phim and Cherubim. This new structure, which is a simplified derivation but not one that goes counter to established
tradition, would satisfy our need for determining a spiritual hierarchy for the four elements. There is, however, a
single duplication found in this list. The Seraphim angelic
name for the attribute of Water, which is Metatron, is also
the archangel for the Sephirah Kether. This could be easily explained by the fact that because Metatron is the chief
of the archangels (occupying the position of Kether), he
would also be a member of the super archangel Seraphim,
representing a bridge between the two structures.

The three levels for the ten Sephiroth are taken from
traditional (Golden Dawn) assignments, which establish
the Godnames, archangels, and angelic choirs. You can find
further details associated with these spiritual entities in any
number of occult and metaphysical resources, so they need
not be described here. As for the Godnames, these have
been already covered in the previous chapter.

A table of the four elements and the associated Godnames, Seraphim, and Cherubim are on the next page.

A table of the ten Sephiroth and the associated Godnames, archangels, and angelic choirs are on the page after
that.

Table of Element Spirits				
Element	Hebrew letter	Godname	Seraphim	Cherubim
Fire	Yod	Ha-Shem (Ehieh)	Seraphiel	Rikbiel
Water	Heh	Shaddai (El Chai)	Metatron	Kerubiel
Air	Vav	Elohim	Yahoel	Auphaniel
Earth	Heh-final	Adonai Ha-Aretz	Uriel	Yophiel

Figure 15: Table of Element spirits

Table of Sephiroth Spirits				
	Sephiroth	Godname	Archangel	Angelic choir
1	Kether	AHYH	Metatron	Hiyoth Haqadesh
2	Chokmah	YH	Ratziel	Auphanim
3	Binah	YHVH ALHYM	Tzaphkiel	Aralim
4	Chesed	AL	Tzadkiel	Chasmolim
5	Geburah	ALHYM GBVR	Kamael	Tarshishim
6	Tiphareth	YHVH ALHYM VDOTh	Raphael	Malakim
7	Netzach	YHVH TzBAVTh	Haniel	Elohim
8	Hod	ALHYM TzBAVTh	Michael	Beni Elohim
9	Yesod	ShDY AL ChY	Gabriel	Alim
10	Malkuth	ADNY MLK	Sandalphon	Eshim

Figure 16: Table of Sephiroth spirits

Theurgy and Invocation

I would like to propose a simple system of theurgy and invocation that could be used by a practicing Qabalist. I will incorporate the classical five stages of magical evocation into this methodology to build up a modern system. While this is not the specific methodology that I employ to perform this operation, it is one that would work quite well, based as it is on a system that I developed early in my studies.

One important consideration that I would like to declare before continuing is that this method would work more efficiently with the various angels associated with the Qabalah than with the evocation of demons. Therefore, I will concentrate on producing a system that addresses that need, while the student can consult with other grimoires to fill in the blanks to work with the goetic demons, if that is his or her desire.

First, let us examine the five classical stages of magical evocation, which were the implied but seldom written-down steps that a magician in the Renaissance would have performed. These are associated with the Latin words *Consecratio, Invocatio, Constrictio, Ligatio,* and *Licentia.*[55]

Consecratio, or *Consecratio Dei,* represented all of the activities that the magician performed to prepare for the work, including sacred baths, asperging the temple and tools with lustral water, burning incense, and reciting psalms, prayers, and orisons to achieve the favor and benediction of the Godhead—a required state prior to performing the work. These activities would be performed even after the magician had sealed himself up in the magic circle, and might include the preparation and sanctification of the circle, vestments, tools, and temple area, as well as the fumigation, reciting psalms and prayers, and engaging in a final bout of contemplative prayer.

Invocatio were the invocations and incantations that the magician declared once he was safely ensconced in the magic circle, fully vested and prepared for the work. All preparations had already been minutely addressed and successfully accomplished, and all that was required at this point was to summon the angel.

---

55. David Rankine and Stephen Skinner, *The Goetia of Dr. Rudd,* 91–94.

However, it was assumed that if the preparations were correct, the timing auspicious, and the integrity and faith of the magician impeccable, then the spirit invoked would materialize in some form or another. The magician could use his talismans and protective lamen to assist in adding greater force to the invocation, but if, after a time, the spirit failed to appear, then the magician had to perform either a single or several exorcisms, burn obnoxious herbs, and generally banish anything that might have been summoned before breaking the magic circle and leaving the work place.

Constrictio was where the magician sought to constrain the manifesting spirit. He also had to verify the spirit's identity, ensuring that it was exactly what the magician had summoned in the first place. Constraining a spirit was a requirement when summoning a demon; but often the magician had to validate an angelic entity as well, at least to verify that he was not being deceived by some lesser spirit or demonic influence. The magician used his special ring, talismans, pentacles, and various words of power to constrain the spirit. Once this was accomplished, the invocation process was considered to be stable, and the magician could move on to the objective of his work.

Ligatio was the act of binding the spirit, usually with an oath, words of power, or threats, to urge it to perform a task suited to its nature and to be accomplished in a specific time frame. Binding a spirit could be considered a kind of pact, except that there was no *quid pro quo*. The spirit obeyed the magician because of his acquired holiness and because of his assumed authority granted by God and his angels. The constraint was performed in a less severe manner with an angel (or not at all), and was extremely important and quite severe with any other spirit, especially a demon.

Licentia was the license to depart that the magician gave to the spirit once it had been properly bound. It was important for the magician to realize that the spirit was to be treated with dignity and respect, and that he would not perform any kind of banishing action if the binding of that spirit was successful. The idea was to condition-ally allow the spirit to return to its natural abode, there to await future summons and willed appearances. The license to depart was therefore quite different from performing a banishing or an exorcism, which would only be performed if the magician had either failed to manifest the spirit or failed to constrain it.

All of the verbiage of these various invocations, con-straints, licenses to depart, exorcisms, and banishments would be kept in the magician's personal grimoire (the infamous black book). Although the magician should memorize all aspects of the operation, he may not have recourse to all of the actions contained in the book, and he might also find himself under extreme duress or supernat-ural attack. Thus having the words written down would be a form of insurance, and it would also be a form of magic itself.

As you can see, these five stages would require quite a bit of time and resources to successfully achieve. However, through the use of the Qabalah, the above five steps can be made into an almost foolproof methodology for performing a theurgistic invocation. The key to this whole process is that the Qabalistic magician already knows the spiritual hierarchy and the matrix of correspondences that will greatly assist this procedure, and ensure that it produces the expected results.

One of the first things that a Qabalistic magician needs is a symbol that represents his spiritual beliefs, authority, and power. This symbol is called the magician's *lamen*, and it traditionally consists of some kind of pentagram or hexagram device drawn on leather, parchment, or fabric, or etched on a piece of precious metal and worn on the person of the celebrant. This lamen should also be consecrated in some manner, either being touched by incense smoke and lustral water, blown upon by one's breath, or blessed with sacred words and signs, or a combination of all of these forms.

The lamen should be a personal creation and not look like anything else that is in print. Basic geometric forms that can be used are the pentagram, hexagram, septagram, octagram, eneagram, Vesica Pisces, or whatever is personally significant. The geometric form should be decorated with sigils, characters, symbols, or other elements that are personally meaningful to the magician. The design can also be colored, using specific symbolic colors that the magician finds important and symbolically representative. The magician draws from various sources, including Qabalistic correspondences, to build up this design. The most important element for the lamen is that it should have the magician's magical name or motto inscribed within it, either using a foreign or magical alphabet, or fashioning it into a sigil form.

Once completed, the magician's lamen represents the power and authority through which she operates, and it becomes the foundation for all magical workings. To help the magician align her spirit and will to this newly developed and crafted design with the mind, she should spend quite a bit of time gazing fixedly at the lamen until its form and structure are completely absorbed into her memory. The magician should be able to project the image of this lamen from her memory onto a blank wall just by staring and focusing her mind.

Two tools that the Qabalistic magician will need to build and design are the dagger and the wand. These can be made to any specification or taste, purchased and customized or made completely from scratch. I will leave the specifics to the imagination of the magician, but there are many examples of these specific weapons. Basically, the dagger is used to aggressively protect and ward the magician, and the wand is used to summon and call spirits. Also, it would be prudent for the magician to have exclusive use of a room.

Other items that the magician will need are incense, an incense burner or brazier, charcoal, lamps and lamp oil, a gallon container filled with consecrated salt water (called *lustral water*), vestments (robe), jewelry, perfumed oil, and a colored cloth scarf to wear around the neck and shoulders. These items should round out the necessary things needed to work simple Qabalistic magic. All of these things must be blessed, consecrated, and kept clean and completely apart from any mundane belongings; they should also be exclusively used for the work and nothing else. To bless the vestments and tools, the magician should use the same simple method used to bless the lamen. Incense, lustral water, making signs, and breathing one's breath into the item should suffice.

The first thing that the celebrant must determine in order to perform a working is to choose a specific angel to invoke. Then a time must be selected for the operation, with certain basic auspices determined in advance, such as that it should be performed at night and with the moon waxing. The operation should also be done during a period of three days and nights, and the magician will have to be completely sequestered during the time of the actual operation.

Once an angel is chosen, then the magician will determine the entire line of the spiritual hierarchy associated with that entity, particularly the Godname of the Sephirah. All of the symbolic correspondences should be noted, particularly the color (for the scarf), incense, perfume, and anything else that would be pertinent. The imagery, symbology, characteristics, and quality of the spirit would also be noted down for use by the magician. A sigil, seal, or character combination also needs to be crafted that can uniquely identify the target spirit, and this should be constructed with paint or ink on a piece of parchment. I use alphabet wheels to craft a sigil representing the name of the spirit that I want to invoke. You can find these alphabet wheels on pages 299 and 300.

Preparation (occurring for at least two of the three days) would include all of the obligations and tasks associated with the first stage of classical theurgy and evocation, which is Consecratio Dei. The focus of this first stage should be upon the spiritual hierarchy, most notably the qualities and characteristics of the Godname. The magician should employ a partial fast, pray, meditate, contemplate, and essentially commune with the Spirit of this Godhead, and thereby become totally immersed within that entity. Other spirits who reside in that linear hierarchy may also be called and communed with once the magician has successfully connected with the specific Godhead.

You can see that learning to master the technique of forging a deep inward connection with aspects of the Deity is quite important to any Qabalistic work, but it makes the process of an invocation far more certain than it would be if this step were omitted. Ensuring that all of these preparations are completed is critical for the next step to be successful. The more time and effort spent in preparation, the better the overall outcome. The key to this operation is acquiring a powerful link with the Godhead associated with the target spirit's hierarchy. Unless or until that link is forged, the invocation should not be performed.

At the appointed time, the magician will perform her final ablutions by taking a bath in consecrated water, anointing herself with the correct perfume, donning the robe with the correctly colored scarf draped over her shoulders, and the lamen worn prominently on her person. The room where the operation is to take place has already been prepared, with the floor carefully cleaned and the circle consecrated with a light misting of lustral water. The consecrated sigil of the angelic spirit is placed in the center of the circle. The lamps are lit, and the magician proceeds to fumigate the area with the proper incense. Then she enters into the circle and proceeds to pray and meditate for a period of time, focusing on that all-important connection with the Godhead.

When the moment is right, the magician will begin with the invocations, knowing that they are being done through that sacred link with the Godhead. It will seem to the magician as if the Godhead itself is speaking through her, instead of the magician acting and speaking her words in vain. The magician should focus now on the qualities and characteristics of the spirit, concentrating on the sigil wherever it has been placed in the circle. Between each of the three basic invocations, the magician should pause for a period of time to gauge its effect. If it is successful, then she will proceed to the next of three stages; if not, then she must abort the working and perform a thorough banishing. This will not be necessary if the magician has successfully contacted and established a powerful link with the Godhead associated with this spirit, since such a connection will make the rest of the invocation process successfully assured.

Whatever transpires between the celebrant and the target spirit should be noted in a notebook kept for that purpose. If there is a specific task that the magician is seeking, then he should write this desire down on parchment, including a specific period for this thing to be accomplished. The task should be given as a command through the Godhead link (during the ligatio stage) to ensure that it will be done without prevarication or deception. The magician should also make certain that such a command is given in a clear and concise manner, making certain that any ambiguity is carefully eliminated. Often, though, it is just as well to seek knowledge and advice or a blessing directly from the spirit, especially if from archangels and super archangels.

Crafting a set of powerful invocations is also an important requirement. The magician should consult the old grimoires to find the proper kind of word choice and tone. I would recommend the *Heptameron* as a good primary resource, but other choices and select grimoire material would work as well. (The *Heptameron* is one of the earliest known grimoires dealing with angel magic.) The *Heptameron* is typically bundled with Agrippa's *Fourth Book of Occult Philosophy*, and that book is still in print in a number of different editions. I have listed the *Fourth Book of Occult Philosophy* in the bibliography, edited by Stephen Skinner. There is some dispute as to whether Agrippa had anything to do with this book, but this version includes the *Heptameron*. The magician may choose to use words of power, such as the infamous barbaric words of evocation (*verba ignota*), or she may even choose to use a sacred language, such as Latin, Greek, or Hebrew.

When using a foreign tongue, it is very important to know exactly what you are saying, so having a good translation as well as knowing how to phonetically pronounce the words is quite critical. Care should also be given to the selection of the various Godnames and the religious tone of the invocation, since each religion would verbalize such pronouncements differently. You may replace the Christian or Jewish elements of a known invocation with elements of your own spiritual pantheon. This action will not in any way destroy either the intent or the power of that invocation. A Pagan or Wiccan practitioner could also use Pagan gods and goddesses as additions to the abstract Godhead for a specific Qabalistic correspondence.

The most important element of Qabalistic theurgy is that the magician uses the innate hierarchy of the Tree of Life to formulate the invocation, and that the highest level, the Godhead, is the primary empowered link for a successful magical outcome. The Qabalist has some advantages over the sorcerer because he is able to make this effective spiritual connection before attempting a magical operation. There is less guesswork and a greater possibility of success, at least in my opinion. If you add to this technique the methodology of Qabalistic pathworking, then you will see that it can be done in a completely comprehensive manner, where the spiritual mechanisms of personal transformation are also harnessed.

fourteen

Systems of Correspondence

In the earlier sections of this book, certain correspondences were given to characterize each of the ten Sephiroth and 22 Pathways of the Tree of Life. These correspondences can also join various unrelated occult items, qualities, and substances together to create a matrix of symbolic associations. Magicians use such a matrix to gather specific spiritual characteristics that they wish to express or realize for an operation, such as an invocation.

Correspondences of the Qabalah represent the qualification of various ingredients or components used to write rituals that would build a unified expression out of those individual qualities. These correspondences are used to inform magicians of the relative components that they may select to construct a ritual, creating a tight set of related symbols and qualities that define the spirit's characteristics. These same correspondences are also used to link spirits within various locations of the Inner Planes.

To make contact with any of these entities, the magician would select and use in a ritual some of the associated correspondences of colors, sounds, herbs, incense, qualities, and characteristics to create an environment attractive for such entities. Then the magician would perform a ritual scrying session, an astral projection, or the greater techniques of invocation and evocation. The magician enters into the domain of the spirit and also channels its powers and knowledge into the mundane world. The correspondences set the tone of the energy signature or character of the spirit, and the structure of the Inner Planes functions as the domain for the hierarchy of spirits and beings. But there is yet more to this kind of working, and the use of talismans, sigils, magical diagrams, and ritual formulas represent the other disciplines incorporated to complete this work.

Qabalah and Tables of Correspondences

Perhaps one of the most difficult topics to either explain or show by example is the systematic use for the many published versions of the Qabalistic tables of correspondences. This shouldn't be a difficult topic to master, considering the fact that we are talking about using published works as a reference and not having to build these many tables of information ourselves. The work has been done for us, but the problem is that the primary version (and for a while, the only available version) was Aleister Crowley's book *Liber 777*.

It has been said that if any student can sit down and make perfect sense out of Crowley's book, then he or she has become very clever and quite adept in understanding the various abstruse symbology of the Qabalah. It could also be said that such a person has tremendous patience and is even able to read Hebrew marginally well. One could fault Crowley for creating a book that only a bright student could make use of without trouble, except for the rumor that he actually purloined this book in manuscript form from MacGregor Mathers (along with a rudimentary Sepher Sephiroth).

What I can say about *Liber 777* is that it is a bit too obscure and requires too much background to make much use of, forcing anyone who regularly uses it into a regimen of distracting precision. A student also has to accept a number of Crowley's personal choices and occult tastes, since he could be quite opinionated, and some of his choices were rather obscure. Another problem that the student will encounter is that Crowley's book is poorly organized with regard to its subject matter. The columns have archaic Roman numerals, and he has the habit of forcing everything into the 32 categories of the Sephiroth and Pathways of the Tree of Life, whether those items fit that pattern or not. The use of a notation such as "31-bis" and "32-bis" because these two paths have the unfortunate role of possessing two meanings (31—Fire and Spirit, and 32—Earth and Saturn) seems rather contrived and artificial to me. I would suggest that these occurrences merely prove that the data does not fit the pattern.

I can't tell you how many hours I have spent using a magnifying glass to ensure that I have correctly spelled the Hebrew words for various angelic and demonic names. I had to print the planetary or astrological signs in pencil next to some of the tabular rows so that it would be more useful to me (and to make certain that I didn't make any mistakes). A regimen of studying and using the book *777* made certain that extracting correspondences was always a tedious and troubling affair, and one that was fraught with the potential for producing errors. Other books have been published since, but they typically were not as comprehensive as Crowley's little book. I would purchase one of these books with the expectation that I could wean myself away from this torturous tome, but, alas, I would soon find myself once again consulting it.

That is not to say that any of these new books lacked something, but that I typically would like to see, if possible, something tying the correspondences back to the Tree of Life. I know that this can't always be done, but I think that it should be done where possible, since my reason for consulting such a reference is to acquire a matrix of corresponding symbolic information. Because I typically perform an invocation through a matrix of symbolic correspondences, having such a handy reference is strategically important to my work as a magician.

My little careworn but carefully kept hard-copy edition of *777* is no longer in print, and in fact it is probably worth a lot of money to a collector. However, there is a paperback edition of this book, entitled *777 and Other Qabalistic Writings of Aleister Crowley*, which is still being sold for a modest sum. This is not one of the more simplistic books authored by Crowley; even so, it is a worthy tome to have on one's library shelf, along with *Book Four*, *Magic in Theory and Practice*, *Magic Without Tears*, and *Gems from the Equinox*.

One book that I have found quite useful for occult and magical references is *The Magician's Companion* by Bill Whitcomb. This book is highly useful, but I have found myself, at times, forgetting that it is even on my bookshelf. I regret to say that it is easily eclipsed by another book, which, I might add, is as comprehensive and relevant as Crowley's book. That work is by far the best reference book that a magician could buy, and could easily supplant Crowley's book. It is written by Stephen Skinner and is entitled *The Complete Magician's Tables*. A hardcover version of this book is still available at a modest cost. I have found myself going back and forth, from Skinner's book to Crowley's book, and I have found them to be equally informative. However, Skinner's book is far easier to use than Crowley's book, and while it conserves the comparison of symbols to the elements of the Tree of Life, it structures the tables according to the requirements of the symbolic category. It also groups the tables by an overall topic, making it relatively easy to find a specific correspondence. I must admit that Skinner's book seldom finds itself on a bookshelf, since it is too valuable and too often consulted.

Another valuable book is *A Dictionary of Angels* by Gustav Davidson, which I find myself often consulting.

Since this book contains an alphabetic listing and brief synopsis of the characteristics of all the angels and demons ever mentioned in the sacred texts, commentaries, folklore, or literature, it represents a powerful and comprehensive collection of occult lore. This book has been instrumental in assisting me in developing the *imago* (image or face) of a specific spirit, so it is one of my most important reference books. The appendix also contains a lot of fascinating lore about the organization of angels and demons, and other interesting information. As far as I am aware, there isn't a better book for cataloguing and descriptively categorizing all of the various angels and demons encountered in occult practices.

I should also include on my list a book that helps me keep astrological meanings and definitions clear and sharp in my head, which is highly important for anyone working planetary or zodiacal magic. That book is *Horoscope Symbols* by Robert Hand. In that book is a concise definition for the planets, signs of the zodiac and the houses. I often find myself going back to it to ensure that I have the correct definition of any of these elements in my mind. (It's surprising to me how easy it is to take these complex but succinct definitions for granted, considering how far they stray from their original meaning.)

Not to be considered a narrow-minded occultist, I often consult a few other books as well. I am usually interested in the mythic motifs of certain Godnames, heroes, heroines, fabulous monsters and mythic creatures, and other cultural icons. It's not unusual for me to find more value in examining the mythic meaning behind certain symbols than comparing them to the Tree of Life.

My reference of choice that I use to examine the myths, legends, and cultural symbols found interlaced in occult studies is the redoubtable two-volume set *Dictionary of Mythology, Folklore and Symbols* by Gertrude Jobes. This is an excellent set of books, and one that I find myself often consulting at various times. Unfortunately, these books were published back in the early 1960s, so they are out of print and now quite expensive. There is a third edition that came out in the 1990s, but I don't know if this is a condensed version of the two-volume set, or just an index. Since the two-book set lists its subjects alphabetically, I have never found myself needing an index.

Another lesser book in the same line (and one that is still available) is *A Dictionary of Symbols* by J. E. Cirlot. I will usually consult this book from time to time, but only when the two volumes by Jobes are unable to fulfill my quest for a specific insight or answer.

Last, but not least, are the resources of a good library or the Internet. Since I have quite an extensive personal occult library, and quite a few books on history, archaeology, anthropology, philosophy, and psychology, I seldom have to make a trip to the local library. However, my collection is certainly not exhaustive, so I do once in a while travel to a large-city library, consulting the electronic catalogue to find the more obscure answers that I am seeking. The Internet is also useful and quite convenient, but it unfortunately mixes a lot of good, solid information with poor scholarship and even urban myth. If I find a significant reference on a site such as Wikipedia, I often attempt to examine the cited references for more solid information. I have found many websites, including Wikipedia, to be full of errors and unsubstantiated information. Still, I suspect that in the future, more and more of the important books and reference materials will be migrated to online facilities for easy use, and that hoarding books will eventually become inconvenient and even unsustainable.

Now that I have discussed the books that I use to gather information about specific symbols of correspondences, what are the kinds of information that I am usually searching for when consulting these books? The following list (which is actually derived from Skinner's topical table of contents) should pretty much demonstrate the kind of information that I find most helpful in writing and composing rituals, and building up a symbolic matrix through which to invoke a spirit:

- Alchemy—symbology (as it relates to the Tree of Life)
- Angels, demons, and various spirits
- Astrology—planets, zodiacal signs, and their various correspondences
- Basic symbols—colors, emblems, seasons, parts of the human body, mind, and soul
- Gematria of various alphabets (sometimes involves examining the occult values of words)
- Gods, goddesses, heros and heroines, and fabulous creatures
- Grimoires—tying various symbology to the spirit lists of the famous grimoires

- Natural magic—animals, plants (herbs), precious stones, metals, perfumes, and incense
- Qabalah—Qabalistic tables and symbolic correspondences
- Religious philosophies and theologies
- Tarot—trumps, court cards, Naib cards and their various correspondences

In addition to compiling this information in various related tables (related by topic or to the Tree of Life), I also like to gather background myths, legends, and other lore to help me fill out my categories, and this is where the ancillary reference books are very helpful.

While tables of correspondences can have as many rows as required to make them intelligible, there is a pattern to the structures that I have found most useful in my work as a writer, and to the work of a practicing ritual magician. These structures are based on the numbers 4, 7, and 12, and can also include multiples of those numbers, such as 16, 21, 36, and 48. Also, these four basic structures are subsets to the ten Sephiroth and the 22 Pathways of the Tree of Life, which can often (but not always) pull them together. Four is the number of the elements, seven is the number of the planets, and 12 is the number of zodiacal signs. Still, there are many other correspondences that can link to these three table structures, or are variations of them, and many of these correspondences can link back to the 32 elements of the Tree of Life.

I have found this universe of corresponding and linking symbology to be one of the more fascinating things about the occult, which excites my intuition and curiosity at all times and in all places. It signifies to me that every-thing is linked into a unified web of meaning and signifi-cance, which has at its center the union of all being as the One. I believe that magic could not work or function as efficiently and nearly miraculously as it does without this unified field of meaningfulness, which lies at the core of all occult insights and teachings.

fifteen

Systems of Numerology

The concept that letters are also numbers may be foreign to our present use of systems of counting and computing, but that was not the case less than two millennia ago. The numbering system that we use today, of Indo-Arabic origin, was also derived from letters, but with the brilliant addition of the zero. It has supplanted earlier and more primitive systems of numeration. However, the Greeks, and then the Hebrews (as well as others), used their alphabets as systems of numeration as well as alphabets. It is possible that this relationship was only deliberately manipulated later on, but a form of letter occultism was developed by the philosophic literati of the time, using specific examples of that obscure relationship between numbers and words, since only certain strategic examples were meaningful, and the rest, merely absurd.

To perform this methodology, broadly called *arithmology* (study of numbers),[56] an occultist had to merely add up the numeric value of the letters in a given word to establish the numeric value of that word. It was also believed that words that had the same numeric value also had the same corresponding meaning. The Greeks were the first to use this kind of word-number interchange, and they called this specific technique *isopsephos.* The word means "equal pebbles" (*iso + psephos*), since the Greeks originally used differently colored pebbles to teach arithmetic. It is very likely that this system of equating words to numbers was in wide use by the Greeks long before it was picked up by the Jews. In fact, the Greeks developed a kind of mysticism that they associated with numbers—hence the term *arithmology.*

As an illustration for the method of performing this kind of word-to-number exchange in Hebrew, let's look at a few famous examples. The Hebrew word AHBH (beloved), which has the individual letter values of 1, 5, 2, and 5, and when added together equals 13, assigns the numeric value of 13 to that word. Also the Hebrew word AChD (unity), which has the values 1, 8, and 4, also computes to the value of 13 when added together. Having revealed this numeric congruency, the occultist would then contemplate upon the subtle relationship between the words *beloved* and *unity*, noting that they could be interchanged as keywords or formulas in a ritual.

---

56. Kieren Barry, *The Greek Qabalah*, 24.

Additionally, the number 13 is also given the qualification of the two words (*beloved* and *unity*), whose numeric values are equivalent, so it now has additional attributes. An occultist would then, using this art of arithmology, produce a book consisting of numbers and their associated words (Sepher Sephiroth, or concordance index). Such a book would show the numeric values of all of the important strategic words or phrases, such as would be found in various Holy Scriptures, as well as the names of the Godhead, angels, demons, and other spirits.

This method of determining the numeric values of words to form numeric correspondences was called by Jewish Qabalists *Gematria*, from the Greek word *grammateia*, meaning "tabulation" (originally used to denote an account book or domestic inventory), or *geometria* (geometry). There isn't an agreement as of yet about which root definition is the correct one.

In addition, there are two other systems of numerology that are used in Qabalah. *Notariqon* is from *notarius*—an ancient method of shorthand writing that Qabalists used to create or define acronyms. *Temurah* is a method of permutation that substitutes letters so as to encrypt or decode words or phrases. There are said to be at least 22 different methods of substitution, one for each letter of the Hebrew alphabet. Temurah is also used to create signatures and sigils from formula words or important names. These are used particularly in the rituals of invocation and evocation. We will now individually explore each system in greater detail.

Gematria

Refer to the table (figure 17) depicting the Hebrew alphabet. You will notice that each Hebrew letter has a numeric value, and that a few have a second value associated with them. The five letters *Kaph, Mim, Nun, Peh*, and *Tzaddi* have different shapes when they occur at the end of a word, so they are given a different and higher numerical value. These are called the *terminal* numerical values, which are used for the terminal form of the letter (as it looks when it occurs at the end of a word).

Having two values for these special five letters allows for the assignment of numerical values of the hundreds, thereby giving some continuity to this archaic system of numeration. In order to examine the possible numeric congruencies that these accumulated values for words and phrases possess, it is necessary to either generate a tabular index from an analysis of hundreds of strategic Hebrew words, or purchase a book in which the work has already been accomplished.

I would recommend the latter approach, since doing this manually is not only difficult but also rife with error. I have already discussed one book that is in print that can help the student build a proper Sepher Sephiroth, and that is the one Aleister Crowley first published years ago, and is now included in the book *777 and Other Qabalistic Writings of Aleister Crowley*. (Another good book on Hebrew Gematria is *Godwin's Cabalistic Encyclopedia*, published by Llewellyn.)

You can use the Hebrew alphabet for deriving the numeric values of any or all specific words whatever the language, or you can use other alphabets for a specific language, such as Greek, Latin, or even the English alphabet.

My simple advice with Gematria is to use it sparingly and for strategic words or phrases where congruity has

Hebrew Letters and Values			
Hebrew Letter	Meaning	Initial Value	Terminal Value
Aleph א	Ox	1	
Beth ב	House	2	
Gimel ג	Camel	3	
Daleth ד	Door	4	
He ה	Window	5	
Vav ו	Nail	6	
Zayin ז	Sword	7	
Cheth ח	Fence	8	
Teth ט	Serpent	9	
Yod י	Hand	10	
Kaph כ	Palm of Hand	20	500
Lamed ל	Ox Goad	30	
Mim מ	Water	40	600
Nun נ	Fish	50	700
Samek ס	Prop	60	
Ayin ע	Eye	70	
Peh פ	Mouth	80	800
Tzaddi צ	Fish Hook	90	900
Qoph ק	Back of Head	100	
Resh ר	Head	200	
Shin ש	Tooth	300	
Tav ת	Tau Cross	400	
Note: A large Aleph = 1,000			

Figure 17: Hebrew alphabet

already been determined through research or other means. This is one method that can be easily abused.

Notariqon

Notariqon consists of two different methods, one for the creation of acronyms, and another for the explosion of acronyms.

In the first example, every letter of a word is used to determine an appropriate word that starts with that letter, so that from the letters of a word, a sentence or phrase is created. In Greek, the letters of the word for fish IChThUS become the initial letters for the words of a phrase, specifically *Iesous Christos Theou hUios Soter* (Jesus Christ, Son of God, the Messiah). So the word *Ichthus* (fish) becomes an acronym or symbol for the whole Christian creed. A Christian could use the sign of the fish to denote this specific theological concept of Christian belief, and it functioned in antiquity as a secret symbol known only to other Christians.

The second method is the reverse of the first, in that the first letters of each word in a phrase are broken out and used to create an acronym. In Latin, the phrase *Iesus Nazarenis Rex Iudeae* (Jesus of Nazareth, King of Judea) becomes the acronym I.N.R.I. This acronym has been used extensively in Christian iconography, theology, and even magic, but it is meaningless without the attribution of those four words.

Creation or reduction of acronyms gives the Qabalist a method to unify various word-components and to create word-formulas by associating words with the letter components of words or phrases. These two methods of

Notariqon are used extensively in the creation and definition of word-formulas, which are used to establish a magical link, and also in unifying all of the ritual components
of a magical ceremony into an integral whole. I have found
these two methods to be extremely important in my own
personal work in developing and writing rituals.

Temurah

Temurah is a system of permutation that uses letter substitution. The Hebrew alphabet can be easily cut in half with
pairs of 11 letters, which can be substituted to form different word associations or to act as a cipher to obscure word-
formulas. The simplest form is the following:

A	B	G	D	H	V	Z	Ch	T	Y	K	(Known as the *Atbash* Cipher)
Th	Sh	R	Q	Tz	Ph	O	S	N	M	L	

From this cipher, it is possible to derive the true name
of the God of the Templars; substituting the letters for
BPhVMTh (Baphomet) with their alternate pair; the word
becomes ShVPhIA (Sophia = Wisdom). Another cipher is
the ALBTh, as follows:

A	B	G	D	H	V	Z	Ch	T	Y	K
L	Th	Sh	R	Q	Tz	Ph	O	S	N	M

There are exactly 24 different ciphers altogether, and
in addition there are also tables of permutation consisting

of 484 squares (22 × 22).[57] The ciphers are less useful than the systems of Notariqon and Gematria. This is because writing with a cipher was necessary for added security measures during the age of the Inquisition, when writing about occult subjects was fraught with risk. Today, these ciphers are no longer deemed important in our enlightened times, but they could be helpful when attempting to uncover secret occult notations that were written in the past age, such as the derivation of Sophia from Baphomet. Still, this method of Temurah can be used by modern magicians to find alternate formulas when they are needed, therefore assisting one in making a permutation of an existing formula and finding a replacement for it that is analogous.

AIQ BKR: The Qabalah of Nine Chambers

The second and more useful method of Temurah is called the AIQ BKR table because its name describes the first two of the nine chambers of the table associated with this system. The AIQ BKR is a table for collapsing numerically associated letters to units of ten, therefore making each letter capable of being associated with the magic squares of the seven planets.

The AIQ BKR table is shown on the next page (figure 18). Once the letters of a spirit's name are reduced to the common values in the cell (usually the lowest values), the name can be made into a sigil by being traced on a magic square. The sigil acts as a unique signature of the spirit, and

---

57. See the table of combinations of Tziruph as found in Bill Whitcomb's *The Magician's Companion*, 441–42.

can be used as a magical link to invoke that spirit into manifestation.

An example: The Spirit of Saturn is ZAZL, which has
the following numerations: 7, 1, 7, and 30. The value for
Lamed (30) is reduced to the value of Gimel (3) so that

Shin	Lamed	Gimel	Resh	Kaph	Beth	Qoph	Yod	Aleph
ש	ל	ג	ר	כ	ב	ק	י	א
300	30	3	200	20	2	100	10	1
Final Mem	Samekh	Vav	Final Kaph	Nun	Heh	Tav	Mem	Daleth
ם	ס	ו	ך	נ	ה	ת	מ	ד
600	60	6	500	50	5	400	40	4
Final Tzaddi	Tzaddi	Teth	Final Peh	Peh	Cheth	Final Nun	Ayin	Zain
ץ	צ	ט	ף	פ	ח	ן	ע	ז
900	90	9	800	80	8	700	70	7

Figure 18: AIQ BKR table

the name can be traced on the square of Saturn, where the
highest number is 9.

On the next page is an example (figure 19) of what that
sigil would look like drawn on the square of Saturn.

AIQ BKR requires the use of what are known as magic
squares, and these squares are associated with the seven
planets: Saturn (3), Jupiter (4), Mars (5), Sun (6), Venus
(7), Mercury (8), and the Moon (9).

Each of these planetary squares is a table consisting of
an exact number of cells across and down as the number
associated with the planet. That number is directly equal to

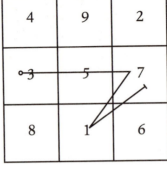

Zazl

Figure 19: Saturn square sigil of ZAZL

the numeration of the Sephiroth, from Binah (Saturn—3) to Yesod (Moon—9). An excellent rendition of these squares can be found in Donald Tyson's translation of Cornelius Agrippa's *Occult Philosophy*, particularly Appendix V (pages 733–51).

Continuing with our brief discussion, as one looks over the other Planetary Squares, it will be noticed that there are numbers that do not appear on the AIQ BKR table. For instance, the square for Jupiter has the values of 11 through 16 that are not represented in any of the AIQ BKR compartments. These are derived numbers that are produced by addition and subtraction (and even multiplication) of the combinations of the original numbers associated with the letters.

Thus the signature of ZAZL could also include the numbers 8 (7 +1), 6 (7 − 1), 4 (3 + 1), and 2 (3 − 1). The additional key numbers represent those numbers that can be derived by totaling the columns horizontally and diagonally. The square of Mercury has two values, one for the horizontal and vertical columns, and one for the diagonal columns. These extra values can be used to make an even more elaborate sigil character for the spirit name.

Magic squares are one way to produce sigils, but they are not the only way. I have made excellent use of what I call alphabetic rings, which are three concentric circles divided into cells into which the letters of an alphabet are placed. Perhaps the most famous ring is the Rose emblem used in the Golden Dawn. On that diagram, the petals of the Rose occupy three concentric rings, where there are three characters in the center ring, seven in the second ring, and 12 in the outer ring. These three concentric rings are then filled with the letters of the Hebrew alphabet, which can be divided into three groups. The Rose emblem with the alphabetic ring is the center piece in the famous magical device of the Rose Cross, worn as a kind of magic lamen in the Golden Dawn.

I have found that you can devise rings that will also accommodate both the Greek and English/Latin alphabets as well. The versatility of these rings has made them much more appealing to me, and I have adopted them exclusively in my magical work. I will reveal these three rings and how to use them in the next section.

Sigil Creation Using Alphabetic Rings

As I have said above, I use alphabetic rings to design and formulate sigils from the names of spirits or important words. This fact has freed me from dealing with magic squares and their inherent complexity, although the sigils that are produced are simple and straightforward.

There are three different alphabetic rings (Hebrew, Greek, and Latin/English) that I can use, and selecting the right one depends upon the language in which the name is written. If the name is an angel or demon, then it is likely (although not always) either of Hebrew derivation or reducible to Hebrew letters. However, some spirit names are obviously Greek; others, Latin; and still others are from some undetermined source. Whenever I am at a loss in attempting to determine the actual language source for a spirit's name, I will opt to use the alphabetic ring for English. The same is true for any Latin-sounding name. So the default ring is the one designed for the English alphabet.

Once you have chosen the ring that you want to use, then you can create the sigil. You may want to use the figures of the alphabetic rings found in this book to craft your own rings on good paper, or you can just directly use the ones in the book. The trick to creating a sigil is to place some tracing paper over the alphabetic ring, and, using a straight edge, link the letters in the cells of the ring, one to the other with penciled lines. Repeating letters in a row can be depicted with a curl or zigzag that slightly extends the line from its point of entering the cell but kept within the boundaries of the cell. The beginning of the sigil is marked with a small circle or a serif line, and the end is unmarked or it can be identified with an arrow or small ring.

Remember that other than using these simple rules, there is no right way or wrong way to craft a sigil. Creating a sigil is an artistic endeavor, so it will always represent your artistic expression which can be uniquely your own.

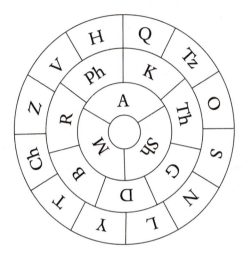

Figure 20: Hebrew alphabet ring

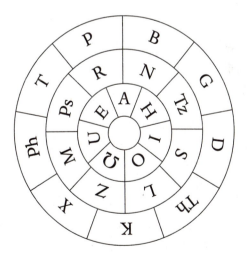

Figure 21: Greek alphabet ring

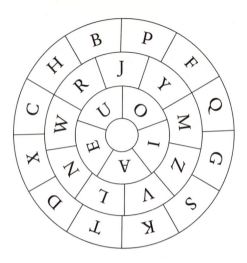

Figure 22: English alphabet ring

Here are the figures of the three alphabetic rings for your consideration and use.

Note that the Hebrew alphabetic ring breaks the Hebrew alphabet into three groups: the mothers (3), double (7), and single letters (12). This is a traditional alphabetic division. The Greek alphabet has seven vowels, eight semi-vowels, and nine voiceless consonants, for a total of 24 letters. The English alphabet has five vowels, nine voiced consonants, and 12 voiceless consonants, for a total of 26 letters. Latin is similar to English because it has five vowels, but only 17 consonants remain for a total of 22 letters. (Two letters, *K* and *Y*, are borrowed from Greek and have no representation in Latin.)

sixteen

Ascension, Transformation, Wisdom, and Gnosis: Putting It All Together

Studying the Qabalah is not just a lot of book reading, memorization, or picking up handy practical techniques for working magic. The themes that it reveals; the esoteric doctrines it explores; and the various Godnames, spirit lists, symbolic tables of correspondences, and practical techniques that it deploys are not the source and core of the spiritual discipline of the Qabalah. Like everything else, the Qabalah is not reducible to being nothing more than the sum of its parts. Qabalah is a living and breathing tradition, and those who do not engage with it to make it come alive for themselves are missing something very crucial and important in their occult studies and practices.

It is quite obvious to anyone who seeks to be proficient in magic that, at some point, you have to put down the books, papers, notes, and other materials, and actually attempt to perform rituals and ceremonies. Nothing is more bizarre, in my opinion, than an armchair magician pretending to be an authority, but what about the armchair Qabalist? That would seem to be okay, as the Qabalah often gets lost in the details of its various and multitudinous amounts of lore. Yet as the discipline of magic requires one to perform rituals and ceremonies, so too does the Qabalah require one to adopt a Qabalistic spiritual discipline.

To be a true adherent of the Qabalah, one must practice and perform Qabalistic operations, exercises, and rites. The key to a true realization and understanding of the Qabalah is that it must become a living and breathing spiritual tradition for anyone who seeks to use it in a manner other than a purely mercenary one. A student of Western occultism and magic can also be a Qabalist without also having to be an adherent of one of the Abrahamic faiths, particularly Judaism and Christianity. Qabalah lends itself quite well to the polytheist, Animist, Gnostic, Theosophist, and Pagan Witch, but it is also quite important to anyone who seeks to work ritual or ceremonial magic. Why do I think that this is true?

Unless your purpose for performing magic is just to enrich and empower yourself without any spiritual considerations or, for that matter, consequences, then you must be seeking some kind of spiritual realization and growth. I have also repeatedly pointed out the fact that spiritualization is a natural outgrowth of magical practices, whether one intends that to happen or not. I believe that transformative experiences and even the accumulation of occult knowledge and spiritual awakening is inescapable. Root doctors and hoodoo specialists become wise and deeply insightful over time, and so do practitioners of ritual and ceremonial magic. A constant and continuous exposure to spirits, various Godheads, and the domain of Spirit in general will have a profound and permanent effect on the practitioner, whether intended or not. However, if magicians deliberately seek to be spiritually transformed and achieve the effects of ascension and gnosis, then it behooves them to have a road map so that they might know where they are, and where they are going.

Qabalah gives the practicing magician a road map to personal transformation, ascension, and ultimately pure gnosis. Not only that, but it also gives the practicing magician a trigger to make those processes happen, whenever and wherever he or she wills it to be. So, it is not only a spiritual road map, but it is also the levers that help the magician to achieve those higher conscious strata of the domain of Spirit. Yet there is one little catch, and that is that the magician must make the various structures and doctrines of the Qabalah into an experiential phenomenon. Also, in order to make full use of the Qabalah as a mechanism to trigger ascension and enlightenment, it must become a *living spiritual tradition*.

How do we make the Qabalah into a living tradition? We make it real by taking the various symbologies and structures, and through meditation, contemplation, pathworking, invocation, and Godhead assumption, make them an awakened and living part of our being. It is through the previously discussed five operations that we are able to fully activate the symbologies and structures of the Tree of the Life. If we superimpose the Tree of Life over our own bodies and activate its various structures within our own being, then that great symbolic structure will become a powerful and dynamic element in our spiritual lives. There is no other way to inculcate the Qabalah into our life except by bringing it literally into our body and mind.

I have proposed exercises and operations to achieve this kind of union, and I can assume that there are many ways of achieving this important goal. Yet I am also quite amazed and amused that some haven't been able to recognize its importance. In fact, it doesn't even matter if a magician chooses another system or discipline over the Qabalah, as long as he or she approaches this alternative methodology with the same design of merging one's spiritual and magical practice with an active metaphysical system of speculation. Without that combined approach, a magical or mystical practice will ultimately produce very little over a long period of time. As my favorite chiropractor[58] is so fond of saying (in regard to the stiffness of my back), "With enough force, even a brick can fly." But I would reply that a structure that is designed to fly requires a lot less force and energy to get it airborne. So it is with a system of magic that has a designed activated system of metaphysical speculation; it will require a lot less time and effort to produce ascension and the gnosis of perfect enlightenment.

---

58. The redoubtable Dr. Adam Klotzek, of Kenwood Chiropractic Arts in Minneapolis, Minnesota.

If my assumption that the ultimate quest for anyone who is practicing ritual or ceremonial magic is to achieve a state of at-one-ment with the Deity is wrong, then all of the other assumptions written here are also wrong and irrelevant. I am writing this section for the sake of those who are actively seeking to become enlightened and a spiritual *master*. To such a practitioner and spiritual adherent, I would recommend the Qabalah as an important tool to wed magic with a system of applied metaphysical speculation. That combination will produce a discipline that is capable of acquiring all that a magician might seek to achieve, whether on the material plane or within the mysterious vaults of the highest spiritual planes. If the Qabalah appeals to you, then your next question (if you don't already know the answer) will be, "How does one learn the Qabalah?" Let's recap and re-examine what we have already covered in order to make certain that the steps needed for a comprehensive knowledge of the Qabalah are fully defined.

How do we approach such a vast and massive discipline, particularly if we are Pagans who are practicing ritual or ceremonial magic? Obviously, we do not need to embrace everything that has ever been published or taught under the rubric of Cabala, Kabbalah, Qabala, or Qabalah. Some of these studies will be relevant, and some of them won't. If we want to understand how the Qabalah evolved over time, we will need to become much more aware of some of the different topics, practices, and beliefs written by those remarkable Jews and Christians who took this wonderful and diverse discipline upon themselves. However, if we just want to learn about the Qabalah and how to use it in our own Pagan-based studies and practices, then some of the more intensely Jewish or Christian perspectives will not be particularly relevant. Let us, then, undertake a subject-matter examination and pull together a very basic curriculum for the average occultist to study the Qabalah. I will also include a few books and materials.

To have a reasonable understanding of the Qabalah, you should attempt to learn the following subjects in the sequential order that they are presented. I will list these subjects from the least to the most difficult, and also from the most to least relevant. At some point, though, to be a truly accomplished Qabalist, you should seek to master all of them.

1. Basic overview of the various elements of the Tree of Life and the practical application of the Qabalah. ("Why is the Qabalah relevant?" "What is the Qabalah?"—build yourself a definition.)

2. Ten Sephiroth—including all of the symbols and correspondences

3. 22 Pathways—including all of the symbols and correspondences (Tree of Life)

4. Four Worlds and the Four Bodies—planes of consciousness and human-related bodies

5. Three Negative Veils, Myth of Creation, and the Origin of Evil (Qliphoth)

6. Practical Qabalah—Gematria, Notariqon, and Temurah—Numerological Analogies, Magical Formulas, Ciphers, and Name-based Sigils, various Magical Squares, and so forth

7. Spiritual Hierarchies and other systems of correspondences

8. Techniques of meditation, contemplation, pathworking, invocation/evocation, Godhead assumption (making the Qabalah an experiential discipline)

9. Greek Qabalah and English Qabalah—and other systems of speculation

10. History of the Qabalah and its evolution—including the different religious-based systems

11. Classical Qabalah—Sepher Yetzirah, Zohar, Sepher Bahir, Cordovero, and Lurian Kabbalah

I would consider items 1 through 8 to be very important and 9 through 11 as topics of interest (but not essential). Eventually, as I have stated, the truly proficient Qabalist will have gained some deeper insights by studying all these other areas, but by then, he or she will have already fully activated a Qabalistic spiritual discipline.

Recommended reading regimen: I would recommend that the following nine books be studied in great detail. You have already read most of my book, so that was at least the first on your list. (All of the following books are currently in print.)

1. *The Chicken Qabalah* (Weiser, 2001)—by Lon Milo DuQuette

2. *Paths of Wisdom* (Thoth Publications, 2007)—by John Michael Greer

3. *The Ladder of Lights* (Red Wheel/Weiser, 1981)—by William G. Gray

4. *A Practical Guide to Qabalistic Symbolism* (Red Wheel/Weiser, 2001)—by Gareth Knight

5. *A Garden of Pomegranates* (Llewellyn, 1995)—by Israel Regardie

6. *Qabalistic Concepts: Living the Tree* (Red Wheel/Weiser, 1997)—by William G. Gray

7. *777 and Other Qabalistic Writings of Aleister Crowley* (Red Wheel / Weiser, 1986)—by Aleister Crowley

8. *The Complete Magician's Tables* (Golden Hoard Press, 2007)—by Stephen Skinner

9. *Kabbalah* (New American Library, 1974)—by Gershom Scholem

In addition to the five operations that I have already covered (and the associated five exercises), all of which are found in chapter 9, I would recommend a technique that is found in a pamphlet published back in 1970: *The Office of the Holy Tree*, written by William G. Gray. Unfortunately, this book is no longer in print, but it can be found in the back of the book *Sangreal Ceremonies and Rituals* (Red Wheel/Weiser, 1986), also written by William G. Gray.

The reason that this book is so important is that it has a Qabalistic spiritual office that is written to express, in prayer form, the essential symbology of the Tree of Life. It is loosely based on the Catholic Office, which is a prayer book that is used for each of the eight prayer-time periods of the day, for every day of the year. Catholic monks, nuns, and prelates of all grades were expected to use the Office as a regimen of prayers, readings, and meditations. It included particularly relevant readings and prayers for specific feast days, religious holidays, and other special religious observances.

A Qabalistic office would incorporate special prayers and meditation topics for each Sephirah and Pathway on the Tree of Life. Thus it would be very useful for anyone who was engaging in a session of contemplation, pathworking, and even forms of Qabalistic theurgy and Godhead assumption. So for these reasons, I highly recommend it.

Once the above topics are pretty well mastered, at least to the point that they are very familiar, you should assemble the required things needed to perform a regimen of daily exercises. There are very few things needed, but these items should be considered important:

- A sequestered room to meditate and perform simple rituals. This room can be adorned with pictures, posters, and paintings, all relevant to the work. It should be kept clean and used just for the spiritual work, but it can be of any size, small or large.

- Oil lamps, incense burner and charcoal, incense, perfumes, blessed salt water (lustral water).

- White robe, special jewelry, consecrated lamen, differently colored scarves, dagger and wand. (Dagger is optional.)

- A journal or notebook—I can't emphasize more strongly the importance of writing down everything that is experienced, dreamed, sensed, transmitted, or otherwise received when engaging in intense Qabalistic workings.

The following exercises and techniques are used in Qabalistic workings:

- Exercises: Qabalistic Cross, Middle Pillar, Opening of the Self, Closing of the Self, Grounding
- Operations: Meditation, Contemplation, Pathworking, Invocation, Godhead assumption

The key to the true Qabalah is to use all of the above practices in a regular schedule, and through them to explore thoroughly the complete list of 11 topics found on pages 306 and 307. Contemplation should be used to realize the deeper elements of the Qabalah, and pathworking should be used to make the Pathways and Sephiroth into a truly experiential phenomenon as well as activate the process of spiritual ascension. Theurgy and Godhead assumption should be used to encounter and intimately experience all of the angels, archangels, super archangels, and Godhead aspects of the Tree of Life. By performing all of these disciplines at various times, I can guarantee that the practicing magician will also ultimately experience the full and profound awakening that is associated with total enlightenment.

Combining the practice of ritual or ceremonial magic with an activated and dynamic regimen of metaphysical speculation and mystical revelation will produce an overall system that will rival anything that the various Eastern traditions can provide. Such a profound and useful combination will truly forge, for the practitioner, a comprehensive yoga of the West.

A Qabalistic Mage

We have now covered everything that you need to begin your journey to master the Qabalah. That might seem like quite an all-consuming endeavor, and indeed it is. Not only do you now know the basics of the Qabalah, but you also know how to teach yourself (and others) the more complex and detailed aspects of this discipline.

I have given you the tools to make this discipline come alive and reveal itself to you. If you never read another book on the subject, at least the five operations and exercises (as found in chapter 9, "Techniques of Mind Control") will help you determine everything else that you might seek to know about the Qabalah. In fact, the only thing that additional books will do is give you more food for thought as you proceed on your spiritual path. The Qabalah can be used in conjunction with spiritual and magical practices to greatly expand their effectiveness, or it can be used alone and without any other practice. This fact by itself should have instructed you on the usefulness of the Qabalah and its utility for one such as you who is following the Western Mystery tradition.

In *The Book of Abramelin*, the author, Abraham von Worms ("Abraham the Jew"), tells his youngest son that he is giving him the wisdom of his knowledge of magic (in the book that he has written) because he must give the knowledge of the Qabalah to his eldest son. So it would seem that he has deemed to divide his wealth and wisdom between his two sons and the eldest receives, of course, the greater share. When I first read this passage, I was quite astounded, since it seemed to say that the knowledge of the Qabalah, in and of itself, was superior to the knowledge of magic. Here is the passage, found in the first book, chapter 9 (p. 34), where Abraham tells his son Lamech:

> *The art of wisdom has its foundation in the secrets of the highest and in the holy Kabbalah, which belongs to your eldest brother Joseph, and not to you.*

It would seem, then, that knowledge of the Qabalah is not only greater than knowledge of magic, but that through it, one could gain everything that magic would give and more. According to *The Book of Abramelin*, a mastery of the Qabalah is superior to the knowledge and practice of magic, and between the two, it is the greater prize by far. This concept becomes even more amazing when we consider that the purpose of *The Book of Abramelin* was to successfully invoke and manifest one's Holy Guardian Angel.

Imagine my amazement when I discovered this great truth only when I was engaged in researching and assembling the material for this book. Prior to that task, I had always assumed that the Qabalah could be practiced as a spiritual discipline by itself, but I was such a big promoter and fan of ritual magic that I hadn't really seen that assumption clearly defined. Assembling and working with the five operations made me realize that the Qabalah is such a powerful spiritual discipline that it alone can guide a seeker to complete enlightenment and at-one-ment with the Deity.

What the Qabalah cannot replace is the daily, weekly, monthly, and seasonal devotions and religious practices. If you choose to use the Qabalah as a system of achieving illumination, then you will also need to deeply engage yourself with your religious beliefs and practices. Qabalah can make these beliefs and practices more meaningful and powerful, but it cannot replace them altogether.

It is also correct that a true adherent to the Qabalah will likely perform theurgistic rituals in order to satisfy one of the five operations, and to gain the knowledge and conversation of the spirits associated with the Qabalistic spiritual hierarchy. This is an important operation, and it should be one that the Qabalist masters along with the other operations and techniques. It is also a bridge and a gateway into the practice and discipline of ritual magic, but these rites and practices can be kept simplistic and direct so that they do not become a distraction to the Great Work.

So, what is the objective of building a spiritual and magical discipline based on the foundation of the Qabalah? The objective, as I have stated numerous times previously, is to achieve complete union with the Godhead; there can be no other objective. This might seem like a very lofty achievement, and perhaps one that can't ever be completed. Not everyone is afforded a life and an understanding that would allow them to become like a god. The number of enlightened teachers and spiritual masters in the world are very few when compared to the population of everyone else throughout time. There would seem to be some very great limitations and barriers confronting someone who would attempt such a feat. However, the mere fact that a person would attempt such an endeavor, even if they should fail to achieve the final goal, would be honorable and quite laudable.

A Qabalistic mage is a person who is seeking self-improvement, spiritual evolution, personal transformation, and self-mastery. Such a person is remarkable no matter what he or she achieves in life. Even partial success would make a student and seeker into a better human being at the very least, a compassionate and inspiring example to humanity at best. Not only that, but unlimited wisdom allows the beneficiary to live life more fully and more completely. A true follower of the Qabalah, regardless of his or her spiritual beliefs and practices, would find that the grace and love of the Deity was always with them, and this would help such a person acquire what others would call a *charmed life*. This is a phenomenon in which a person constantly experiences the benefits of good fortune, health, and a life lived with meaning and purpose. I can say without any doubt that I have experienced this very phenomenon from time to time, and I know it is possible to realize it thoroughly and completely.

I am not advocating that anyone who takes up the practice and discipline of the Qabalah will automatically gain a charmed life, but it is something that I have seen time and again, and it has made me a believer. Someone who lives their life with a strong, practical, and spiritual discipline is able to see and take advantage of good opportunities, and to endure the calamities and misfortune that might otherwise cause permanent despair and even self-destruction. If you will assume this kind of spiritual discipline, it will make a profound difference in your life; so, for this reason, I am a strong advocate of developing and maintaining an occult spiritual life.

We begin our lives with whatever our parents and our station in life can afford us, and from there we must rely on ourselves alone and unaided. We can be given everything we need and more, but what we do with it is solely up to our own initiative, regardless of virtues or flaws. However, this comprehensive beginners' book seeks to give you something that you might not have received from anyone else, and that is a road map to enlightenment and spiritual mastery. I can't tell you exactly how to attain this goal, but I can at least give you the tools to accomplish this end for yourself. The rest, of course, is up to you. Like the legacy that you received in life when you were born, however great or humble, what you do with your gifts and advantages is your own personal fate. Yet by sharing with you the knowledge that I have received over decades of study and practice, perhaps you might gain something that was not part of your birthright or inheritance. Whether you received any spiritual or occult inclination or abilities from your ancestors, you now have in your hands the means to becoming a spiritual master and a Qabalistic mage.

May you use this knowledge to maximize your potential and realize your highest ambition. And may the Godhead that you serve bless you and make the perilous path of life straight and without obstacles.

Bright Blessings to you—
Frater Barrabbas

glossary

Absolute Spirit: Another way of defining the One or the spiritual source.

Aggadah: Biblical textual analyses that were concerned with non-legal and homiletic themes.

Aion: Greek for "time" (also Latin, *Aeon*), representing periods or epochs of time. Later, it became a term for hypostatized beings representing the ultimate spiritual source of the universe.

Bereshith: Hebrew for "In the beginning..."—the first word of the biblical chapter of Genesis. Root word is RVSh (head) with conjunctive prefix "B" (in), which means, literally, "in the head."

Cosmogony: Theory or model about the origin of the universe or how it was created.

Cosmology: The evolution, structure, and constituent parts of the universe.

Decans: Ten-degree segment of the zodiac. There are a total of 36 decans, three for each sign of the zodiac.

Deresh: A method of textual analysis used in the Talmud consisting of a comparative analysis—i.e., comparing different texts using the same words, and employing a biblical concordance to accomplish that end.

Din: Hebrew word for "judgment," also a method of textual analysis used in the Talmud to analyze and define legal dictates in the Hebrew Bible.

Ein Sof Aur: A triple pre-existing nothingness, called the Three Negative Veils, which were named *Ein* (Nothing), *Ein Sof* (Limitless Nothing), and *Ein Sof Aur* (Limitless Light).

Emanation: To issue from a source.

Epistemology: Nature and scope of knowledge.

Evolution: Growth, typically used to define a phenomenon of expanding spiritual and intellectual awareness associated with spiritual and magical practices.

Four Qabalistic Worlds: Four levels of the created universe as defined through the domain of consciousness.

Gnosis: Intuitive wisdom gained through direct experience with the Godhead.

Gnosticism: Various Jewish and Christian religious sects that stipulated that one could not know God without having direct experiences and developing a personal relationship with that Deity.

Godhead: Attribute of the Deity representing a finite facet of the greater but unnamed One.

Great Chain of Being: Interrelated spiritual hierarchy, in which all things are connected to everything else. (Sources from Plato, Aristotle, and Neoplatonism.)

Haikhalot: Hebrew word for "palaces," being the seven palaces where resides the Godhead in early forms of the Qabalah.

Halakha: Biblical textual analyses that were concerned with Jewish religious law.

Heterodoxy: Opposite of orthodoxy, representing a synthesis of ideas and beliefs that are not natural for a given religious system. Known today as *eclecticism.*

Higher Self: The God/dess within the individual human being. Also called the *Atman* by Indian sages.

Holy Guardian Angel: Considered the personal angel that protects and guides each human being. Some believe that the HGA is synonymous with the Higher Self.

Hypostasis: Giving an abstract concept or a monotheistic attribute of the Deity a fully developed and seemingly independent personality and characteristics. Example: Sophia, the Greek word for "wisdom," became an independent goddess among some Gnostics.

Immanent: Opposite of transcendent, represents the aspect of the Deity that is intimate and essential to the individual human being.

Inner Planes: Other-world domain where spirits and various Godheads reside.

Involution: Descent of the spiritual essence of the Godhead to imbue the material and unspiritual world with the essence of Spirit and the potential of consciousness.

Left-Hand Path: Also, *Left-Hand Occultism*—is based on an inversion of the rightful order and lawfulness as established by status-quo spirituality, so it is often seen as a form of diabolism or demonolatry (worship of demons).

Logos: Greek word for "word"—specific meaning is that it is divine directive of the Absolute Spirit (Word of God).

Macrocosm: A cosmic level of being.

Merkabah: Chariot Throne of God, protected by Seraphim and pulled by the Cherubim, and whose wheels of fire (Ophanim) are also angelic beings who drive the chariot. A good emblem of this concept is found in the Chariot Tarot trump.

Meta-data: A specific description (or set of descriptions) about a certain data element.

Meta-hierarchy: A hierarchy that pulls other unique and distinct hierarchies together into a single larger hierarchy.

Meta-knowledge: Defined as information that is used to organize and define a body of information.

Meta-system: A system that is used to describe or organize a system.

Microcosm: Human level of being, as opposed to the Godhead (Macrocosm).

Midrash: From the Hebrew word that means "to investigate" or "to study." A deep textual analysis of the various passages in the Hebrew Bible.

Mishnah: From the Hebrew word that means "repetition." Orally transmitted lore regarding various legal considerations, traditions, and even folklore written into a series of biblical commentaries.

Monad: A unitary spiritual perspective. Symbolized as the first being, or the One.

Negative Veils: A mysterious source depicted as a triple preexisting nothingness (see *Ein Sof Aur*).

Neoplatonism: A religious and mystical philosophy that appeared in the third century CE, based on the teachings and writings of Plato and his followers. Focused on the specific cosmological and spiritual aspects of Platonic beliefs.

Neopythagoreanism: A blending of the philosophies in antiquity of Pythagoras's concept of divine numbers with Plato's concept of ideals, so that pure numbers were equated as the thoughts (ideals) of the Godhead.

Nephesh: Animal soul or emotional body.

Neschamah: Intuitive self, personal spirit.

Ontology: Nature of reality.

Operant Link: A magical mechanism consisting of a sigil device and strategic associations taken from tables of correspondences (such as color, incense, perfume, etc.).

Pardes: Persian word for "orchard," "garden," or "paradise," represented by the acronym for Peshat, Remez, Deresh, and Sod methods of textual analysis (PaRDeS).

Peshat: A method of textual analysis used in the Talmud consisting of simple or literal interpretations.

Pleroma: Greek word for "wholeness." Represents the repository of all spiritual beings and forces.

Qabalah iyyunit: Type of Qabalah consisting of mystical speculation and ecstatic practices.

Qabalah Ma'asit: Type of Qabalah consisting of practical occultism and theurgy.

Qliphoth: Hebrew word for a shell or the outer covering of some kind of fruit or nut.

Remez: A method of textual analysis used in the Talmud consisting of a deep textual analysis performed through an examination of hints.

Right-Hand Path: Orthodoxy, or lawful spiritual practices; also, status-quo spirituality. Emphasis on Light, Good, Lawful, Piety, and a masculine-based perspective.

Ruach: Hebrew for "breath"; also, spirit.

Sod: A method of textual analysis used in the Qabalah consisting of an analysis of hidden meanings, mysteries, or secrets. (This methodology was excluded from the Talmud.)

Talmud: Collection of various analytical texts consisting of the Mishnah, Gemara, Tosfta, and other commentaries. There are two Talmuds—Jerusalem and Babylonian.

Targum (Targunim, pl.): Various books of the Hebrew Bible translated into Aramaic.

Ten Sephiroth: From the Hebrew *Sephirah*, meaning "number" (although not the typical word for that term).

Tenakh: An acronym for the three parts of the Hebrew Bible: Torah, Nevi'im, and Khetuvim, or TNKh. (*Khetuvim*—the lesser books, such as the Psalms, Proverbs, Job, Song of Songs, Ruth, and others. *Nevi'im*—books of the Prophets, including Joshua, Kings, and Judges.)

Theurgistic ascension: Used of various Godhead formulations and magical practices to achieve union with the One.

Theurgy: From the Greek for "God-work." Form of magic that allows the practitioner to assume and act in concert with various aspects of the Godhead.

Torah: Hebrew word for "instruction." First five books of the Hebrew Bible—Genesis, Exodus, Leviticus, Numbers, and Deuteronomy.

Tree of Life: Etz Chaim—symbol or glyph that contains the 32 elements of the Qabalah: namely, the 10 Sephiroth and the 22 Pathways.

22 Pathways: Paths between the Sephiroth on the Tree of Life. Pathways are represented by the 22 Hebrew letters and the Major Arcana of the Tarot.

Universal Mind: Derived from the philosophy of Hegel, representing the universal higher mind or source of all being.

Western Mystery tradition: Collection of mystical and esoteric knowledge as found in all esoterically defined religions of the Western world.

Yechidah: Individual Monad or Atman residing within a person.

bibliography

Barry, Kieren. *The Greek Qabalah*. York Beach, ME: Samuel Weiser, 1999.

Cirlot, J. E. *A Dictionary of Symbols*. Translated by Jack Sage. Mineola, NY: Dover Publications, 2002. (Other editions are also available.)

Crowley, Aleister. *777 and Other Qabalistic Writings of Aleister Crowley*. New York: Samuel Weiser, 1986. (First published in 1955.)

———. *The Book of Thoth*. New York: Samuel Weiser, 1972.

Dan, Joseph. *Kabbalah: A Very Short Introduction*. Oxford: Oxford University Press, 2006.

Davidson, Gustav. *A Dictionary of Angels*. New York: Free Press, 1971.

Drob, Sanford L. *Symbols of the Kabbalah: Philosophical and Psychological Perspectives*. Northvale, NJ: Jason Aronson, 2000.

DuQuette, Lon Milo. *The Chicken Qabalah of Rabbi Lamed Ben Clifford: Dilettante's Guide to What You Do and Do Not Need to Know to Become a Qabalist*. York Beach, ME: Weiser, 2001.

Fortune, Dion. *The Mystical Qabalah*. London: Ernest Benn, 1974.

Freedman, Daphne. *Man and the Theogony in the Lurianic Cabala*. Piscataway, NJ: Gorgias Press, 2006.

Godwin, David. *Godwin's Cabalistic Encyclopedia* (third edition). Woodbury, MN: Llewellyn, 2008.

Gray, William G. *The Ladder of Lights*. Toddington, UK: Helios, 1981.

———. *Qabalistic Concepts: Living the Tree*. York Beach, ME: Red Wheel/ Weiser, 1997.

———. *Sangreal Ceremonies and Rituals*. York Beach, ME: 1986.

Greer, John Michael. *Paths of Wisdom*. Loughborough, UK: Thoth Publications, 2007.

Hand, Robert. *Horoscope Symbols*. Atglen, PA: Schiffer, 1981.

Holtz, Barry W., ed. *Back to the Sources: Reading the Classical Jewish Texts*. New York: Simon & Schuster, 1984.

Knight, Gareth. *A Practical Guide to Qabalistic Symbolism* (vols. I–II). York Beach, ME: Red Wheel/Weiser, 2001. (First published in 1965 by Helios Ltd.)

Niditch, Susan. *Ancient Israelite Religion*. New York: Oxford University Press, 1997.

Patai, Raphael. *The Hebrew Goddess*. Detroit, MI: Wayne State University Press, 1990.

Rankine, David, and Stephen Skinner. *The Goetia of Dr. Rudd*. London: Golden Hoard Press, 2007.

Regardie, Israel. (Chic Cicero and Sandra Tabatha Cicero, eds.) *A Garden of Pomegranates: Skrying on the Tree of Life*. St. Paul, MN: Llewellyn, 1999.

———. *The Middle Pillar: The Balance Between Mind and Magic*. St. Paul, MN: Llewellyn, 2002.

Scholem, Gershom. *Kabbalah*. New York: New American Library, 1974.

Skinner, Stephen. *The Complete Magician's Tables*. Singapore: Golden Hoard Press, 2007. (Distributed by Llewellyn Worldwide.)

Skinner, Stephen, ed. *The Fourth Book of Occult Philosophy* (by H. C. Agrippa). Berwick, ME: Ibis Press, 2005.

Tyson, Donald, ed., and James Freake, trans. *Three Books of Occult Philosophy* (by H. C. Agrippa). St. Paul, MN: Llewellyn, 1997.

Von Worms, Abraham. *The Book of Abramelin: A New Translation*. Edited and translated by Georg Dehn and Steven Guth. Berwick, ME: Ibis Press, 2006.

Wallis, R. T. *Neoplatonism*. London: Bristol Classical Press, 2002.

Whitcomb, Bill. *The Magician's Companion*. St. Paul, MN: Llewellyn, 1993.

Yates, Frances A. *Giordano Bruno and the Hermetic Tradition*. Chicago: University of Chicago Press, 1991.

index

Four Worlds, 15, 21, 31–34, 45, 47, 134, 140–142, 181–183, 204, 207, 255, 257, 306

G
Gabriel, 92, 100, 112, 113, 115, 119, 257–259, 263
Geburah, 89, 90, 100–103, 108, 121–123, 125–128, 135, 138, 142, 151, 152, 165, 166, 172–174, 187, 209, 213, 263
Gematria, 15, 65, 66, 79, 245, 284, 289–291, 294, 306
glyphs, 35, 42, 44, 71, 97, 192, 194, 203, 323
Gnosticism, 11, 22, 65, 67–69, 79, 99, 172, 201, 225, 302
Godhead assumption, 199, 209, 220, 221, 250, 303, 307, 309, 310
Godnames, 88–94, 100, 182, 202, 209, 212–215, 217, 220, 221, 225, 226, 229, 232, 233, 238, 241–244, 247, 248, 251, 254, 259–263, 271, 274, 282, 301
Gray, William, 80, 140
grounding, 131, 209, 215, 216, 220, 221, 234, 310

H
Haikhalot, 11, 319
ha-Kohen, Isaac, 68, 99
Hebrew, 4, 11, 20–23, 30, 32, 34, 38–40, 50, 54–56, 61, 63, 64, 70, 76, 77, 96, 108, 109, 134, 136, 142, 147–149, 151, 152, 157, 159, 162, 181, 182, 202, 213, 226, 230–232, 234, 236, 238, 240, 245, 262, 274, 279, 280, 288–291, 293, 297–300, 317–319, 321–323
Hod, 74, 91, 92, 100–103, 112, 113, 116–118, 121, 122, 135, 138, 142, 145, 152, 187, 210, 241, 258, 263
hypostasis, 238, 319

S

To Write to the Author

If you wish to contact the author or would like more information about this book, please write to the author in care of Llewellyn Worldwide Ltd., and we will forward your request. Both the author and publisher appreciate hearing from you and learning of your enjoyment of this book and how it has helped you. Llewellyn Worldwide Ltd. cannot guarantee that every letter written to the author can be answered, but all will be forwarded. Please write to:

Frater Barrabbas
℅ Llewellyn Worldwide
2143 Wooddale Drive
Woodbury, MN 55125-2989

Please enclose a self-addressed stamped envelope for reply,
or $1.00 to cover costs. If outside the USA, enclose
an international postal reply coupon.

GET MORE AT LLEWELLYN.COM

Visit us online to browse hundreds of our books and decks, plus sign up to receive our e-newsletters and exclusive online offers.

- • Free tarot readings • Spell-a-Day • Moon phases
- • Recipes, spells, and tips • Blogs • Encyclopedia
- • Author interviews, articles, and upcoming events

GET SOCIAL WITH LLEWELLYN

Find us on Facebook
www.Facebook.com/LlewellynBooks

Follow us on twitter™
www.Twitter.com/Llewellynbooks

GET BOOKS AT LLEWELLYN

LLEWELLYN ORDERING INFORMATION

Order online: Visit our website at www.llewellyn.com to select your books and place an order on our secure server.

Order by phone:
- • Call toll free within the U.S. at 1-877-NEW-WRLD (1-877-639-9753)
- • Call toll free within Canada at 1-866-NEW-WRLD (1-866-639-9753)
- • We accept VISA, MasterCard, and American Express

Order by mail:
Send the full price of your order (MN residents add 6.875% sales tax) in U.S. funds, plus postage and handling to: Llewellyn Worldwide, 2143 Wooddale Drive Woodbury, MN 55125-2989

POSTAGE AND HANDLING

STANDARD (U.S. & Canada):
(Please allow 12 business days)
$25.00 and under, add $4.00.
$25.01 and over, FREE SHIPPING.

INTERNATIONAL ORDERS (airmail only):
$16.00 for one book, plus $3.00 for each additional book.

Visit us online for more shipping options.
Prices subject to change.

FREE CATALOG!

To order, call
1-877-NEW-WRLD
ext. 8236
or visit our website

The Complete
Magician's Tables

the most complete tabular set of Magic, Kabbalistic, Angelic, Astrologic, Alchemic, Demonic, Geomantic, Grimoire, Gematria, I Ching, Tarot, Pagan Pantheon, Plant, Perfume and Character Correspondences in more than 777 Tables

Stephen Skinner

The Complete Magician's Tables
STEPHEN SKINNER

Anyone practicing magic will want this comprehensive book of magician's correspondences. Featuring four times as many tables than Aleister Crowley's *Liber 777*, this is the most complete collection of magician's tables available. This monumental work documents thousands of mystical links—spanning Pagan pantheons, Qabalah, astrology, tarot, I Ching, angels, demons, herbs, perfumes, and more!

The sources of this remarkable compilation range from classic grimoires such as the *Sworn Book* to modern theories of prime numbers and atomic weights. Data from Peter de Abano, Abbot Trithemius, Albertus Magnus, Agrippa, and other prominent scholars are referenced here, in addition to hidden gems found in unpublished medieval grimoires and Qabalistic works.

Well organized and easy to use, *The Complete Magician's Tables* can help you understand the vast connections making up our strange and mysterious universe.

978-0-7387-1164-5, 432 pp., 7¼ x 10   **$49.95**

GODWIN'S
CABALISTIC
ENCYCLOPEDIA

Complete Guidance to Both Practical and Esoteric Applications

3rd Edition
Enlarged and Revised

DAVID GODWIN

Godwin's Cabalistic Encyclopedia

Complete Guidance to Both
Practical and Esoteric Applications

DAVID GODWIN

One of the most valuable books on the Cabala is back, with a new and more usable format. This book is a complete guide to Cabalistic magick and Gematria in which every demon, angel, power, and name of God ... every Sephirah, path, and plane of the Tree of Life ... and each attribute and association is fully described and cross-indexed by the Hebrew, English, and numerical forms.

All entries are now incorporated into one comprehensive dictionary. There are hundreds of new entries and illustrations, making this book even more valuable for Cabalistic pathworking and meditation. It now has many new Hebrew words and names, as well as the terms of Freemasonry, the entities of the Cthulhu mythos, and the Aurum Solis spellings for the names of the demons of the *Goetia*. It contains authentic Hebrew spellings and a new introduction that explains the uses of the book for meditation on Godnames.

The Cabalistic schema is native to the human psyche, and *Godwin's Cabalistic Encyclopedia* is a valuable reference tool for all Cabalists, magicians, scholars, and scientists of all disciplines.

978-1-56718-324-5, 832 pp., 6 x 9 $39.95

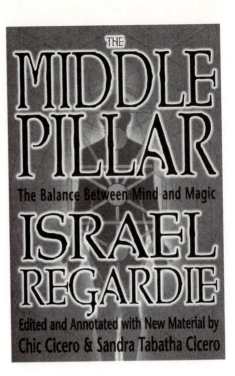

THE
MIDDLE
PILLAR

The Balance Between Mind and Magic

ISRAEL
REGARDIE

Edited and Annotated with New Material by
Chic Cicero & Sandra Tabatha Cicero

The Middle Pillar:
The Balance Between Mind and Magic
formerly *The Middle Pillar*
ISRAEL REGARDIE
EDITED BY CHIC CICERO AND
SANDRA TABATHA CICERO

Break the barrier between the conscious and unconscious mind through the Middle Pillar exercise, a technique that serves as a bridge into magic, chakra work, and psychology. This classic work introduces a psychological perspective on magic and occultism while giving clear directions on how to perform the Qabalistic Cross, The Lesser Banishing Ritual of the Pentagram, the Middle Pillar exercise, along with its accompanying methods of circulating the light, the Vibratory Formula, and the building up of the Tree of Life in the aura.

The Ciceros, who knew Regardie personally, have made his book much more accessible by adding an extensive and useful set of notes, along with chapters that explain Regardie's work in depth. They expand upon it by carrying it into a realm of new techniques that are directly related to Regardie's core material. Especially valuable is the chapter on psychology, which provides a solid frame of reference for Regardie's numerous remarks on this subject.

978-1-56718-140-1, 312 pp., 6 x 9 $17.95

A
GARDEN
OF
POMEGRANATES
Skrying on the Tree of Life
ISRAEL
REGARDIE

Edited and Annotated with New Material by
Chic Cicero & Sandra Tabatha Cicero

A Garden Of Pomegranates
Skrying on the Tree of Life
ISRAEL REGARDIE
EDITED BY CHIC CICERO AND
SANDRA TABATHA CICERO
(Annotated with new material)

When Israel Regardie wrote *A Garden of Pomegranates* in 1932, he designed it to be a simple yet comprehensive guidebook outlining the complex system of the Qabalah and providing a key to its symbolism. Since then it has achieved the status of a classic among texts on the Hermetic Qabalah. It stands as an extraordinary introductory guide for magicians on this complex system, with an emphasis on direct experience through meditation on the 22 paths.

Now, Chic Cicero and Sandra Tabatha Cicero—Golden Dawn Adepts and personal friends of the late Regardie—have made the book even more useful for today's occult students, with full annotations, critical commentary, and explanatory notes. They have added practical material in the form of pathworkings, suggested exercises, and daily affirmations—one for each Sephirah and each path. Brief rituals, meditations, and Qabalistic mantras complement Regardie's section on Gematria and other forms of numerical Qabalah.

978-1-56718-141-8, 552 pp., 6 x 9 $21.95

LLEWELLYN'S SOURCEBOOK SERIES

Three Books of Occult Philosophy

written by
Henry Cornelius Agrippa
of Nettesheim

Completely Annotated, with
Modern Commentary

The Foundation Book
of Western Occultism

Translated by James Freake

Edited and Annotated by
Donald Tyson

Three Books of Occult Philosophy
EDITED BY DONALD TYSON

Three Books of Occult Philosophy by Henry Cornelius Agrippa (1486–1535) is the single most important text in the history of Western occultism. Even today, occultists use the techniques first described here, although rarely giving credit to it.

The Hermetic Order of the Golden Dawn's systems of the Kabbalah, geomancy, elements, and seals and squares of the planets are all taken, in a large measure, from Agrippa—but for 500 years, *Three Books of Occult Philosophy* was almost impossible to find.

Donald Tyson took on the Herculean task of digging out the original, correcting the errors, and fully annotating the entire work. As a result, not only is this new edition easily available to scholars, but it is now fully understandable by people today. The ancient magics, in their original form, live again.

Other than the annotations, there are also extensive appendices on such topics as the elements, the magical squares, the humors, and more. Biographical and geographical dictionaries and the general index make accessing and understanding information in this book easier than ever.

This is the ultimate version of the book that is the ultimate book on magic. If you are interested in any form of magic or occultism, you must get *Three Books of Occult Philosophy*.

978-0-87542-832-1, 1024 pp., 7 x 10 $49.95